S0-BCR-641

TRANSMETROPOLITAN
the new scum

WARREN ELLIS
WRITER

DARICK ROBERTSON
PENCILLER

RODNEY RAMOS
KEITH AIKEN

INKERS

NATHAN EYRING

COLORIST

CLEM ROBINS

LETTERER

Original covers by

darick robertson

and

geoff darrow

TRANSMETROPOLITAN
created by
warren ellis
and
darick robertson

Karen Berger • VP-Executive Editor   Stuart Moore and Shelly Roeberg • Editors-original series   Cliff Chiang • Assistant Editor-original series   Michael Wright • Editor-collected edition

Robbin Brosterman • Senior Art Director   Paul Levitz • President & Publisher   Georg Brewer • VP-Design & Retail Product Development   Richard Bruning • Senior VP-Creative Director

Patrick Caldon • Senior VP-Finance & Operations   Chris Caramalis • VP-Finance   Terri Cunningham • VP-Managing Editor   Alison Gill • VP-Manufacturing   Jim Lee • Editorial Director-WildStorm

Rich Johnson • VP-Book Trade Sales   Hank Kanalz • VP-General Manager, WildStorm   Lillian Laserson • Senior VP & General Counsel   Gregory Noveck • Senior VP-Creative Affairs

David McKillips • VP-Advertising & Custom Publishing   John Nee • VP-Business Development

Cheryl Rubin • Senior VP-Brand Management   Bob Wayne • VP-Sales & Marketing

TRANSMETROPOLITAN: THE NEW SCUM

Published by DC Comics. Cover and compilation Copyright © 2000 Warren Ellis and Darick Robertson. All Rights Reserved.

Originally published in single magazine form as TRANSMETROPOLITAN 19-24, VERTIGO: WINTER'S EDGE 3. Copyright © 1999, 2000 Warren Ellis and Darick Robertson. All Rights Reserved.

All characters, their distinctive likenesses and related elements featured in this publication are trademarks of DC Comics. The stories, characters, and incidents featured in this

publication are entirely fictional. DC Comics does not read or accept unsolicited submissions of ideas, stories or artwork.

DC Comics, 1700 Broadway, New York, NY 10019 • A Warner Bros. Entertainment Company

Printed in Canada. Fifth Printing. ISBN: 978-1-56389-627-9.

Cover illustration by Darick Robertson. Cover color by Nathan Eyring. Logo design by Gregory Homs.

WARREN ELLIS writes and DARICK ROBERTSON pencils

THE NEW SCUM

one: NEW HOME

ODNEY RAMOS inker
NATHAN EYRING color&separations
CLEM ROBINS letterer
CLIFF CHIANG assistant editor
STUART MOORE editor

TRANSMETROPOLITAN CREATED BY WARREN ELLIS & DARICK ROBERTSON

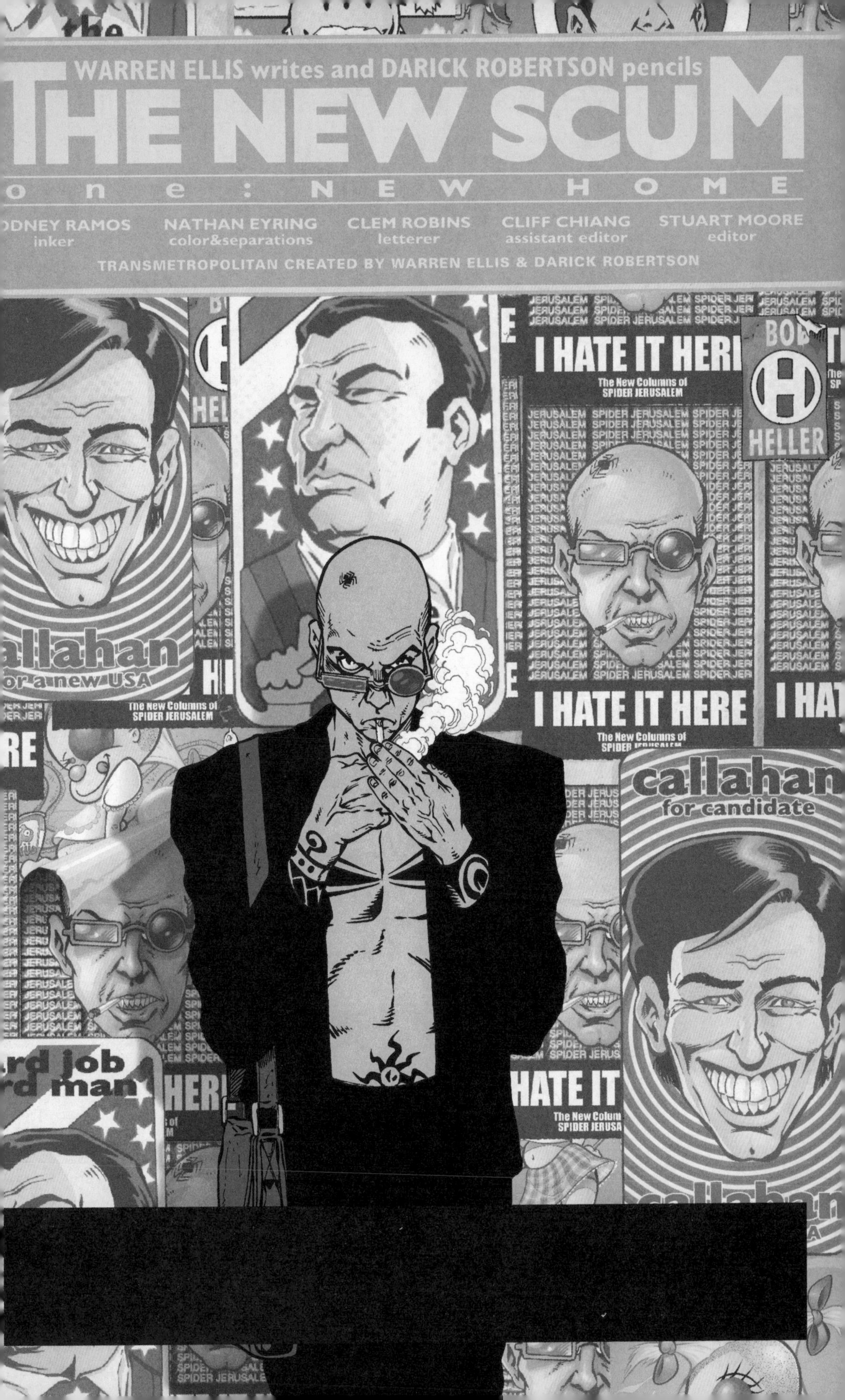

I HATE IT HERE
The New Columns of SPIDER JERUSALEM
BOB HELLER
callahan for a new USA
I HATE IT HERE
The New Columns of SPIDER JERUSALEM
callahan for candidate

[redacted]

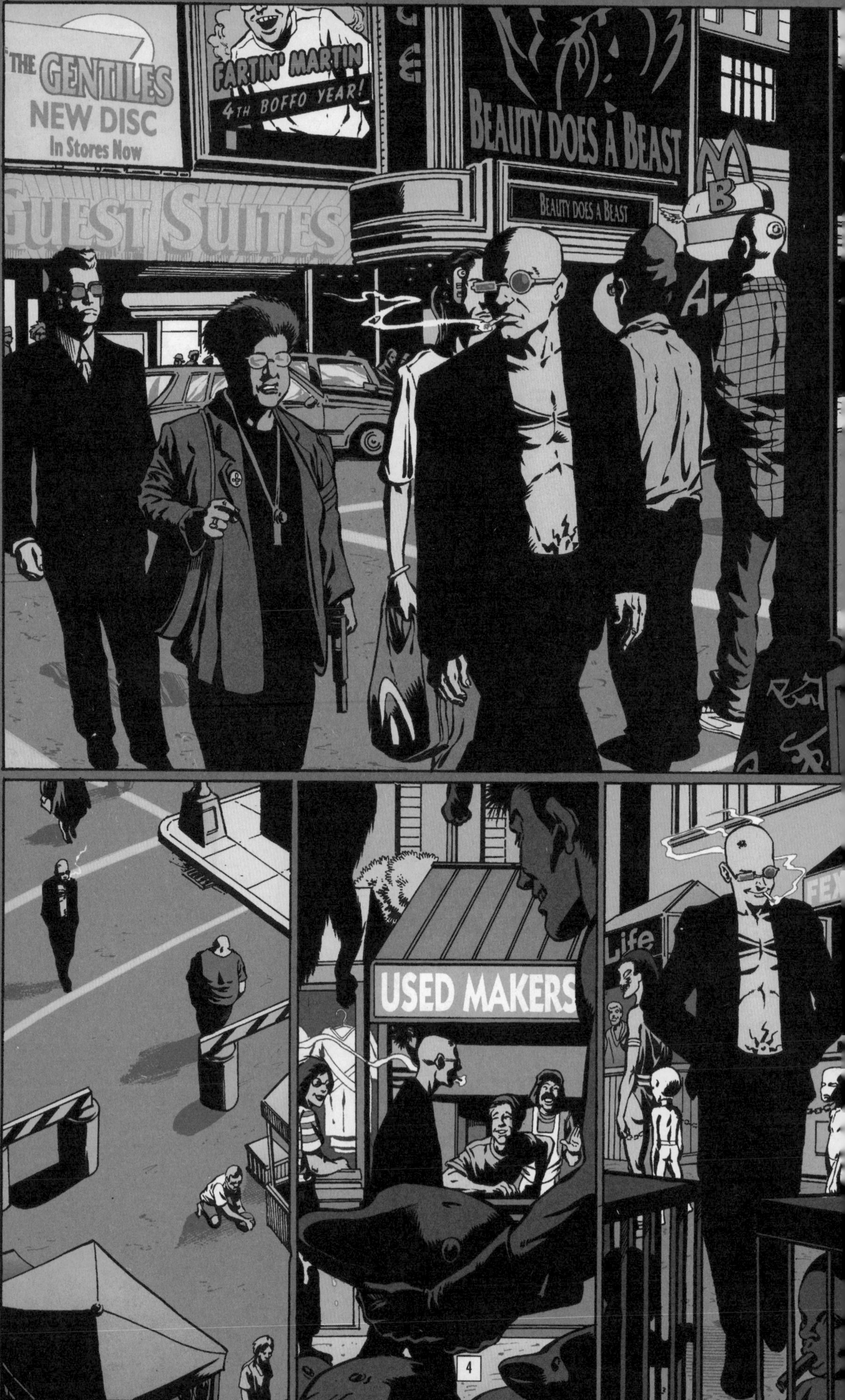
THE GENTILES NEW DISC
In Stores Now
FARTIN' MARTIN
4TH BOFFO YEAR!
BEAUTY DOES A BEAST
GUEST SUITES
BEAUTY DOES A BEAST
USED MAKERS
Life

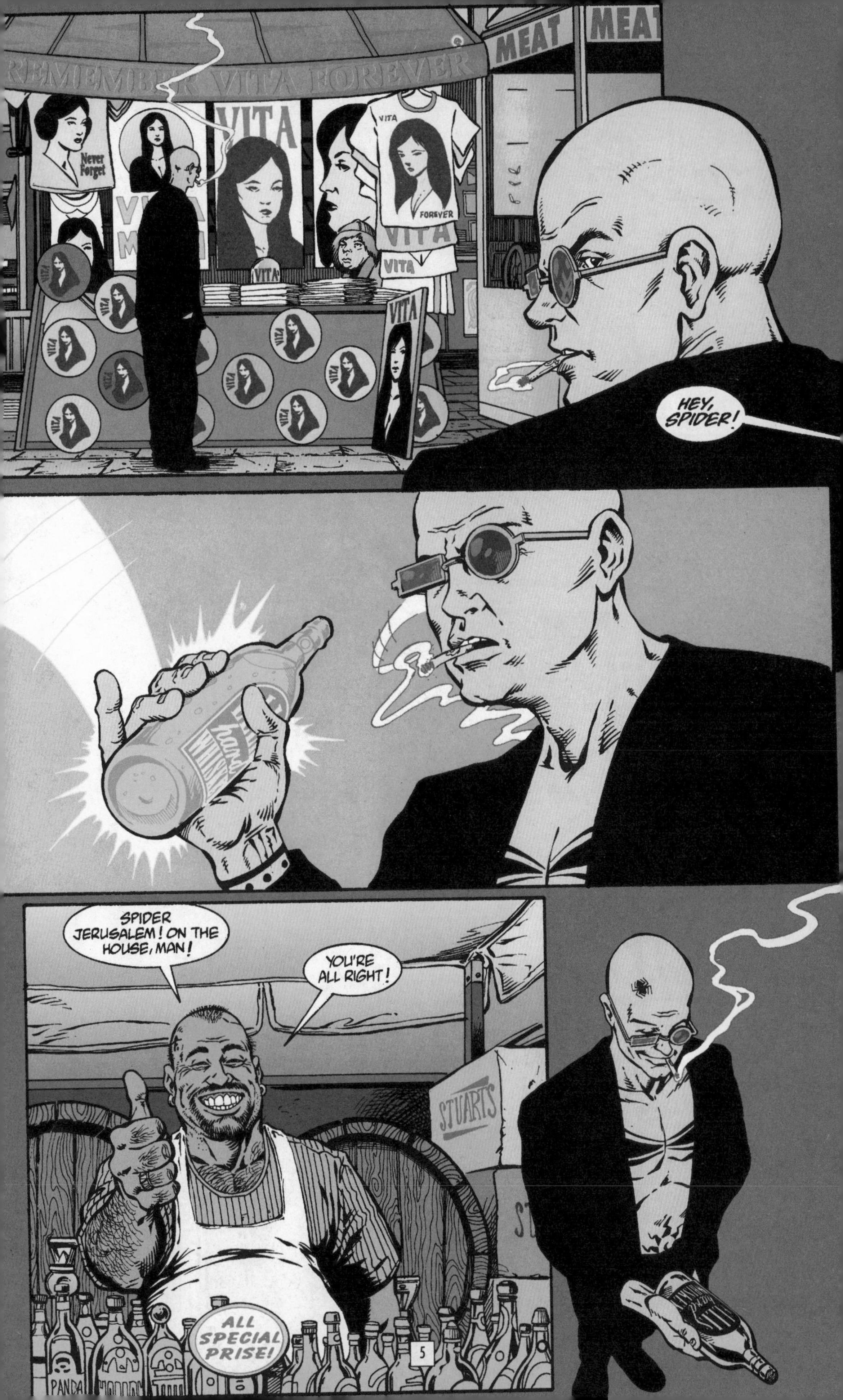
REMEMBER VITA FOREVER
MEAT
MEAT
Never Forget
VITA
VITA
FOREVER
HEY, SPIDER!
SPIDER JERUSALEM! ON THE HOUSE, MAN!
YOU'RE ALL RIGHT!
STUARTS
ALL SPECIAL PRISE!

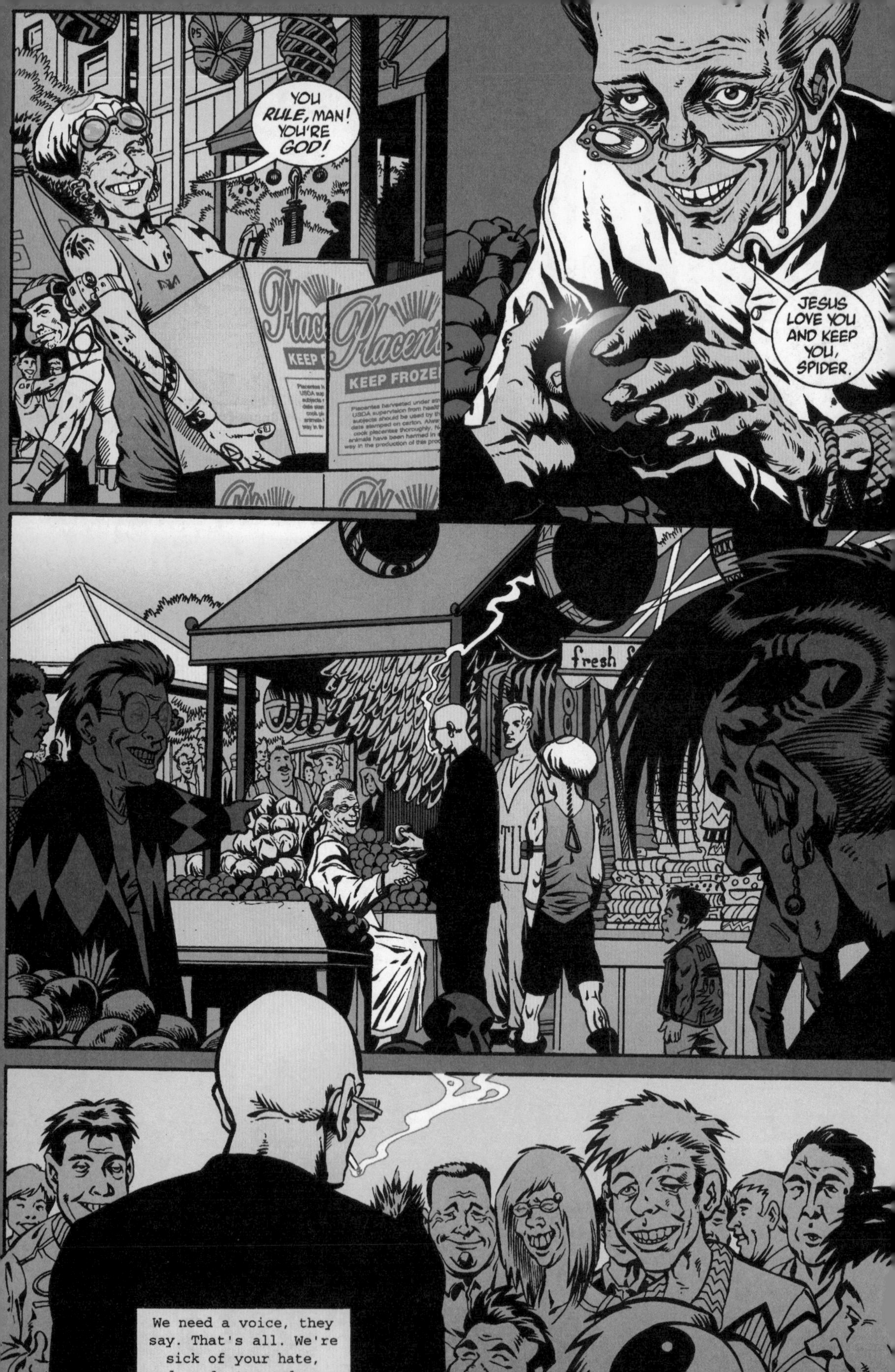
YOU RULE, MAN! YOU'RE GOD!
JESUS LOVE YOU AND KEEP YOU, SPIDER.
We need a voice, they say. That's all. We're sick of your hate, and we don't need your pity. We need a VOICE.

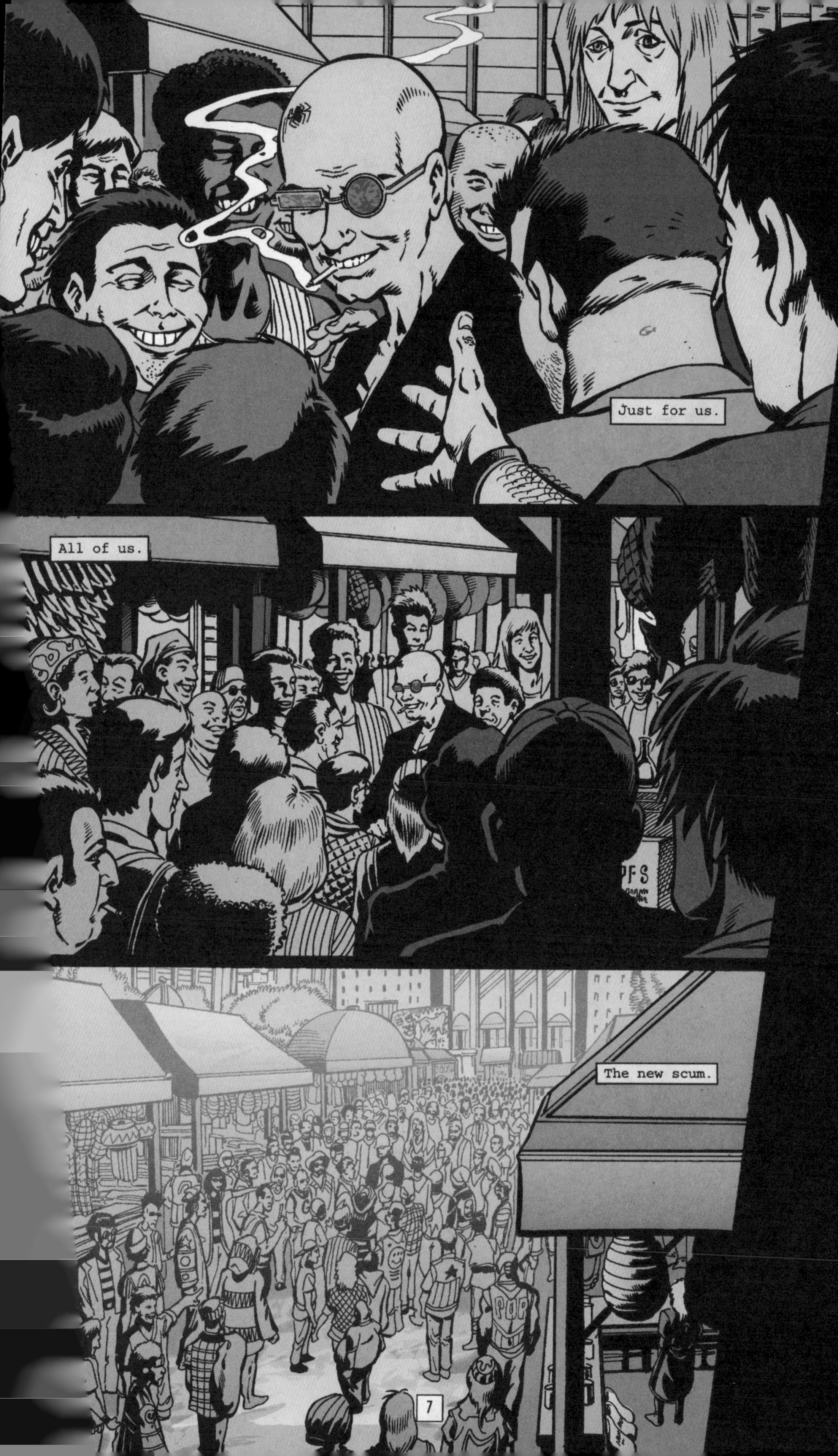
Just for us.
All of us.
The new scum.

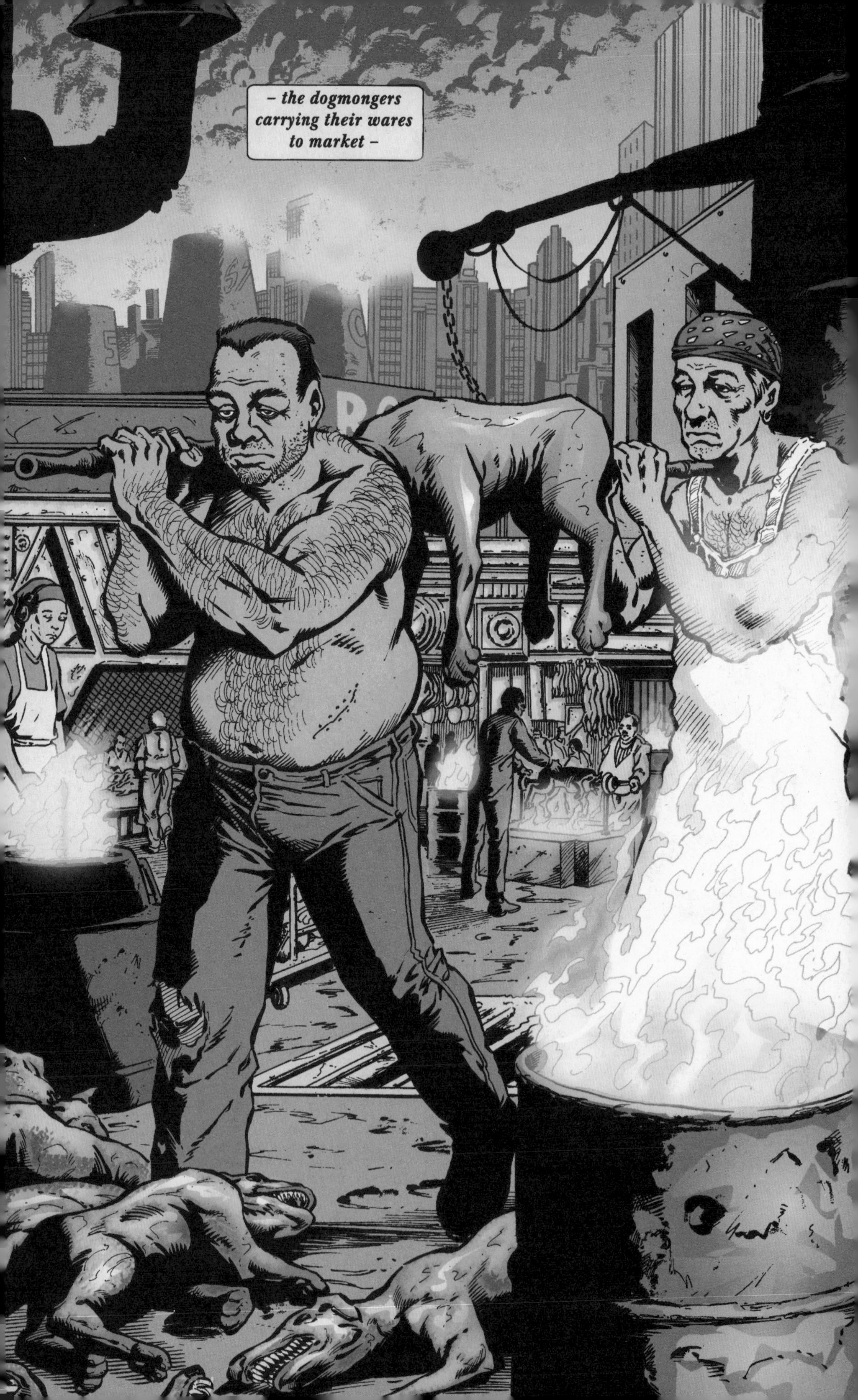
– the dogmongers carrying their wares to market –

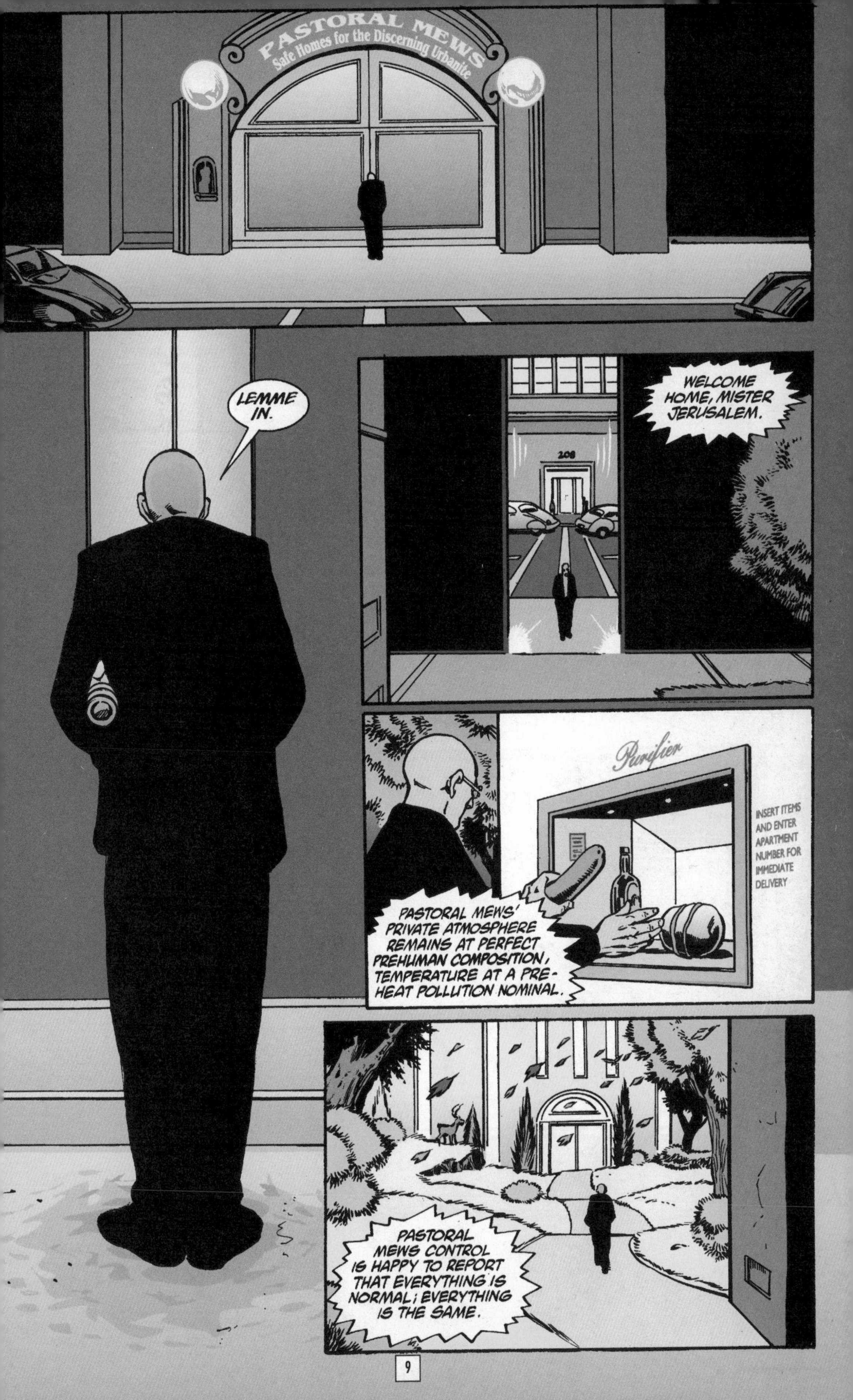
PASTORAL MEWS
Safe Homes for the Discerning Urbanite
LEMME IN.
WELCOME HOME, MISTER JERUSALEM.
208
Purifier
INSERT ITEMS AND ENTER APARTMENT NUMBER FOR IMMEDIATE DELIVERY
PASTORAL MEWS' PRIVATE ATMOSPHERE REMAINS AT PERFECT PREHUMAN COMPOSITION, TEMPERATURE AT A PRE-HEAT POLLUTION NOMINAL.
PASTORAL MEWS CONTROL IS HAPPY TO REPORT THAT EVERYTHING IS NORMAL; EVERYTHING IS THE SAME.

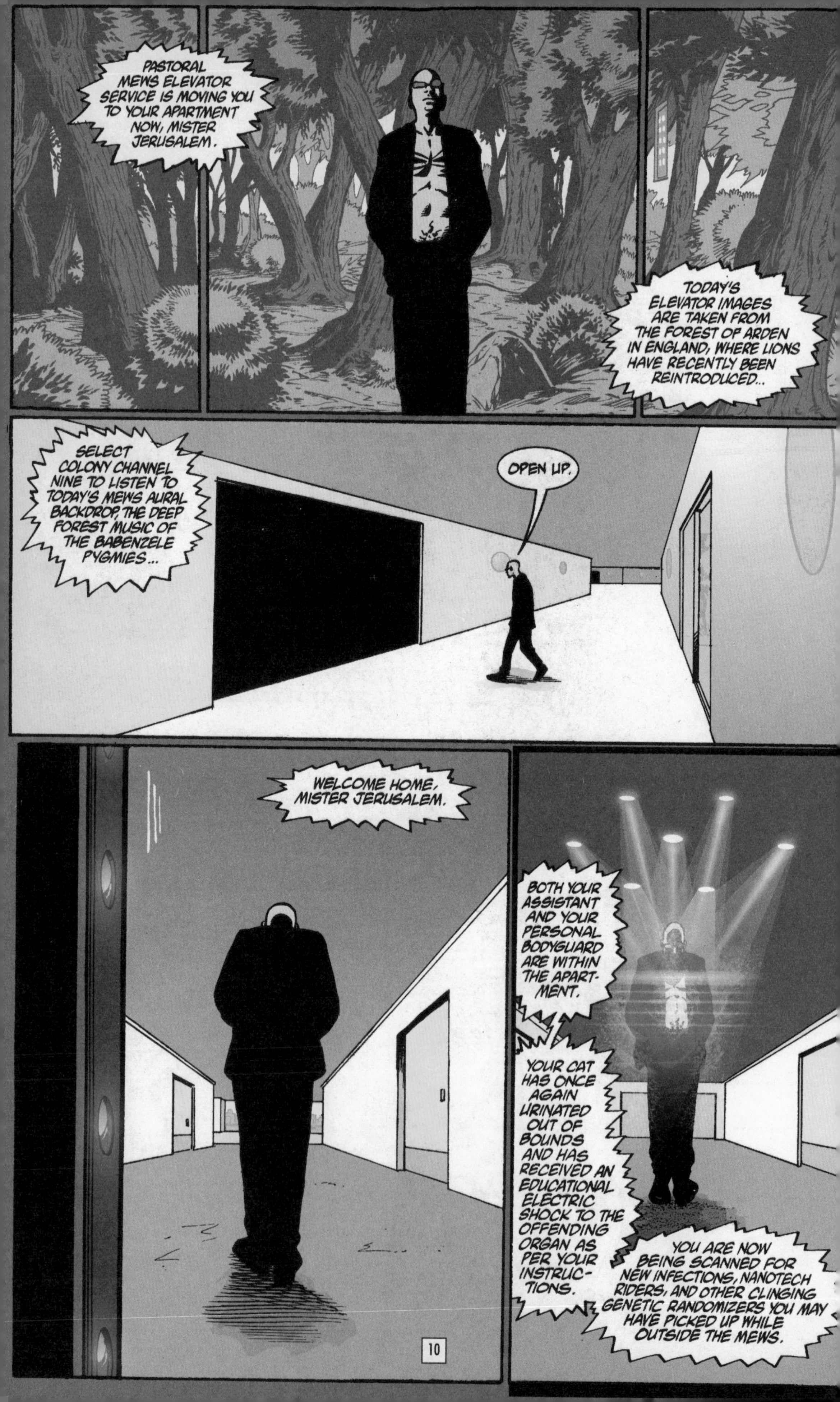
PASTORAL MEWS ELEVATOR SERVICE IS MOVING YOU TO YOUR APARTMENT NOW, MISTER JERUSALEM.
TODAY'S ELEVATOR IMAGES ARE TAKEN FROM THE FOREST OF ARDEN IN ENGLAND, WHERE LIONS HAVE RECENTLY BEEN REINTRODUCED...
SELECT COLONY CHANNEL NINE TO LISTEN TO TODAY'S MEWS AURAL BACKDROP, THE DEEP FOREST MUSIC OF THE BABENZELE PYGMIES...
OPEN UP.
WELCOME HOME, MISTER JERUSALEM.
BOTH YOUR ASSISTANT AND YOUR PERSONAL BODYGUARD ARE WITHIN THE APARTMENT.
YOUR CAT HAS ONCE AGAIN URINATED OUT OF BOUNDS AND HAS RECEIVED AN EDUCATIONAL ELECTRIC SHOCK TO THE OFFENDING ORGAN AS PER YOUR INSTRUCTIONS.
YOU ARE NOW BEING SCANNED FOR NEW INFECTIONS, NANOTECH RIDERS, AND OTHER CLINGING GENETIC RANDOMIZERS YOU MAY HAVE PICKED UP WHILE OUTSIDE THE MEWS.

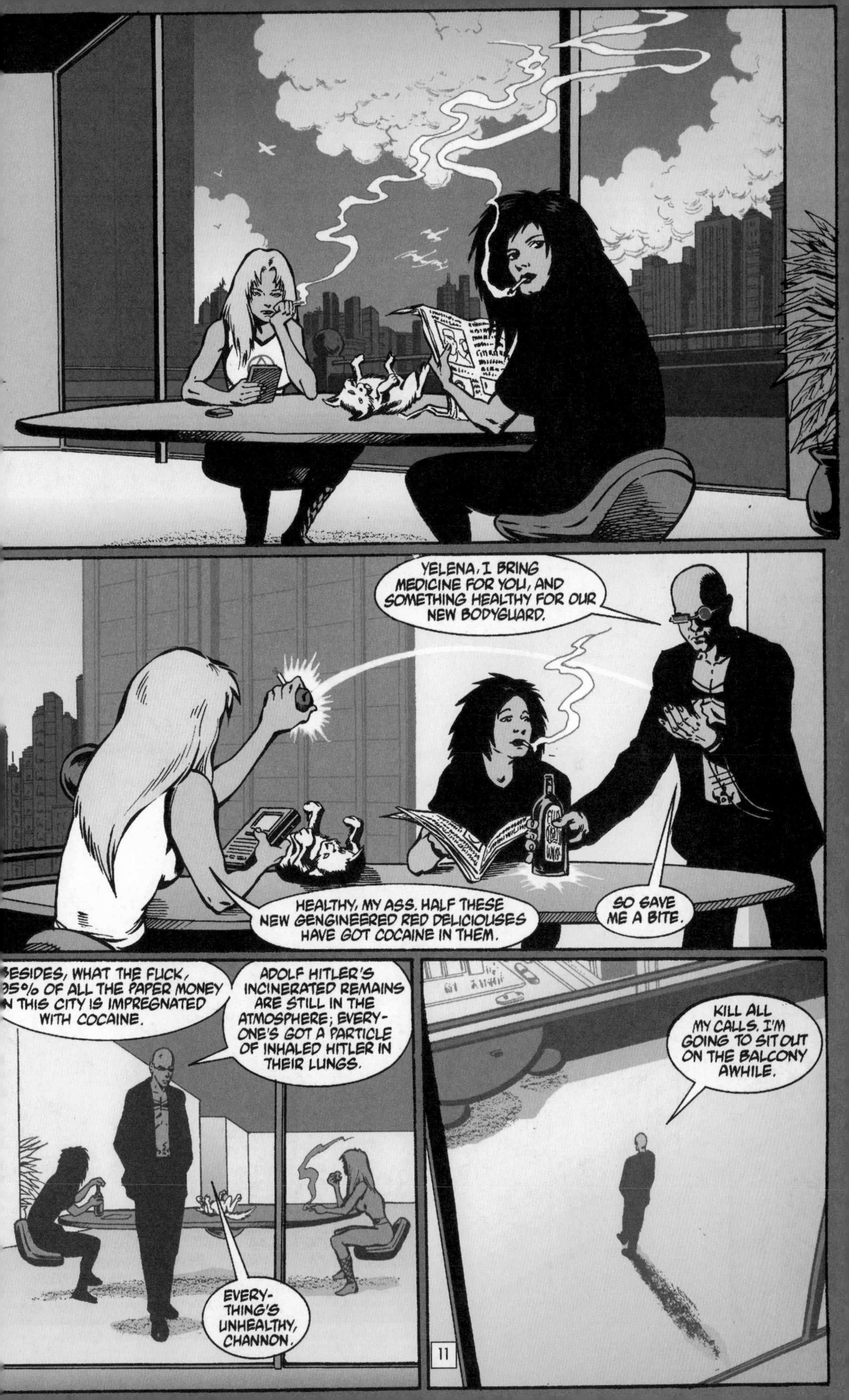
YELENA, I BRING MEDICINE FOR YOU, AND SOMETHING HEALTHY FOR OUR NEW BODYGUARD.
HEALTHY, MY ASS. HALF THESE NEW GENGINEERED RED DELICIOUSES HAVE GOT COCAINE IN THEM.
SO SAVE ME A BITE.
BESIDES, WHAT THE FUCK, 95% OF ALL THE PAPER MONEY IN THIS CITY IS IMPREGNATED WITH COCAINE.
ADOLF HITLER'S INCINERATED REMAINS ARE STILL IN THE ATMOSPHERE; EVERYONE'S GOT A PARTICLE OF INHALED HITLER IN THEIR LUNGS.
EVERYTHING'S UNHEALTHY, CHANNON.
KILL ALL MY CALLS. I'M GOING TO SIT OUT ON THE BALCONY AWHILE.
11

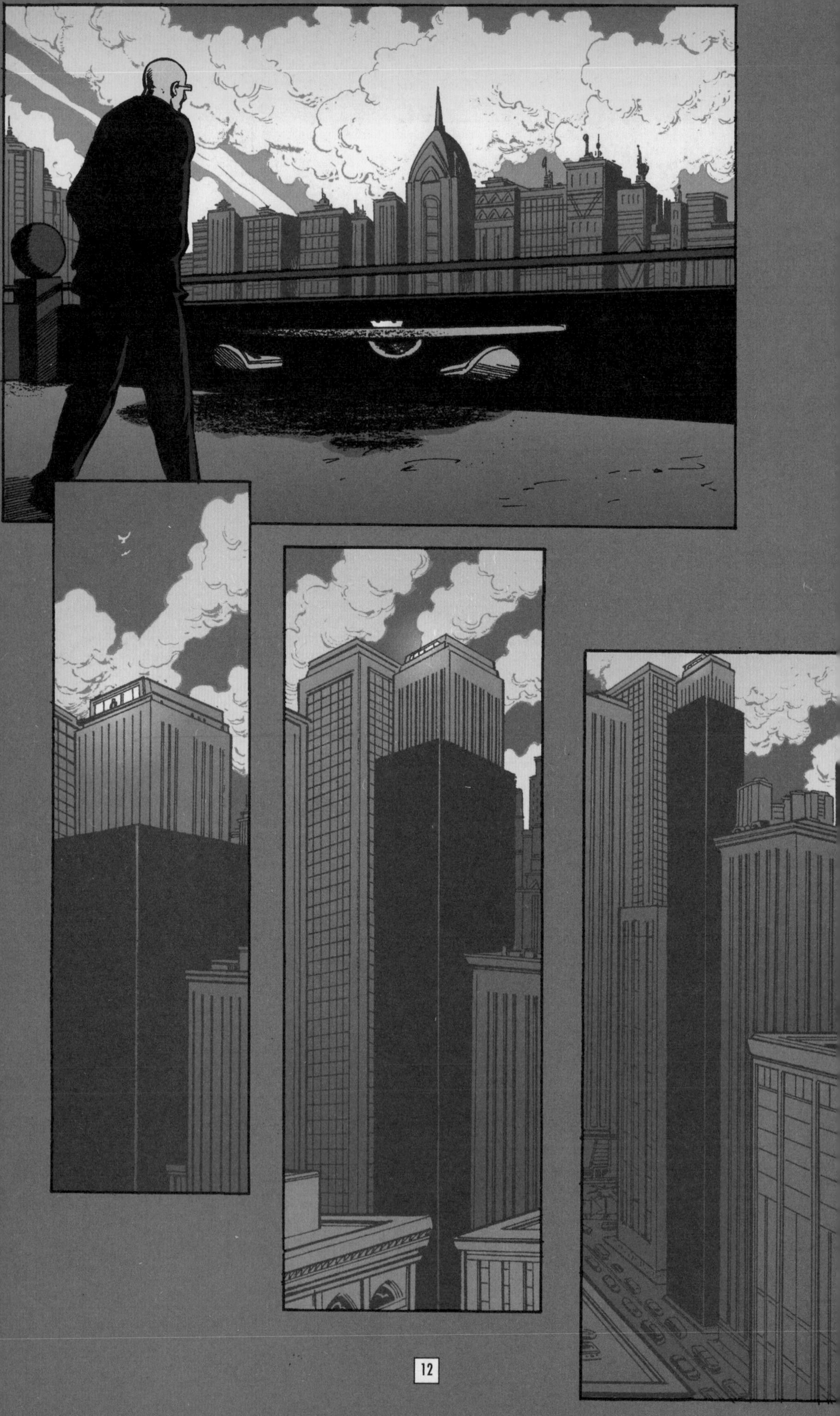

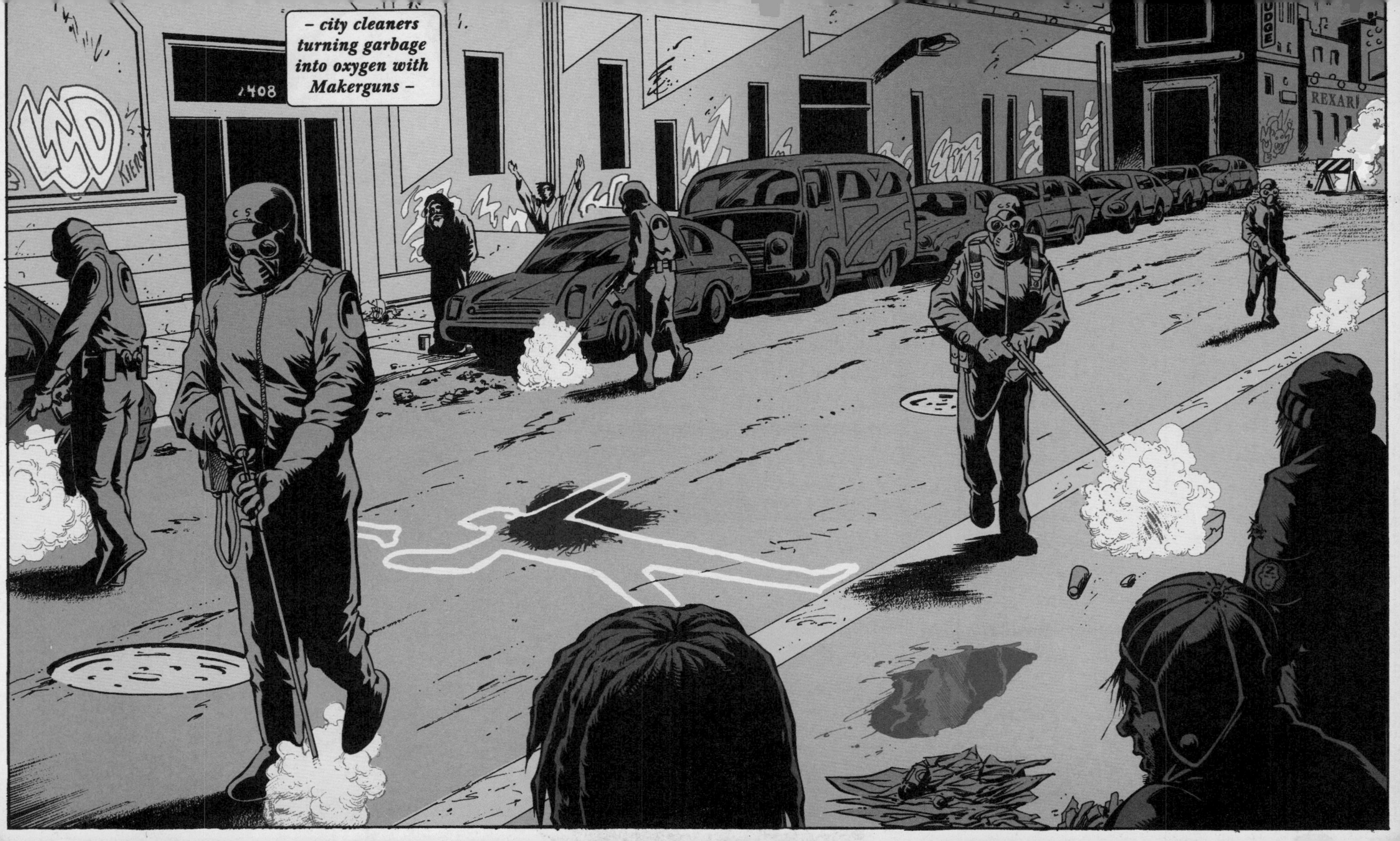
– city cleaners turning garbage into oxygen with Makerguns –
1408
LCD
REXAR

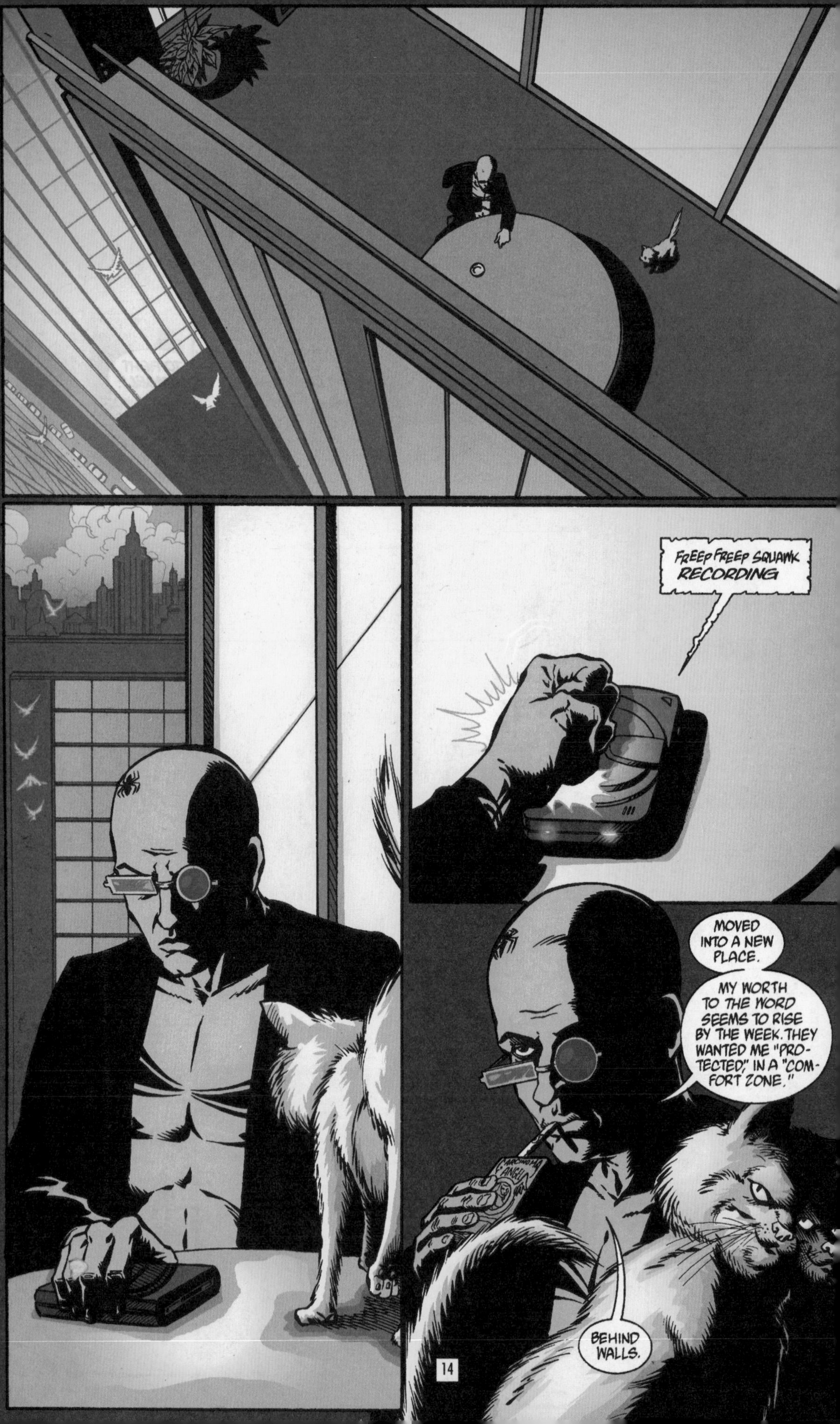

FREEP FREEP SQUAWK
RECORDING
MOVED INTO A NEW PLACE.
MY WORTH TO THE WORD SEEMS TO RISE BY THE WEEK. THEY WANTED ME "PROTECTED," IN A "COMFORT ZONE."
BEHIND WALLS.

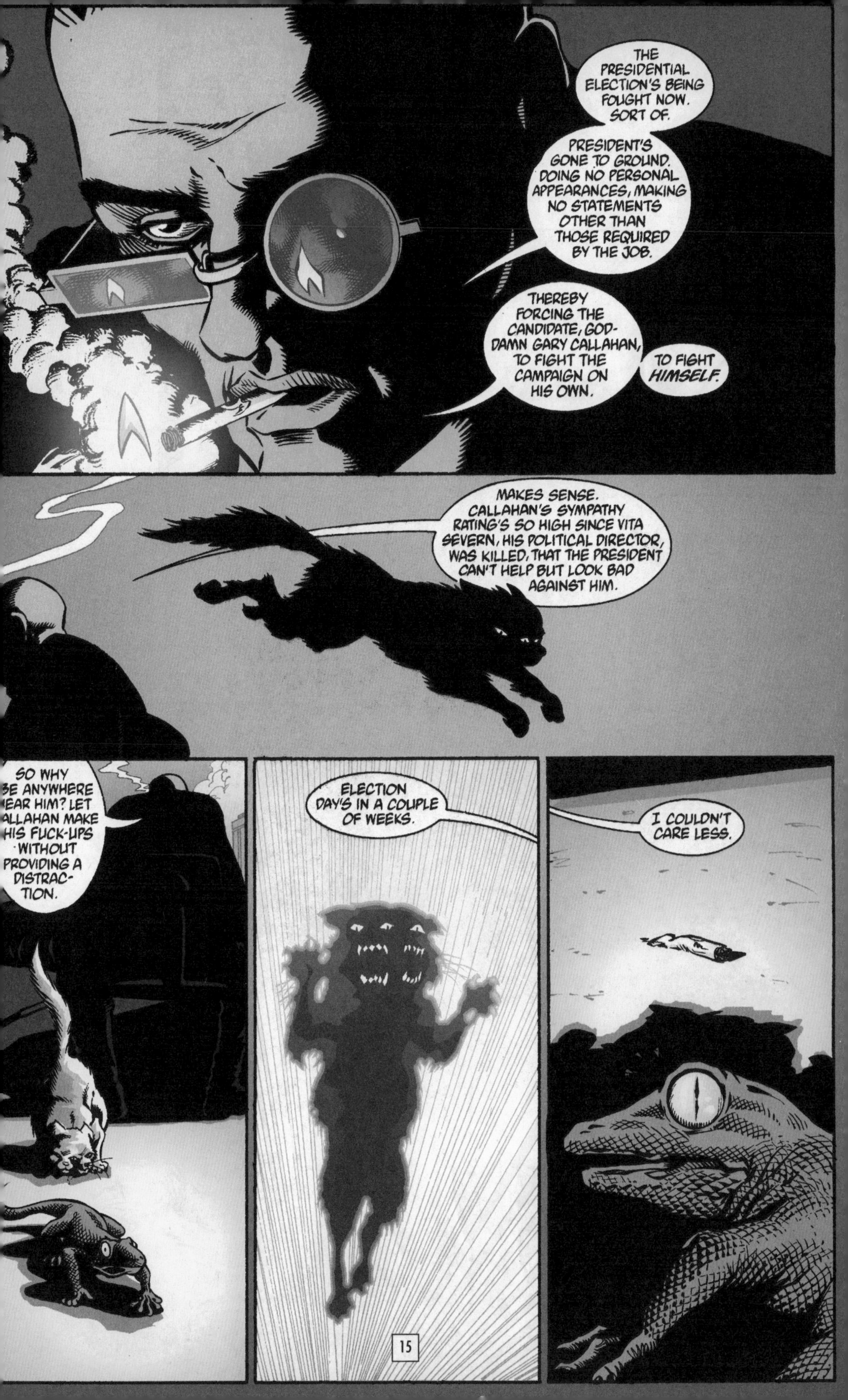
THE PRESIDENTIAL ELECTION'S BEING FOUGHT NOW. SORT OF.
PRESIDENT'S GONE TO GROUND. DOING NO PERSONAL APPEARANCES, MAKING NO STATEMENTS OTHER THAN THOSE REQUIRED BY THE JOB.
THEREBY FORCING THE CANDIDATE, GOD-DAMN GARY CALLAHAN, TO FIGHT THE CAMPAIGN ON HIS OWN.
TO FIGHT *HIMSELF.*
MAKES SENSE. CALLAHAN'S SYMPATHY RATING'S SO HIGH SINCE VITA SEVERN, HIS POLITICAL DIRECTOR, WAS KILLED, THAT THE PRESIDENT CAN'T HELP BUT LOOK BAD AGAINST HIM.
SO WHY BE ANYWHERE EAR HIM? LET ALLAHAN MAKE HIS FUCK-UPS WITHOUT PROVIDING A DISTRAC-TION.
ELECTION DAY'S IN A COUPLE OF WEEKS.
I COULDN'T CARE LESS.

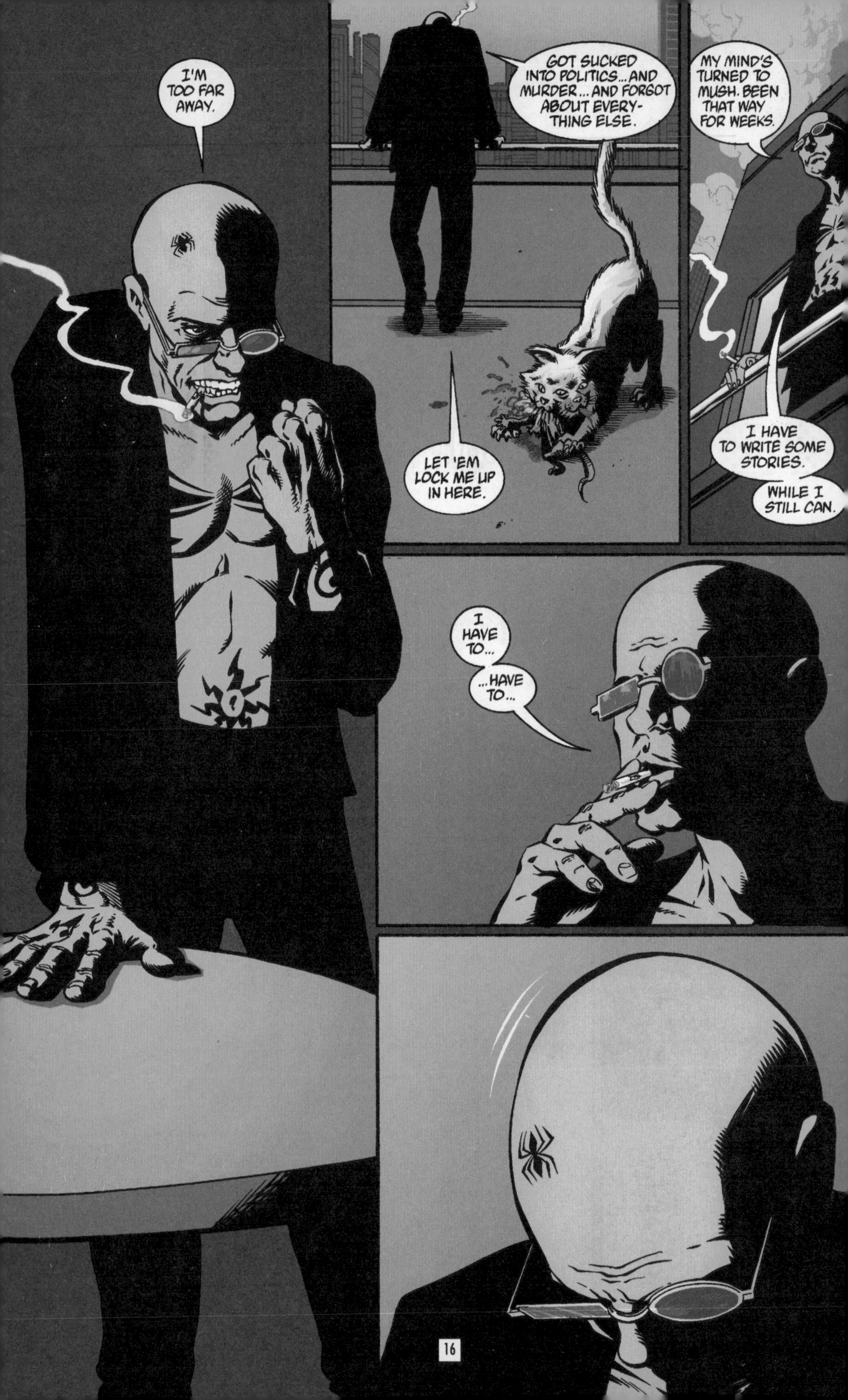
I'M TOO FAR AWAY.
GOT SUCKED INTO POLITICS... AND MURDER... AND FORGOT ABOUT EVERYTHING ELSE.
LET 'EM LOCK ME UP IN HERE.
MY MIND'S TURNED TO MUSH. BEEN THAT WAY FOR WEEKS.
I HAVE TO WRITE SOME STORIES.
WHILE I STILL CAN.
I HAVE TO...
...HAVE TO...

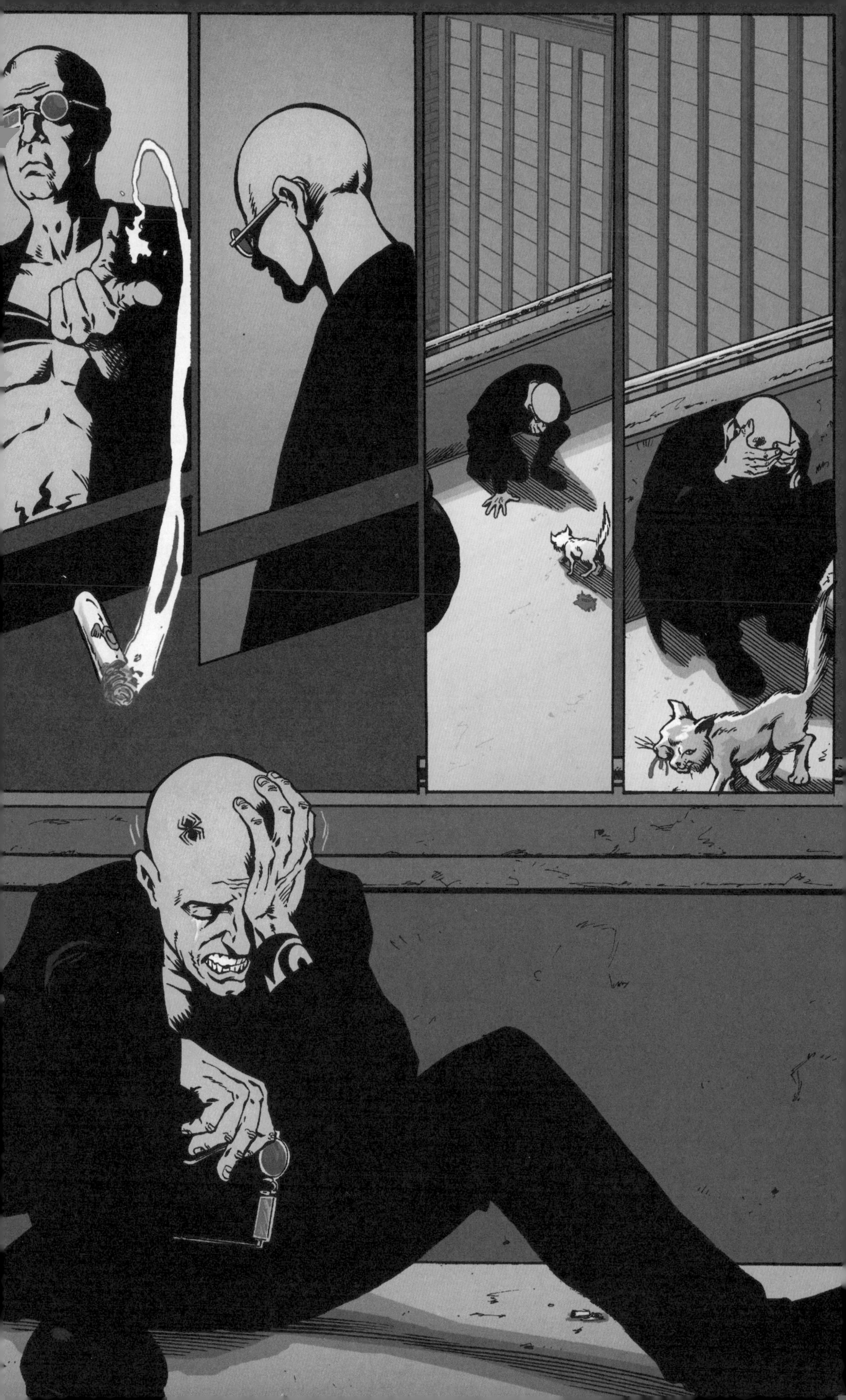

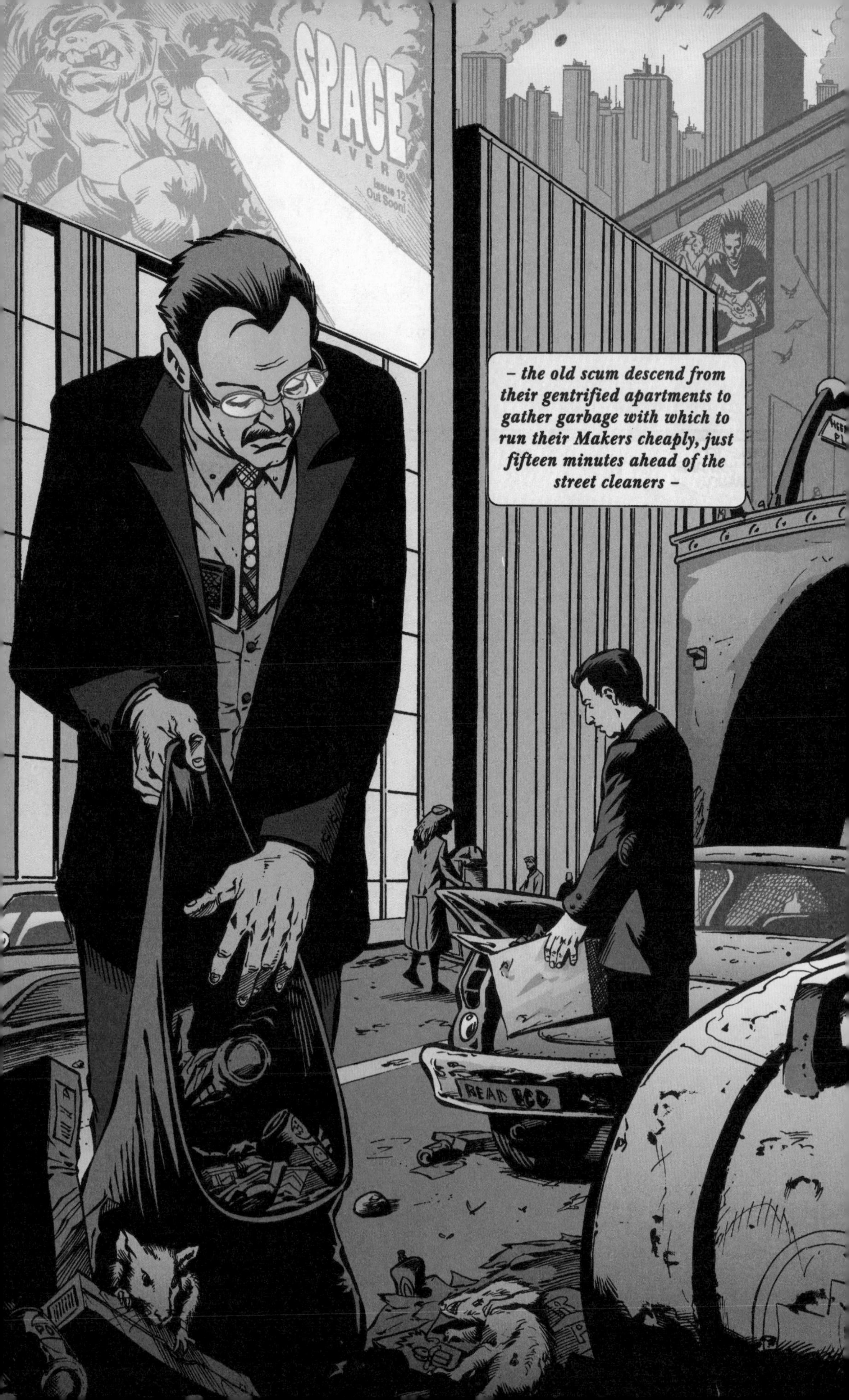
SPACE BEAVER ®
Issue 12 Out Soon!
– the old scum descend from their gentrified apartments to gather garbage with which to run their Makers cheaply, just fifteen minutes ahead of the street cleaners –
READ ECO

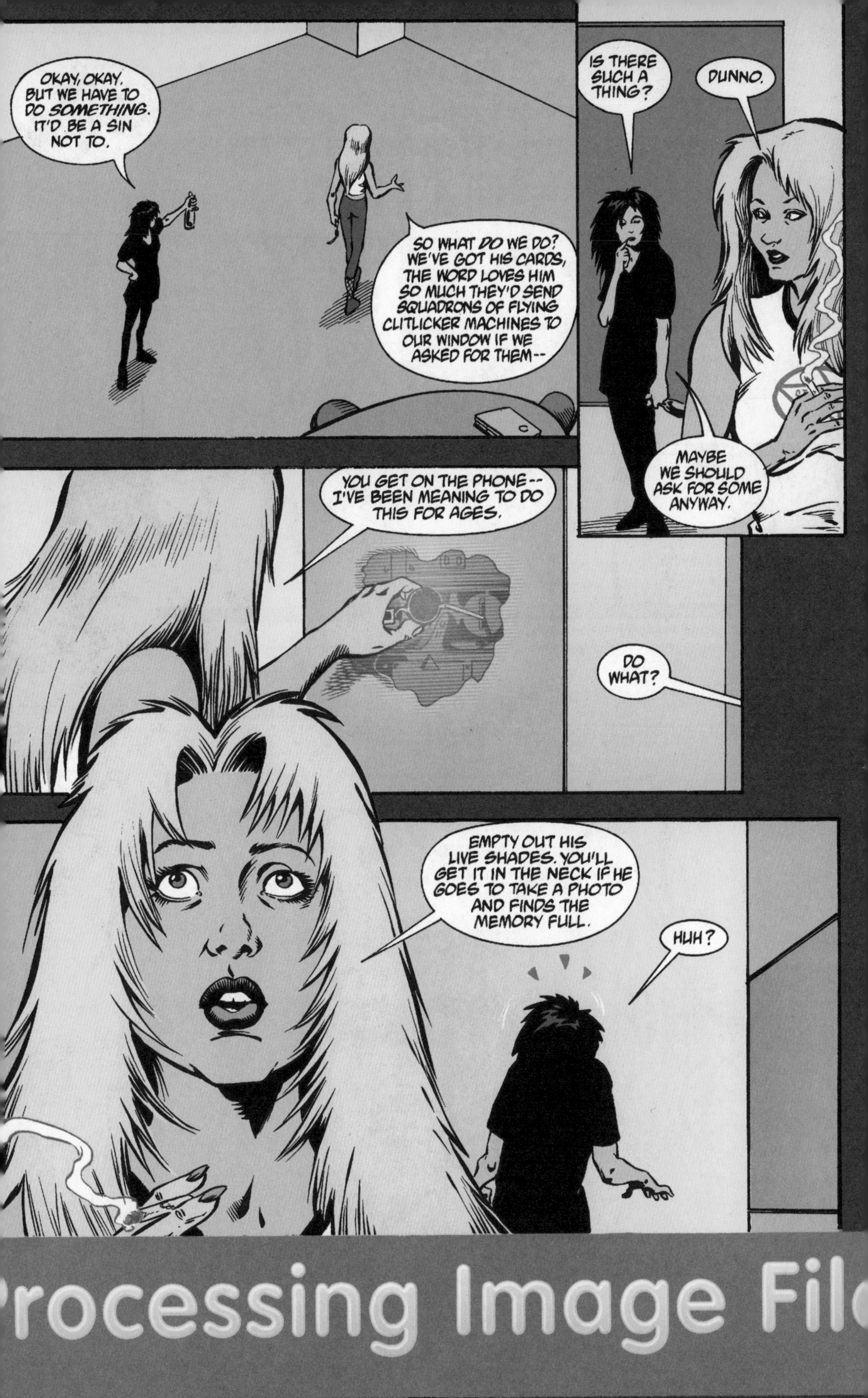
OKAY, OKAY. BUT WE HAVE TO DO SOMETHING. IT'D BE A SIN NOT TO.
SO WHAT DO WE DO? WE'VE GOT HIS CARDS, THE WORD LOVES HIM SO MUCH THEY'D SEND SQUADRONS OF FLYING CLITLICKER MACHINES TO OUR WINDOW IF WE ASKED FOR THEM--
IS THERE SUCH A THING?
DUNNO.
MAYBE WE SHOULD ASK FOR SOME ANYWAY.
YOU GET ON THE PHONE-- I'VE BEEN MEANING TO DO THIS FOR AGES.
DO WHAT?
EMPTY OUT HIS LIVE SHADES. YOU'LL GET IT IN THE NECK IF HE GOES TO TAKE A PHOTO AND FINDS THE MEMORY FULL.
HUH?
Processing Image File

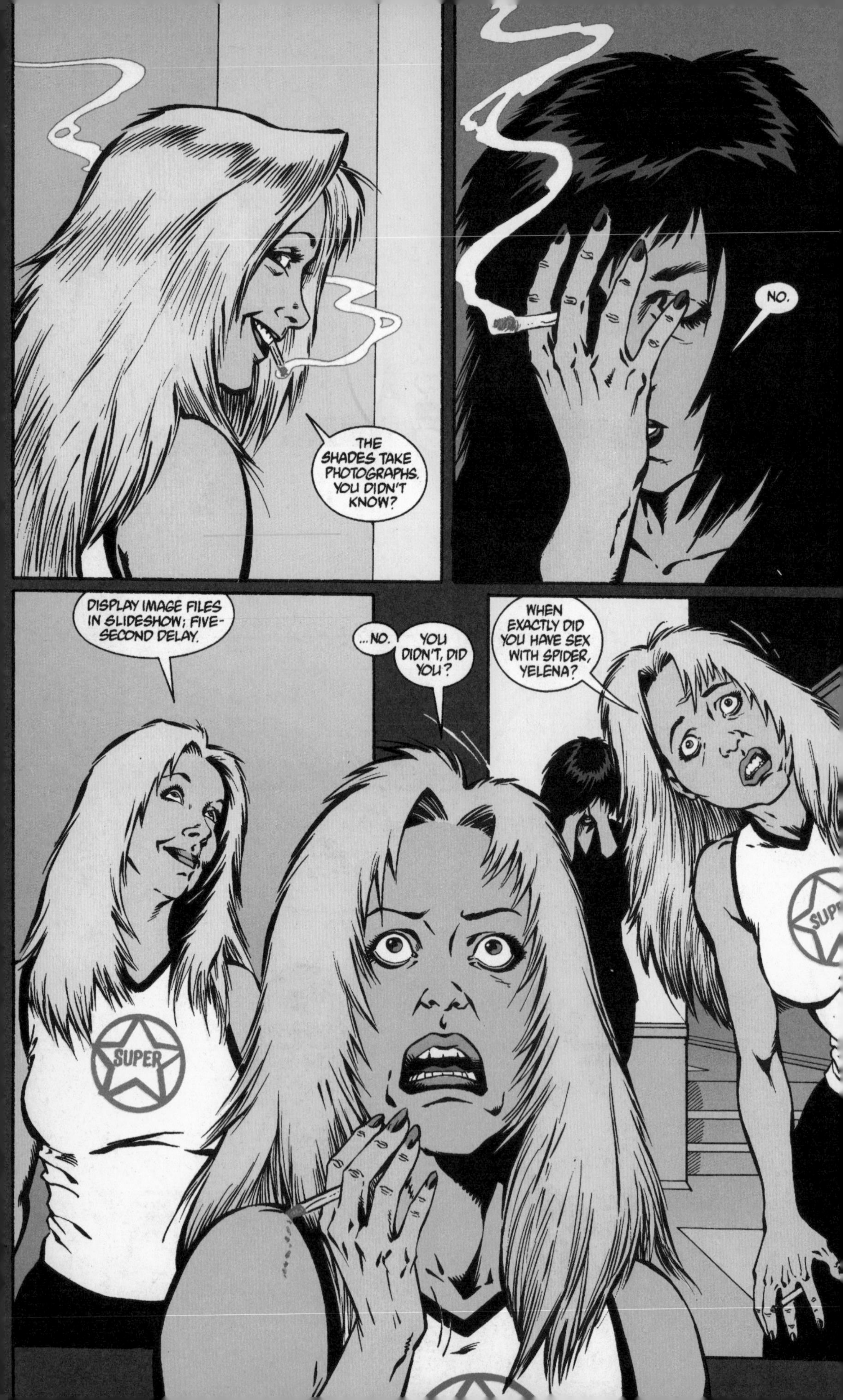
THE SHADES TAKE PHOTOGRAPHS. YOU DIDN'T KNOW?
NO.
DISPLAY IMAGE FILES IN SLIDESHOW; FIVE-SECOND DELAY.
...NO.
YOU DIDN'T, DID YOU?
WHEN EXACTLY DID YOU HAVE SEX WITH SPIDER, YELENA?
SUPER
SUPER

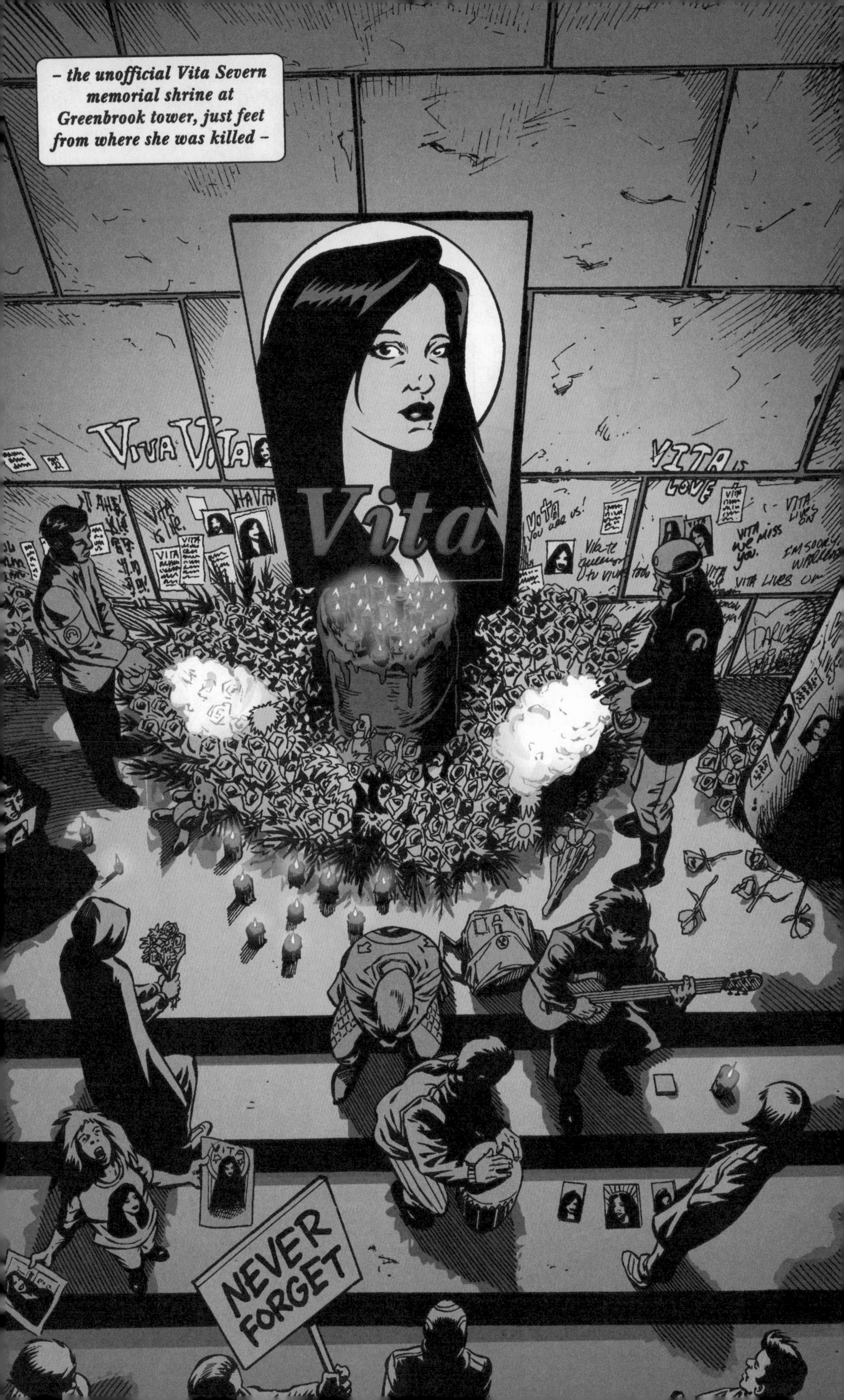
– the unofficial Vita Severn memorial shrine at Greenbrook tower, just feet from where she was killed –
VIVA VITA
Vita
VITA IS LOVE
VITA we miss you.
VITA LIVES ON
NEVER FORGET

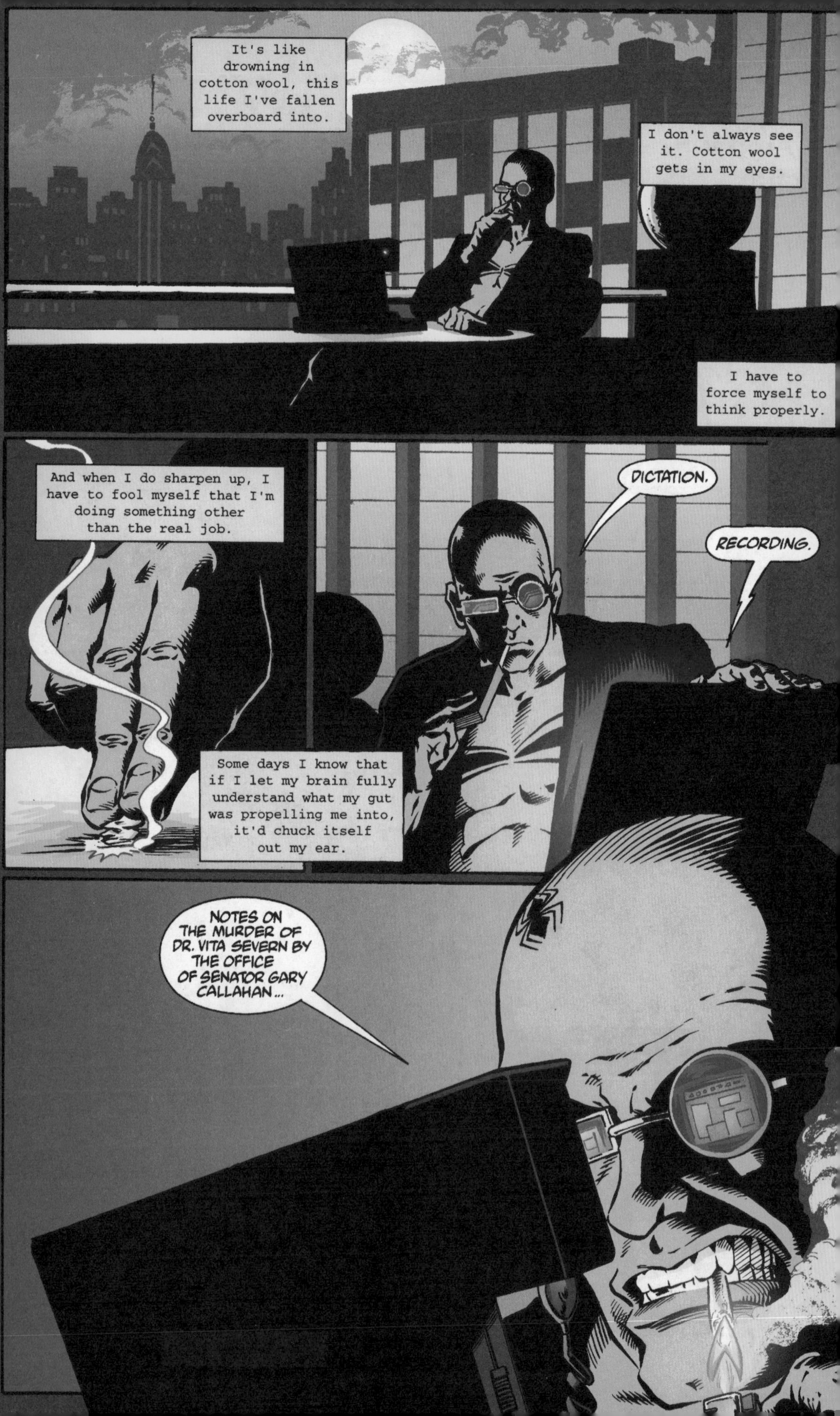
It's like drowning in cotton wool, this life I've fallen overboard into.
I don't always see it. Cotton wool gets in my eyes.
I have to force myself to think properly.
And when I do sharpen up, I have to fool myself that I'm doing something other than the real job.
DICTATION.
RECORDING.
Some days I know that if I let my brain fully understand what my gut was propelling me into, it'd chuck itself out my ear.
NOTES ON THE MURDER OF DR. VITA SEVERN BY THE OFFICE OF SENATOR GARY CALLAHAN...

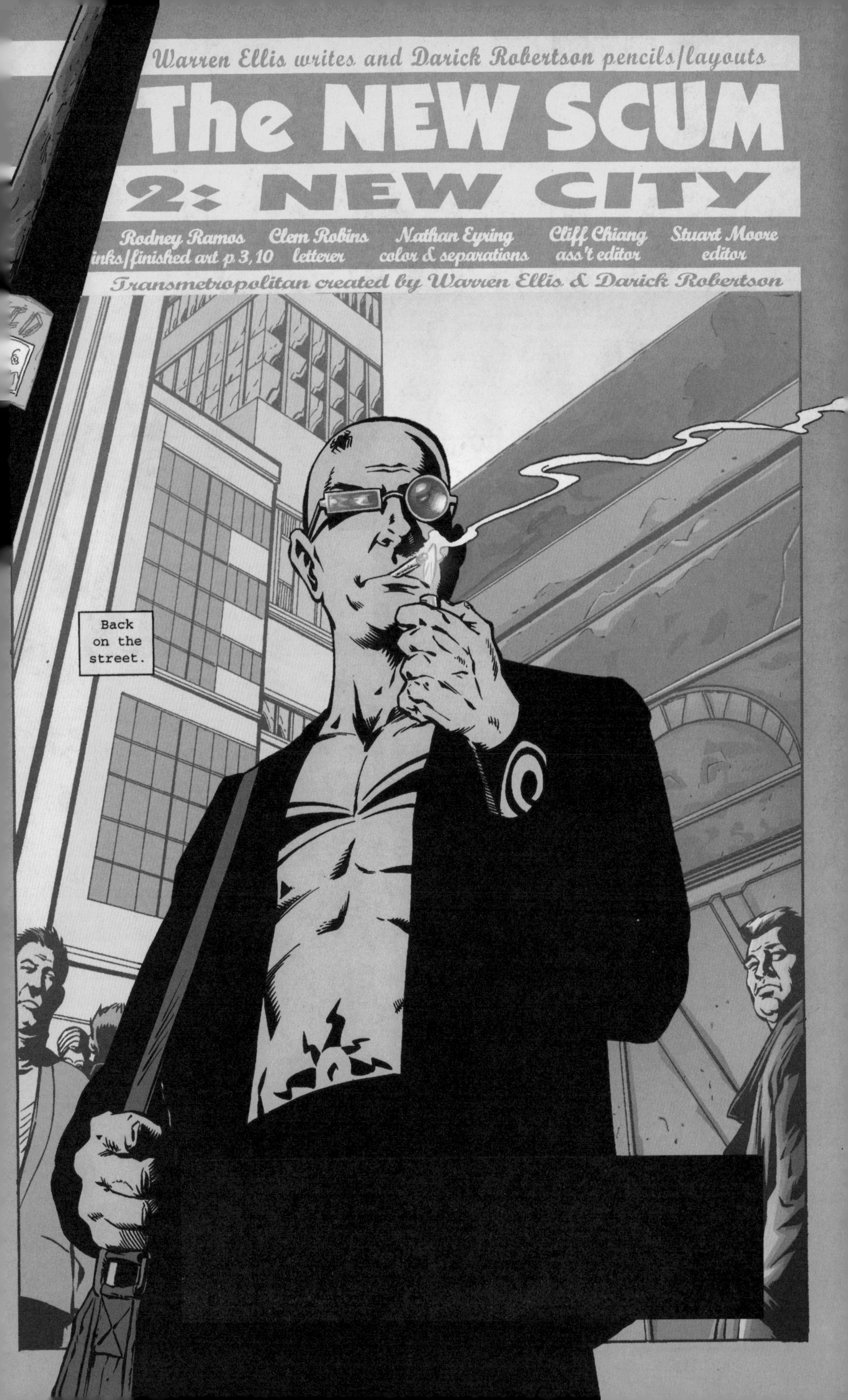
Warren Ellis writes and Darick Robertson pencils/layouts
The NEW SCUM
2: NEW CITY
Rodney Ramos inks/finished art p. 3, 10
Clem Robins letterer
Nathan Eyring color & separations
Cliff Chiang ass't editor
Stuart Moore editor
Transmetropolitan created by Warren Ellis & Darick Robertson
Back on the street.

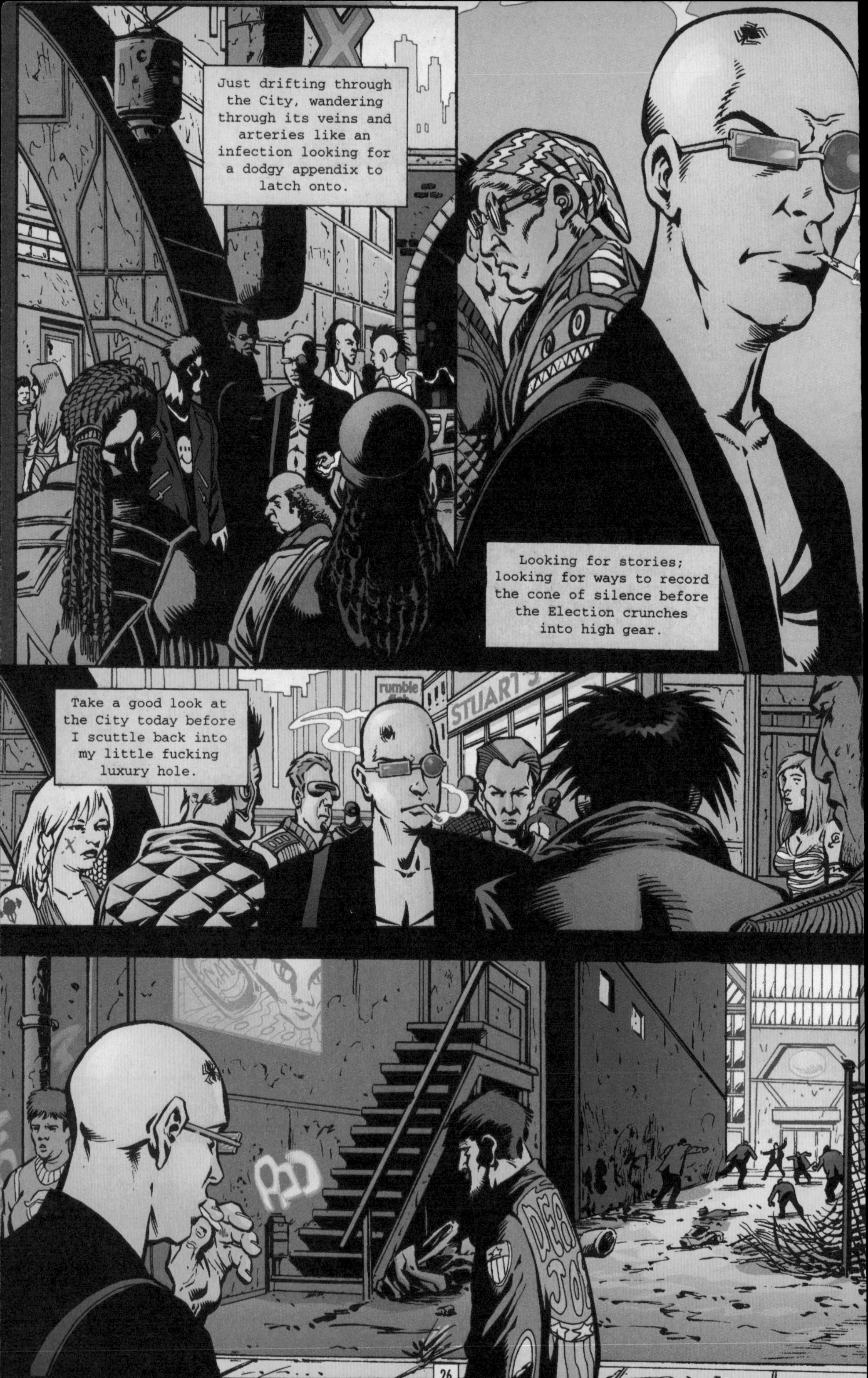
Just drifting through the City, wandering through its veins and arteries like an infection looking for a dodgy appendix to latch onto.
Looking for stories; looking for ways to record the cone of silence before the Election crunches into high gear.
rumble
STUART'S
Take a good look at the City today before I scuttle back into my little fucking luxury hole.

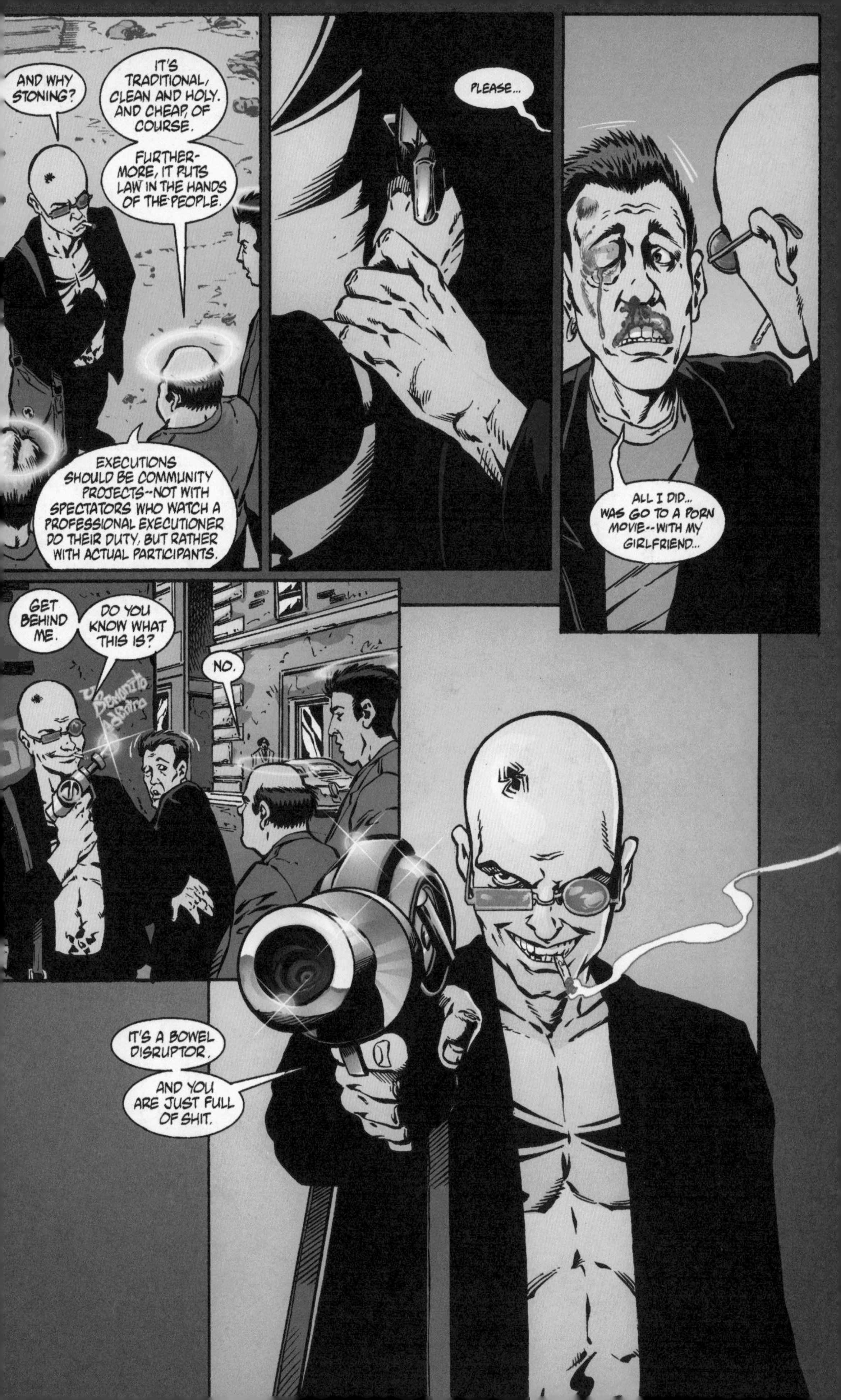
AND WHY STONING?
IT'S TRADITIONAL, CLEAN AND HOLY. AND CHEAP, OF COURSE.
FURTHER-MORE, IT PUTS LAW IN THE HANDS OF THE PEOPLE.
EXECUTIONS SHOULD BE COMMUNITY PROJECTS--NOT WITH SPECTATORS WHO WATCH A PROFESSIONAL EXECUTIONER DO THEIR DUTY, BUT RATHER WITH ACTUAL PARTICIPANTS.
PLEASE...
ALL I DID... WAS GO TO A PORN MOVIE--WITH MY GIRLFRIEND...
GET BEHIND ME.
DO YOU KNOW WHAT THIS IS?
NO.
IT'S A BOWEL DISRUPTOR.
AND YOU ARE JUST FULL OF SHIT.

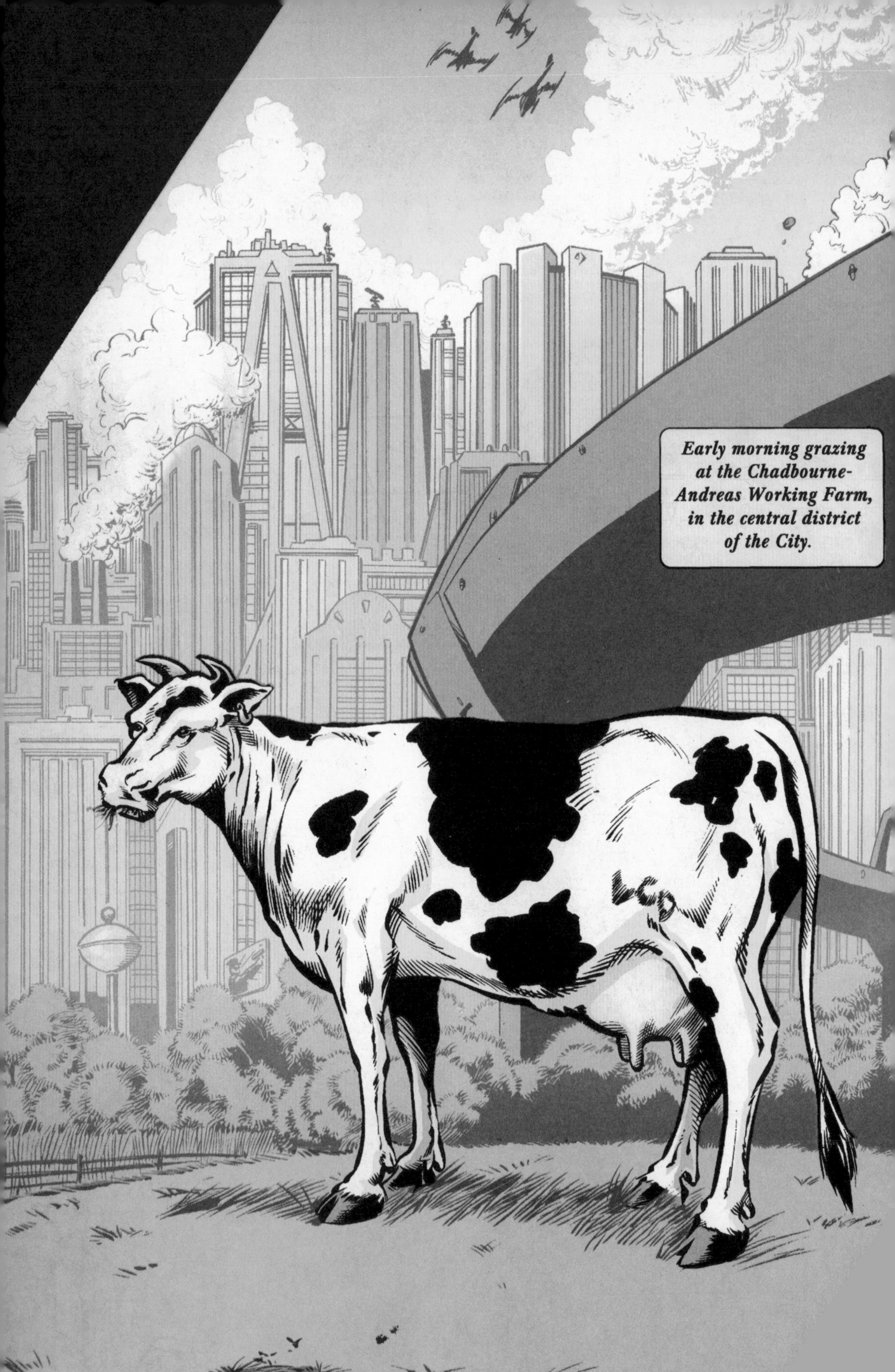
Early morning grazing at the Chadbourne-Andreas Working Farm, in the central district of the City.

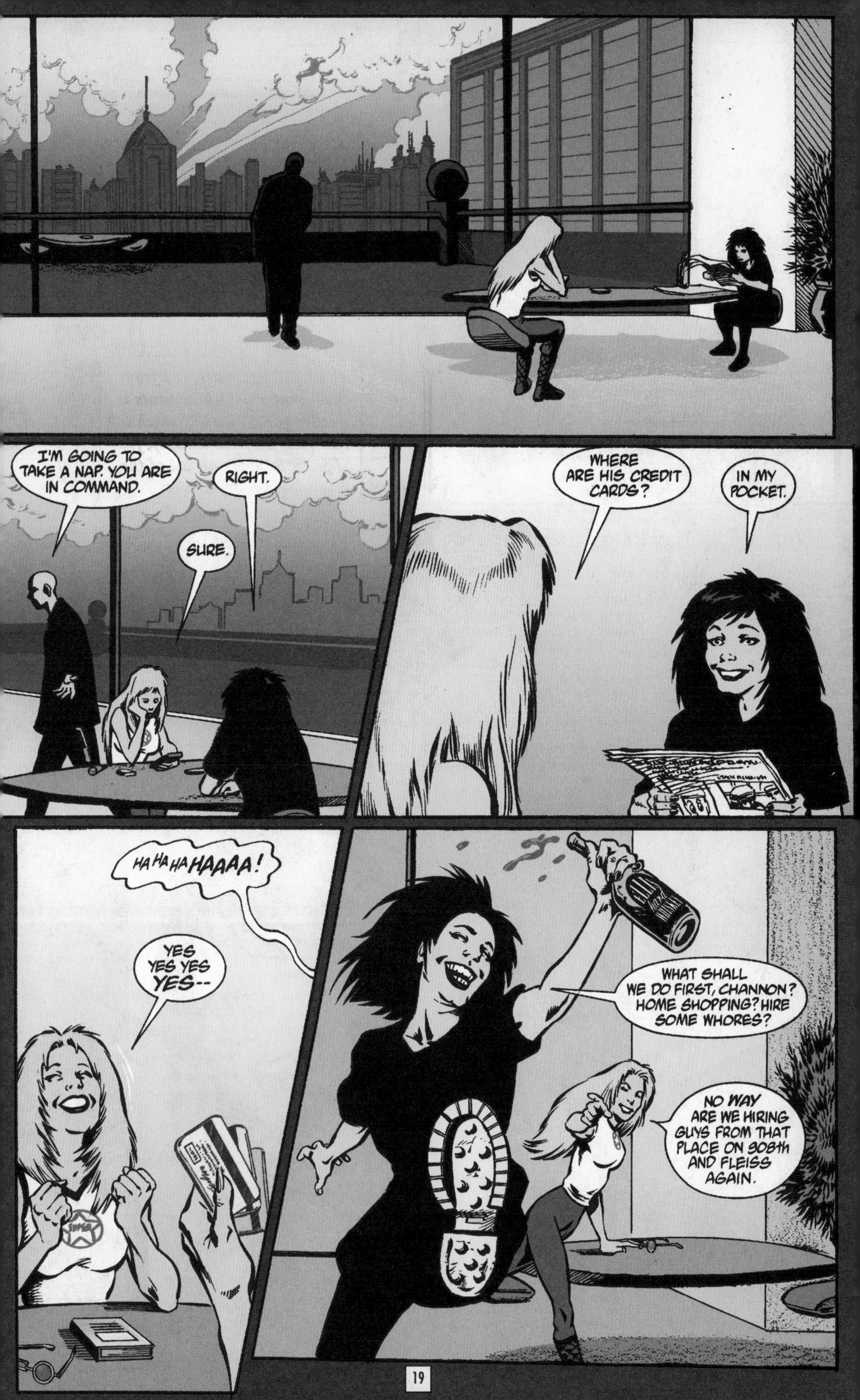
I'M GOING TO TAKE A NAP. YOU ARE IN COMMAND.
RIGHT.
SURE.
WHERE ARE HIS CREDIT CARDS?
IN MY POCKET.
HA HA HA HAAAA!
YES YES YES YES--
WHAT SHALL WE DO FIRST, CHANNON? HOME SHOPPING? HIRE SOME WHORES?
NO WAY ARE WE HIRING GUYS FROM THAT PLACE ON 908th AND FLEISS AGAIN.

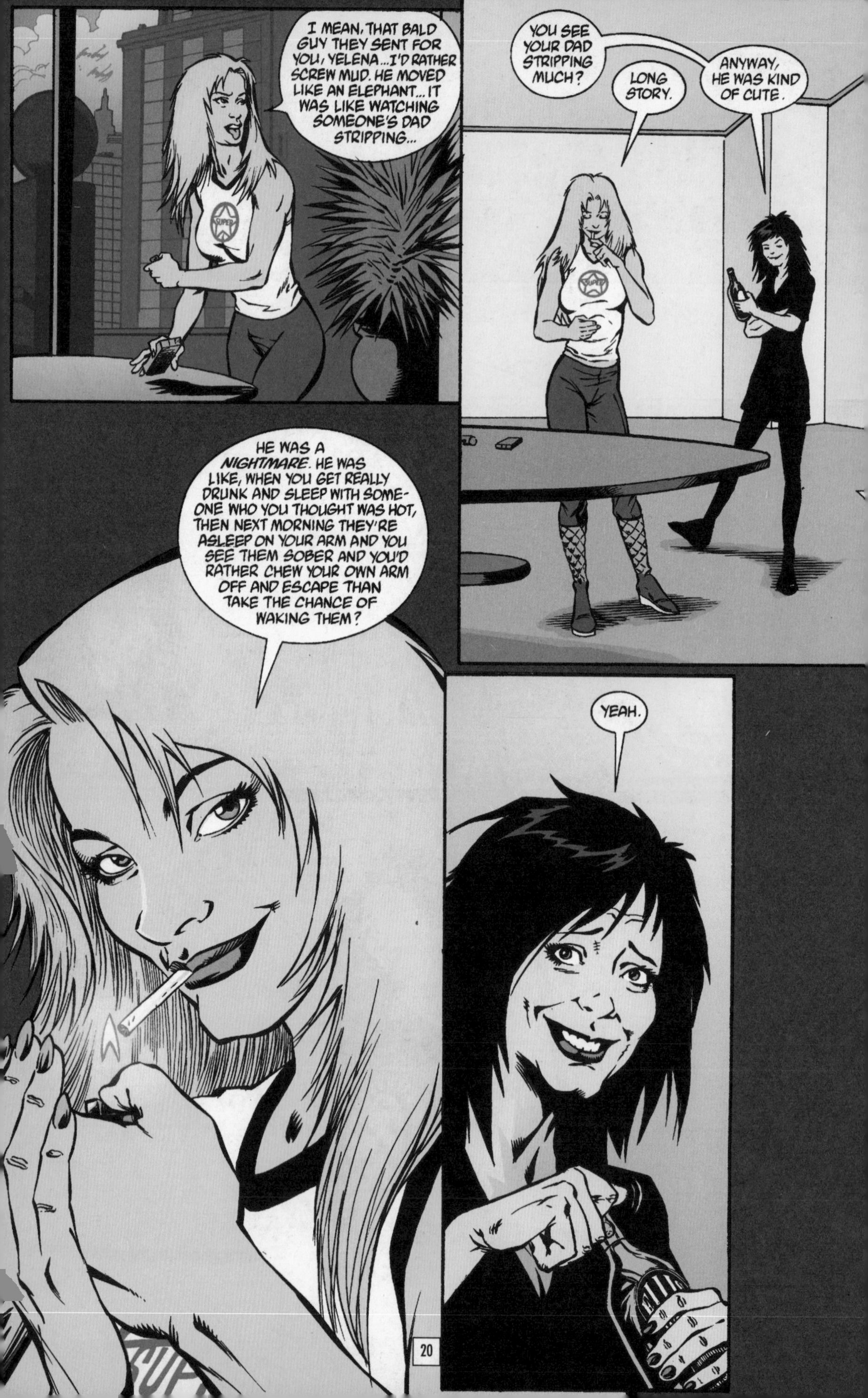
I MEAN, THAT BALD GUY THEY SENT FOR YOU, YELENA...I'D RATHER SCREW MUD. HE MOVED LIKE AN ELEPHANT... IT WAS LIKE WATCHING SOMEONE'S DAD STRIPPING...
YOU SEE YOUR DAD STRIPPING MUCH?
LONG STORY.
ANYWAY, HE WAS KIND OF CUTE.
HE WAS A NIGHTMARE. HE WAS LIKE, WHEN YOU GET REALLY DRUNK AND SLEEP WITH SOME-ONE WHO YOU THOUGHT WAS HOT, THEN NEXT MORNING THEY'RE ASLEEP ON YOUR ARM AND YOU SEE THEM SOBER AND YOU'D RATHER CHEW YOUR OWN ARM OFF AND ESCAPE THAN TAKE THE CHANCE OF WAKING THEM?
YEAH.

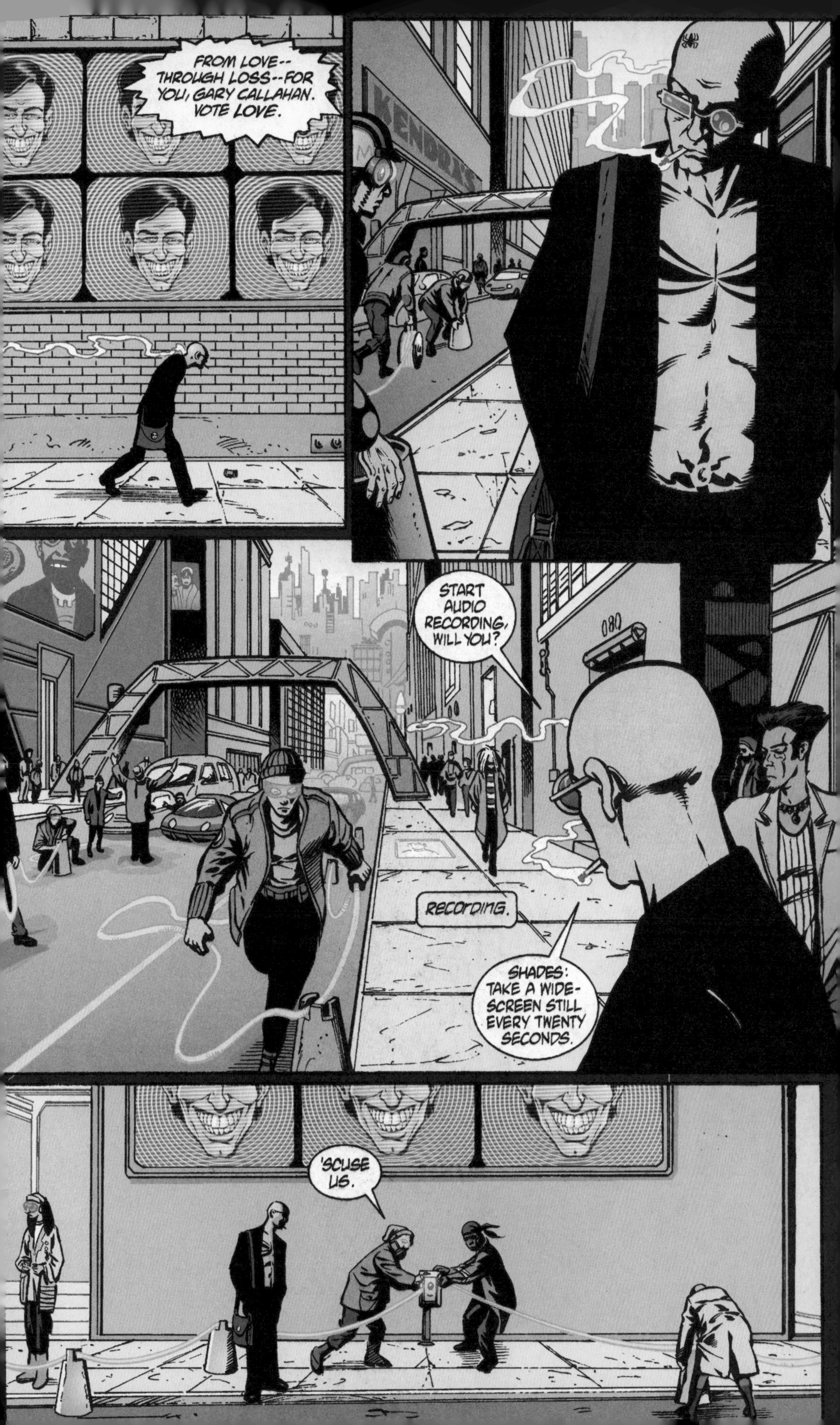
FROM LOVE--
THROUGH LOSS--FOR
YOU, GARY CALLAHAN.
VOTE LOVE.
START AUDIO RECORDING, WILL YOU?
RECORDING.
SHADES: TAKE A WIDE-SCREEN STILL EVERY TWENTY SECONDS.
'SCUSE US.

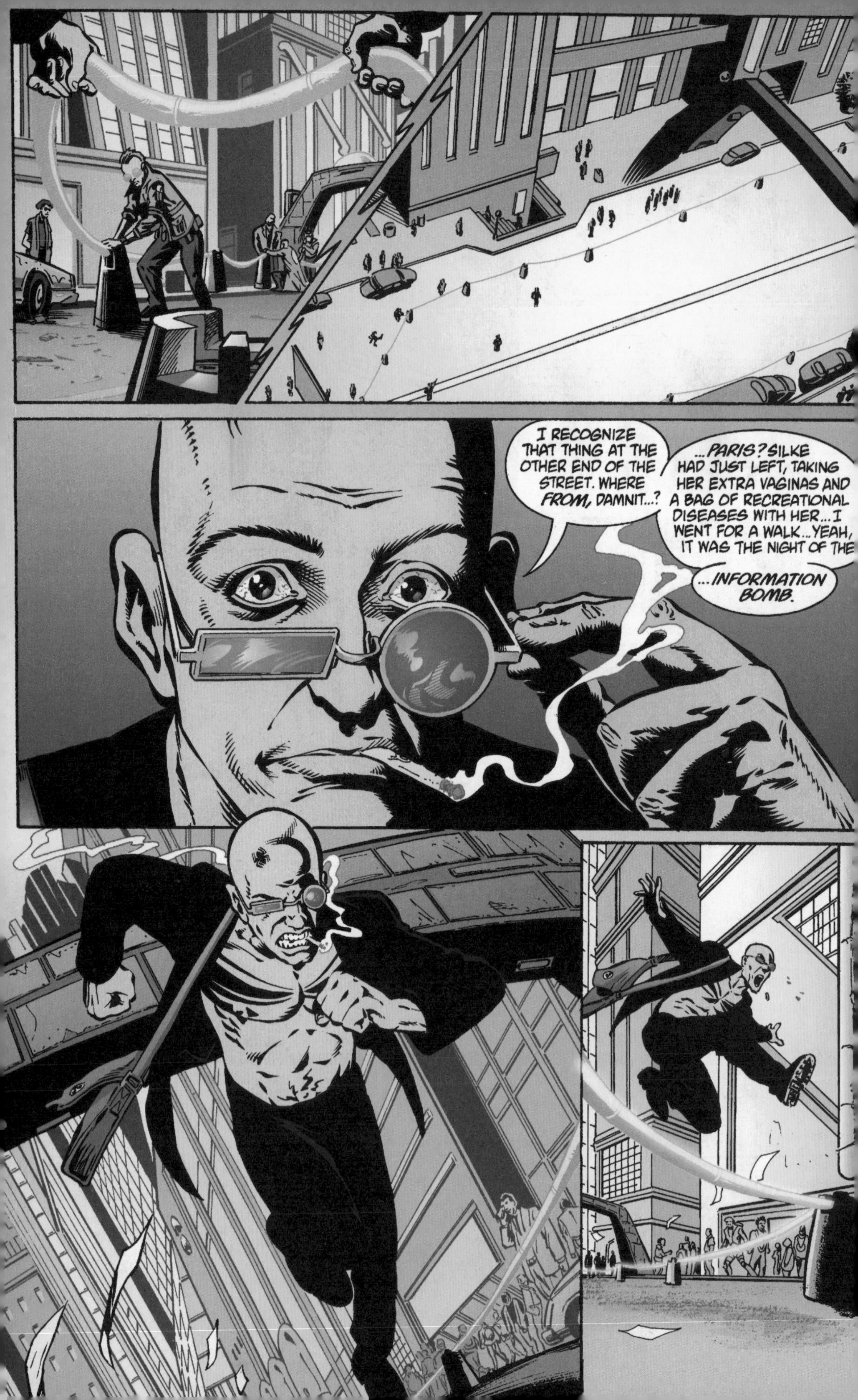
I RECOGNIZE THAT THING AT THE OTHER END OF THE STREET. WHERE *FROM,* DAMNIT...?
...*PARIS?* SILKE HAD JUST LEFT, TAKING HER EXTRA VAGINAS AND A BAG OF RECREATIONAL DISEASES WITH HER...I WENT FOR A WALK...YEAH, IT WAS THE NIGHT OF THE
...*INFORMATION BOMB.*

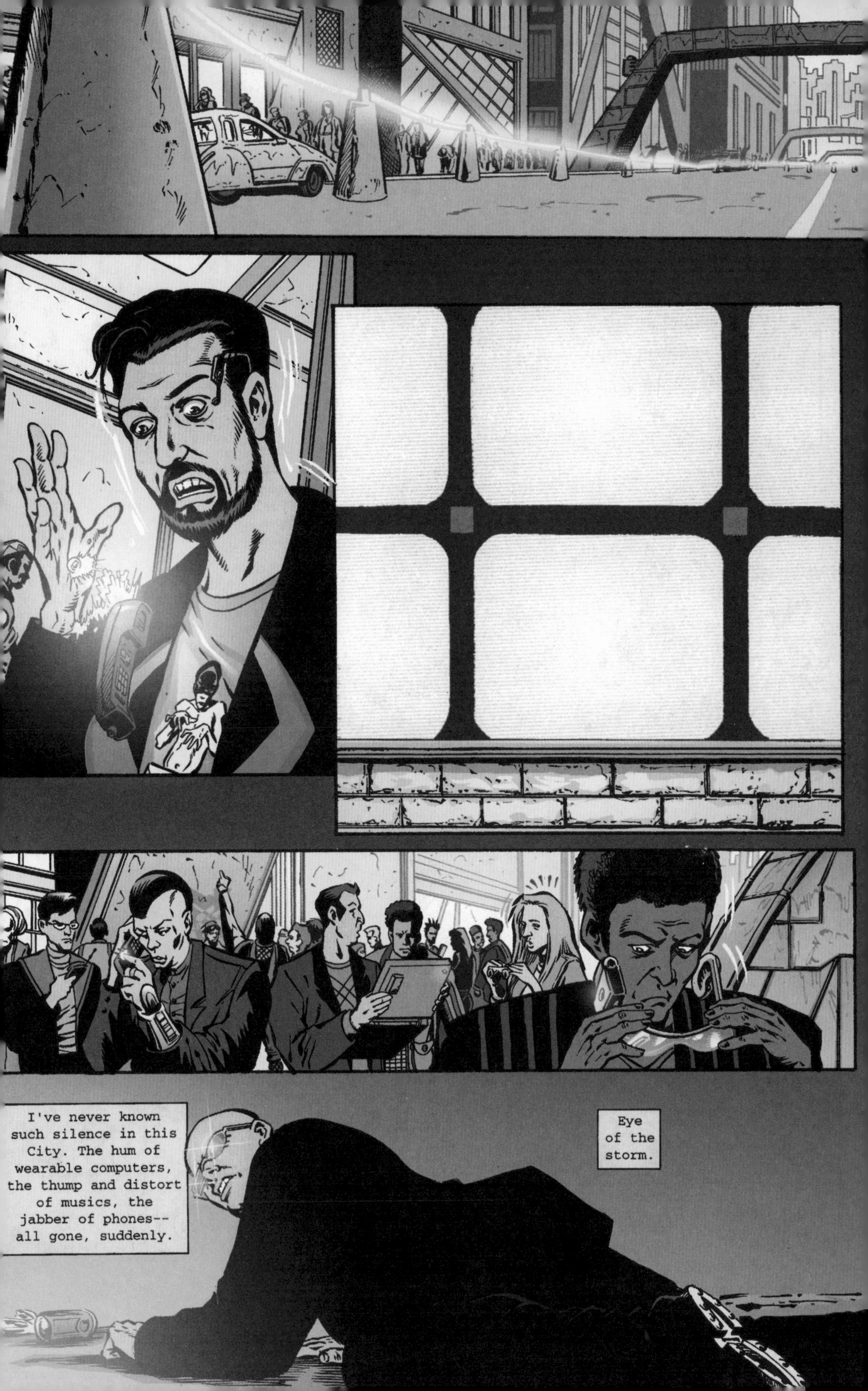
I've never known such silence in this City. The hum of wearable computers, the thump and distort of musics, the jabber of phones--all gone, suddenly.
Eye of the storm.

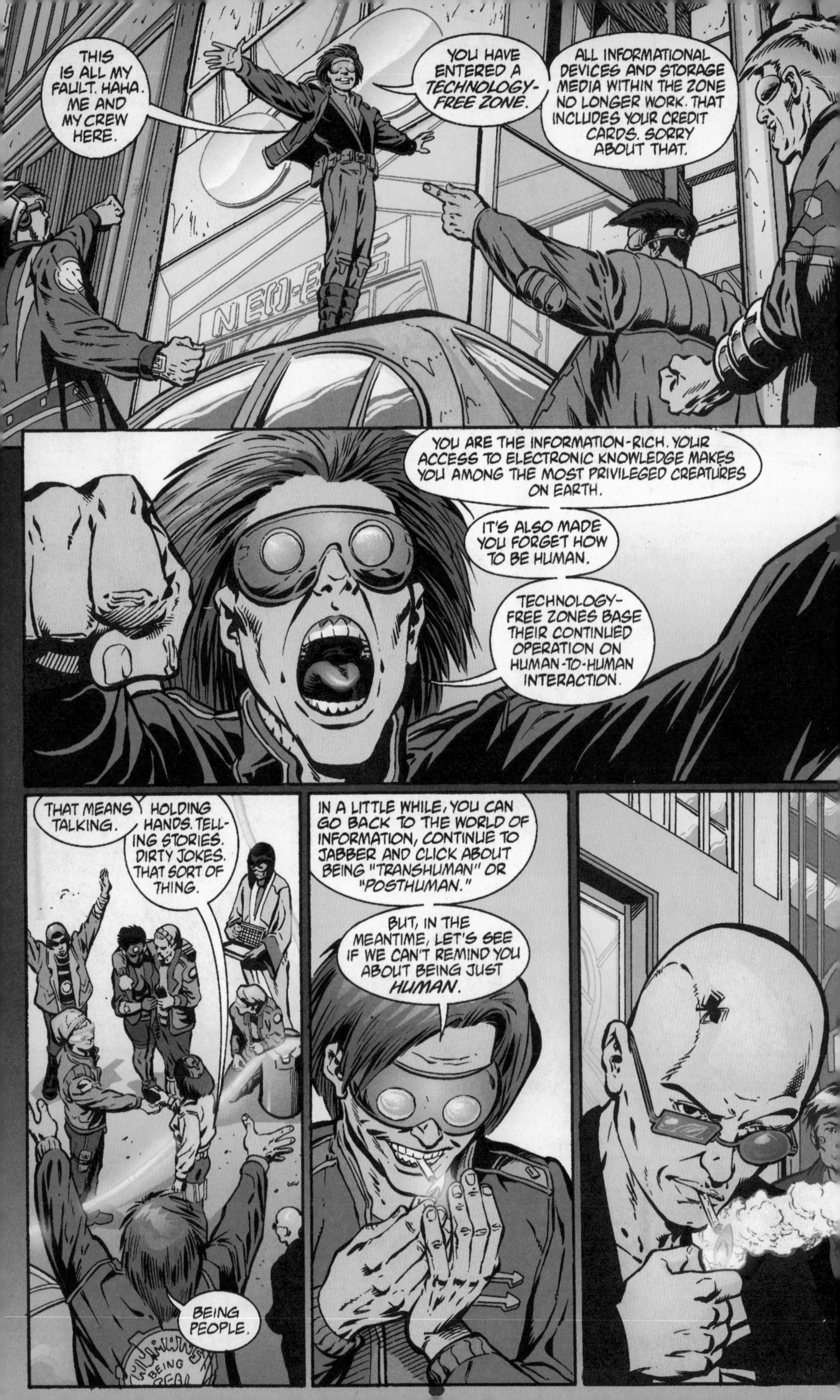
THIS IS ALL MY FAULT. HAHA. ME AND MY CREW HERE.
YOU HAVE ENTERED A TECHNOLOGY-FREE ZONE.
ALL INFORMATIONAL DEVICES AND STORAGE MEDIA WITHIN THE ZONE NO LONGER WORK. THAT INCLUDES YOUR CREDIT CARDS. SORRY ABOUT THAT.
YOU ARE THE INFORMATION-RICH. YOUR ACCESS TO ELECTRONIC KNOWLEDGE MAKES YOU AMONG THE MOST PRIVILEGED CREATURES ON EARTH.
IT'S ALSO MADE YOU FORGET HOW TO BE HUMAN.
TECHNOLOGY-FREE ZONES BASE THEIR CONTINUED OPERATION ON HUMAN-TO-HUMAN INTERACTION.
THAT MEANS TALKING.
HOLDING HANDS. TELLING STORIES. DIRTY JOKES. THAT SORT OF THING.
BEING PEOPLE.
IN A LITTLE WHILE, YOU CAN GO BACK TO THE WORLD OF INFORMATION, CONTINUE TO JABBER AND CLICK ABOUT BEING "TRANSHUMAN" OR "POSTHUMAN."
BUT, IN THE MEANTIME, LET'S SEE IF WE CAN'T REMIND YOU ABOUT BEING JUST HUMAN.

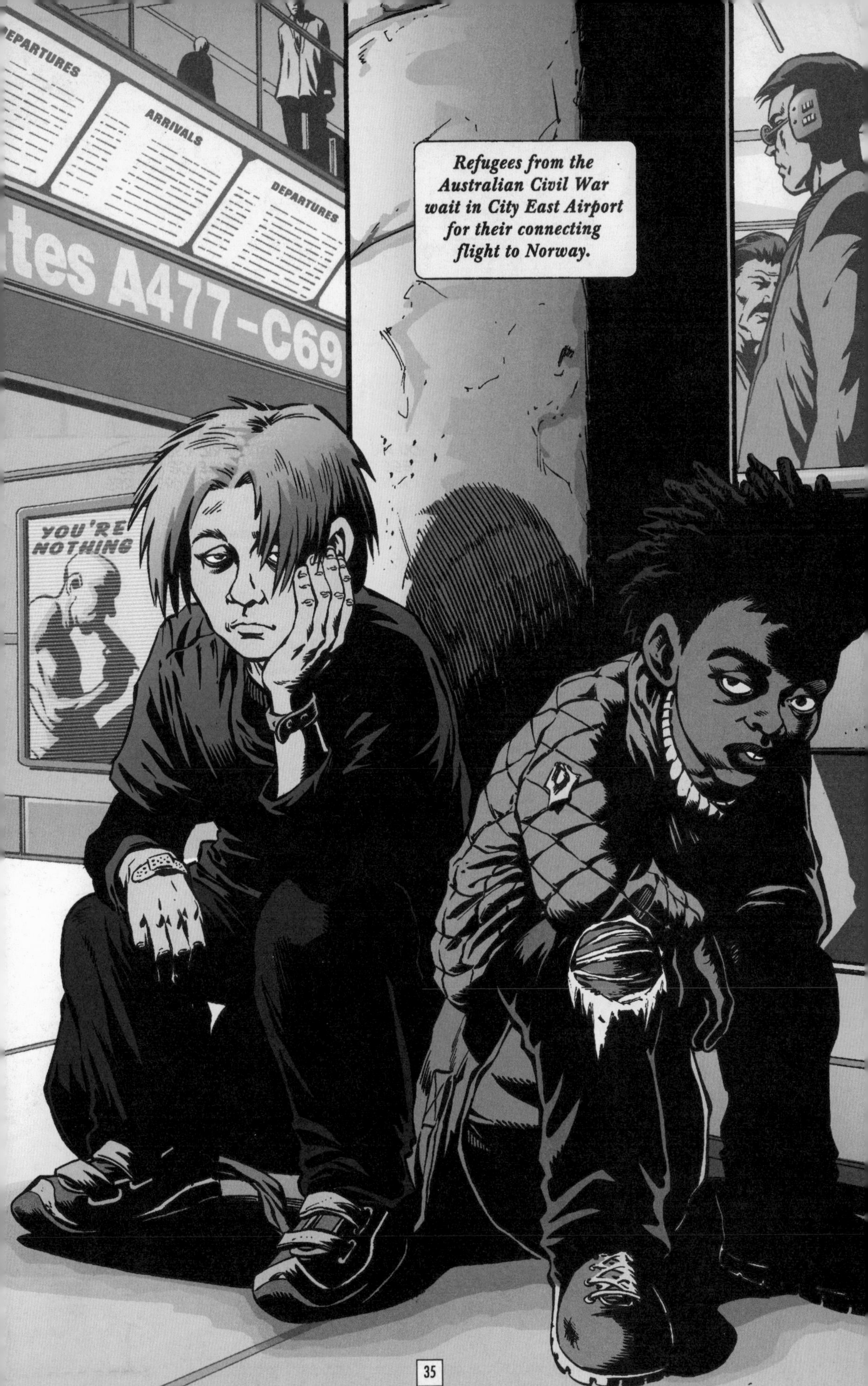

DEPARTURES
ARRIVALS
DEPARTURES
tes A477-C69
Refugees from the Australian Civil War wait in City East Airport for their connecting flight to Norway.
YOU'RE NOTHING

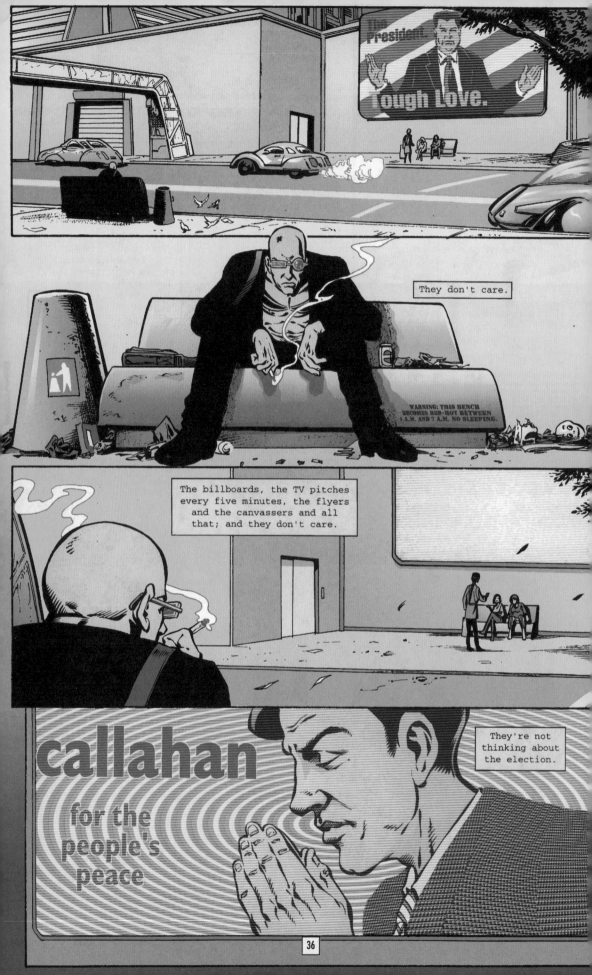

President. **Tough Love.**

They don't care.

WARNING: THIS BENCH BECOMES RED-HOT BETWEEN 4 A.M. AND 7 A.M. NO SLEEPING.

The billboards, the TV pitches every five minutes, the flyers and the canvassers and all that; and they don't care.

callahan
for the people's peace

They're not thinking about the election.

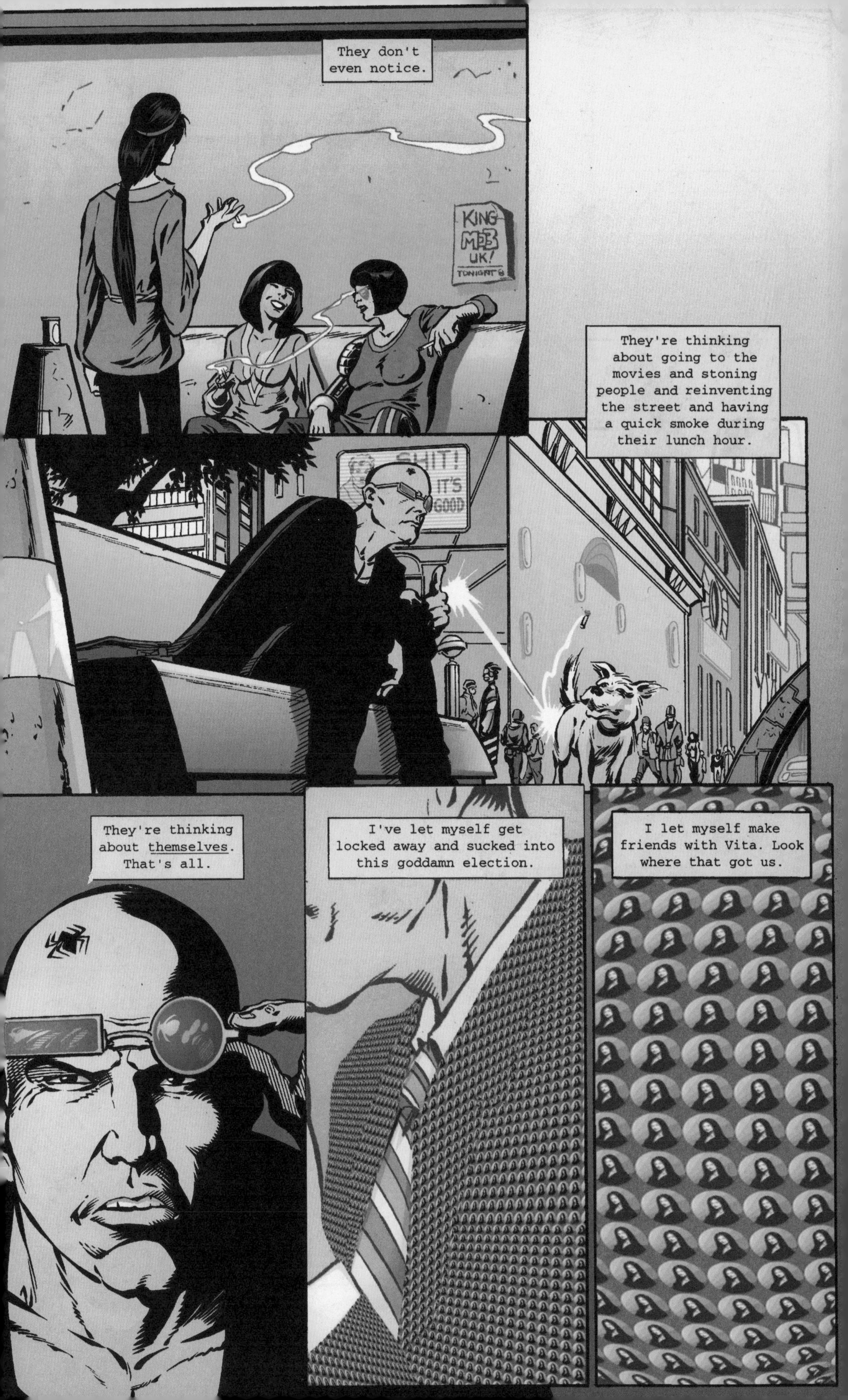
They don't even notice.
KING MB3 UK! TONIGHT
They're thinking about going to the movies and stoning people and reinventing the street and having a quick smoke during their lunch hour.
SHIT! IT'S GOOD
They're thinking about themselves. That's all.
I've let myself get locked away and sucked into this goddamn election.
I let myself make friends with Vita. Look where that got us.

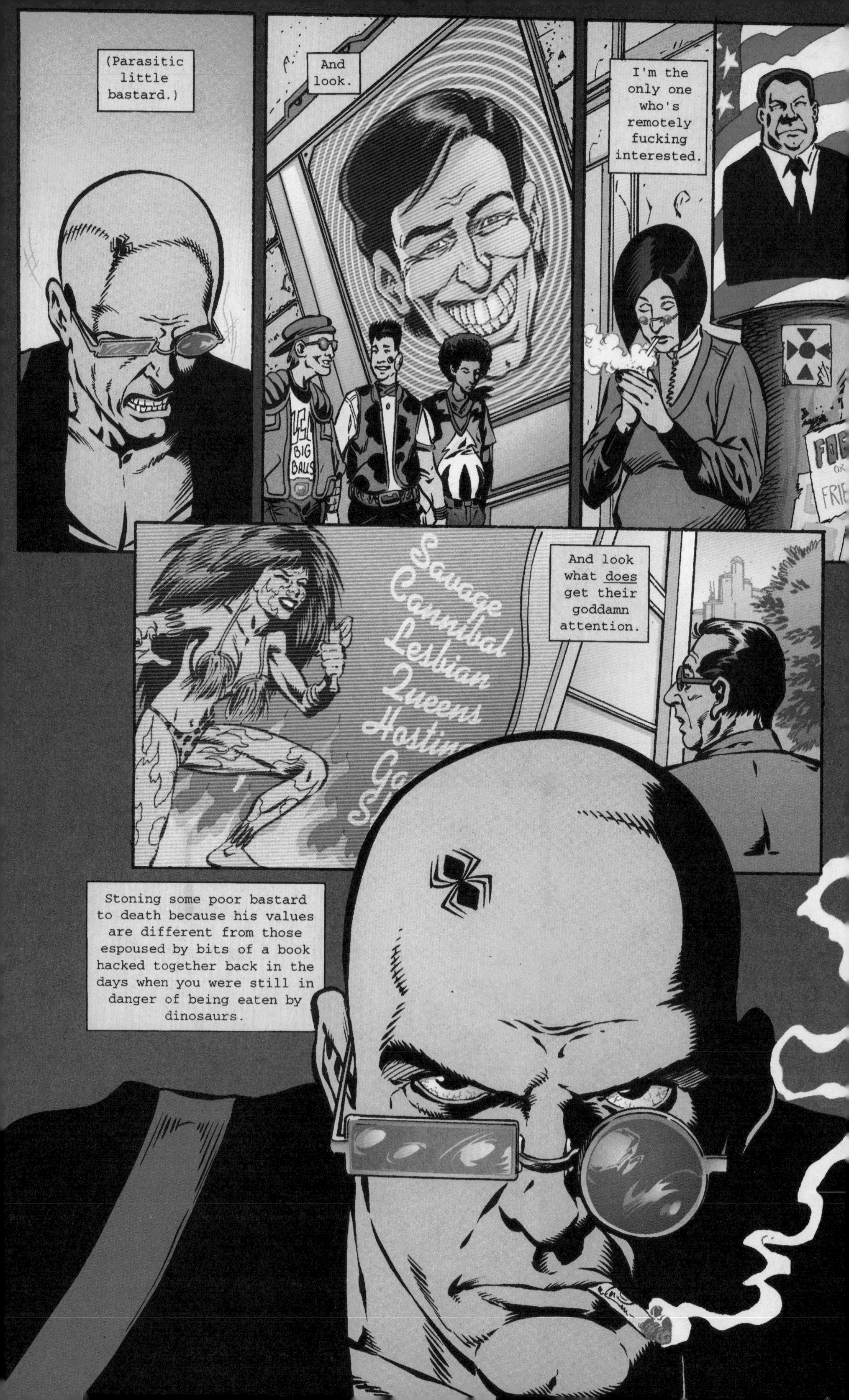
(Parasitic little bastard.)
And look.
BIG BALLS
I'm the only one who's remotely fucking interested.
And look what does get their goddamn attention.
Savage Cannibal Lesbian Queens Hostin
Stoning some poor bastard to death because his values are different from those espoused by bits of a book hacked together back in the days when you were still in danger of being eaten by dinosaurs.

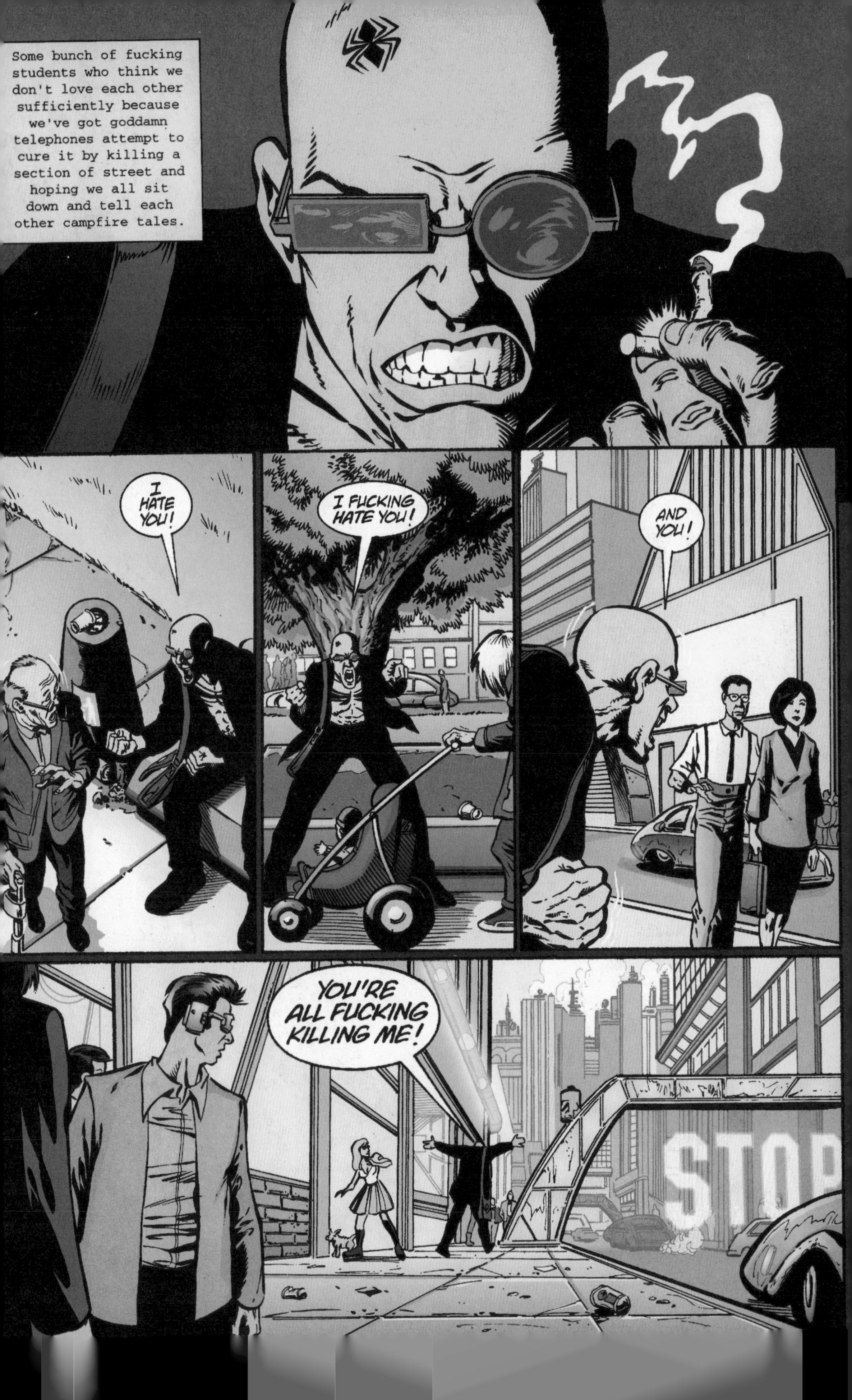
Some bunch of fucking students who think we don't love each other sufficiently because we've got goddamn telephones attempt to cure it by killing a section of street and hoping we all sit down and tell each other campfire tales.
I HATE YOU!
I FUCKING HATE YOU!
AND YOU!
YOU'RE ALL FUCKING KILLING ME!
STOP

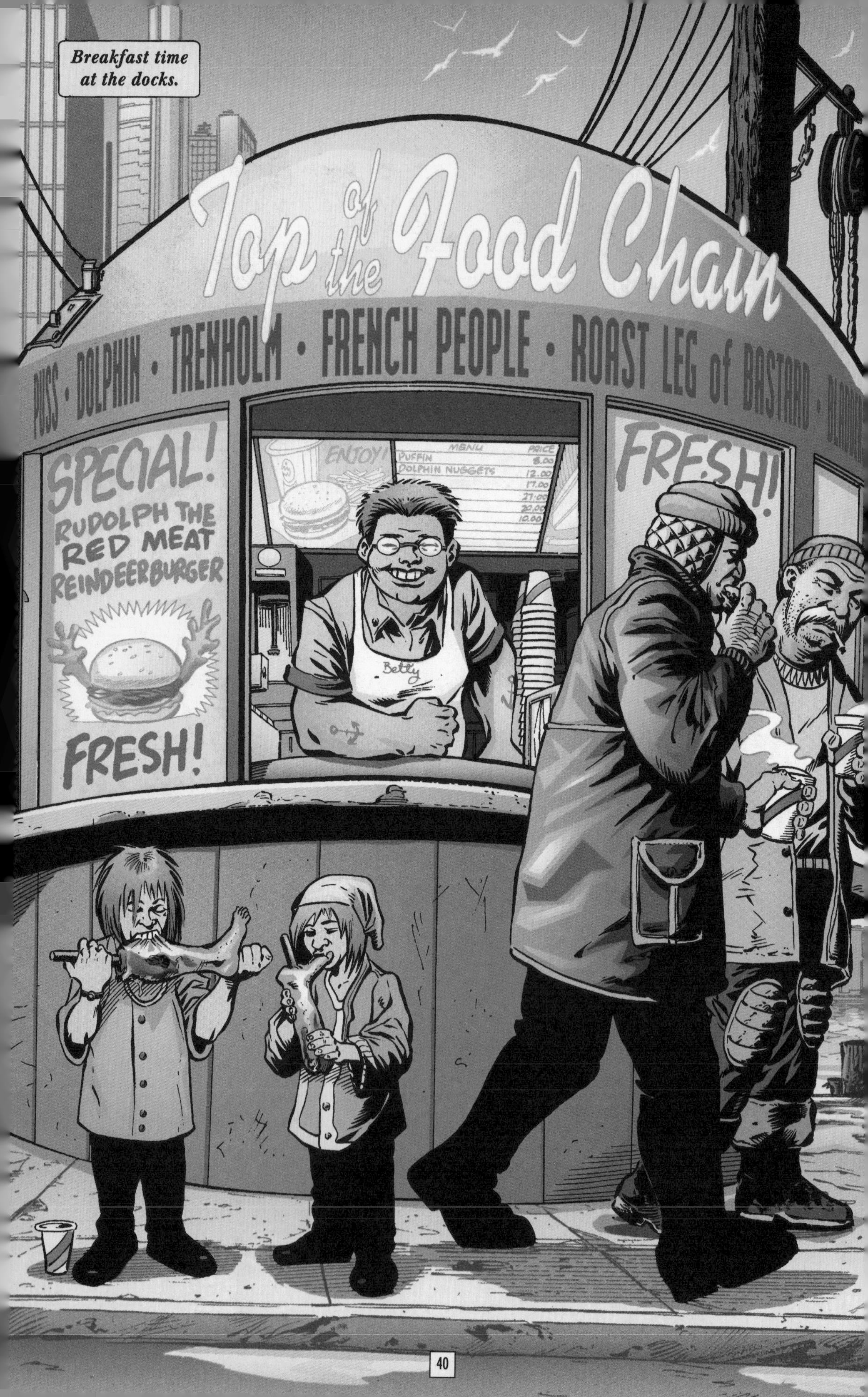
Breakfast time at the docks.
Top of the Food Chain
PUSS • DOLPHIN • TRENHOLM • FRENCH PEOPLE • ROAST LEG of BASTARD •
SPECIAL! RUDOLPH THE RED MEAT REINDEERBURGER FRESH!
ENJOY!
MENU PRICE
PUFFIN 8.00
DOLPHIN NUGGETS 12.00
17.00
27.00
20.00
10.00
FRESH!
Betty

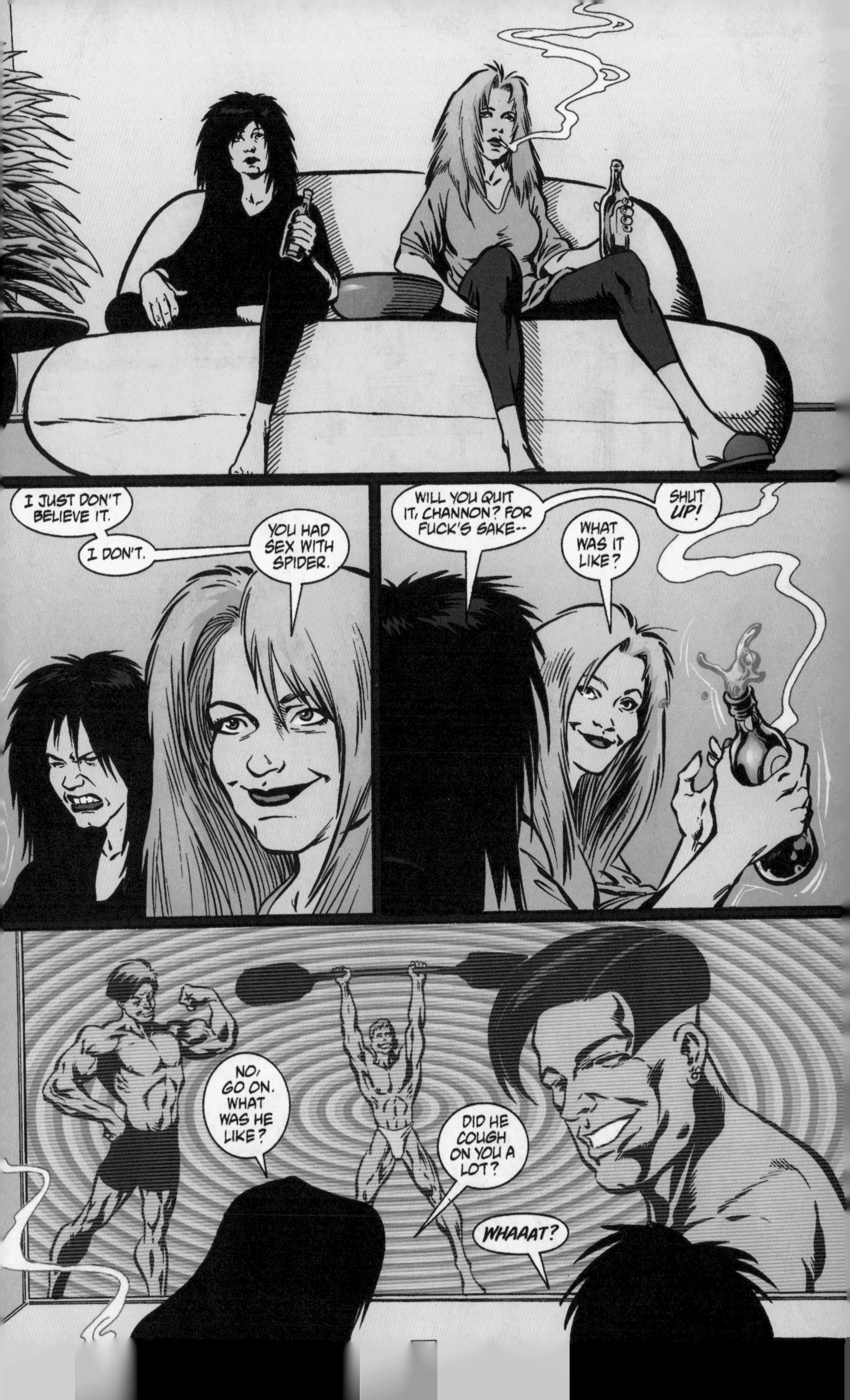
I JUST DON'T BELIEVE IT.
I DON'T.
YOU HAD SEX WITH SPIDER.
WILL YOU QUIT IT, CHANNON? FOR FUCK'S SAKE--
SHUT UP!
WHAT WAS IT LIKE?
NO, GO ON. WHAT WAS HE LIKE?
DID HE COUGH ON YOU A LOT?
WHAAAT?

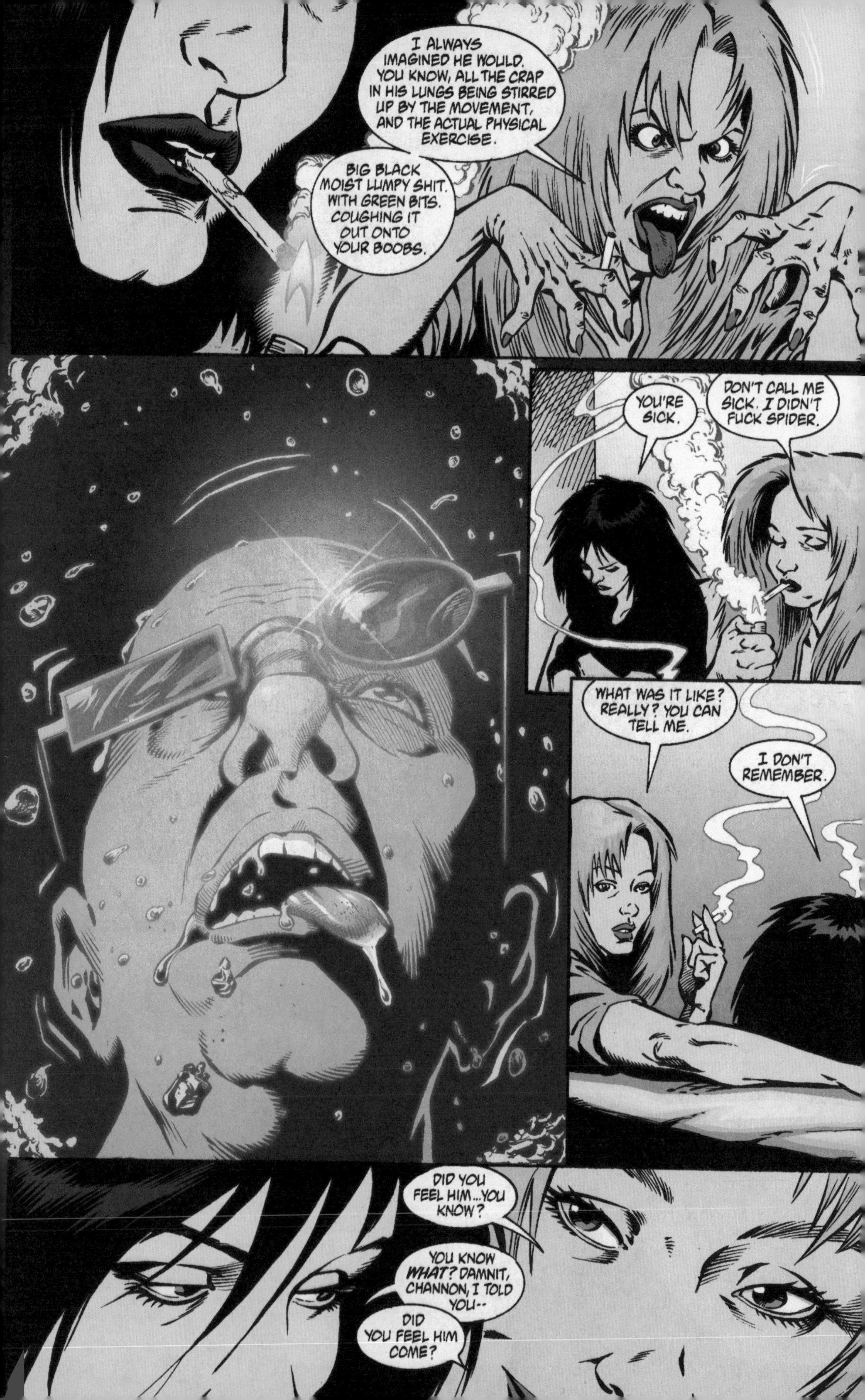
I ALWAYS IMAGINED HE WOULD. YOU KNOW, ALL THE CRAP IN HIS LUNGS BEING STIRRED UP BY THE MOVEMENT, AND THE ACTUAL PHYSICAL EXERCISE.
BIG BLACK MOIST LUMPY SHIT. WITH GREEN BITS. COUGHING IT OUT ONTO YOUR BOOBS.
YOU'RE SICK.
DON'T CALL ME SICK. I DIDN'T FUCK SPIDER.
WHAT WAS IT LIKE? REALLY? YOU CAN TELL ME.
I DON'T REMEMBER.
DID YOU FEEL HIM...YOU KNOW?
YOU KNOW WHAT? DAMNIT, CHANNON, I TOLD YOU--
DID YOU FEEL HIM COME?

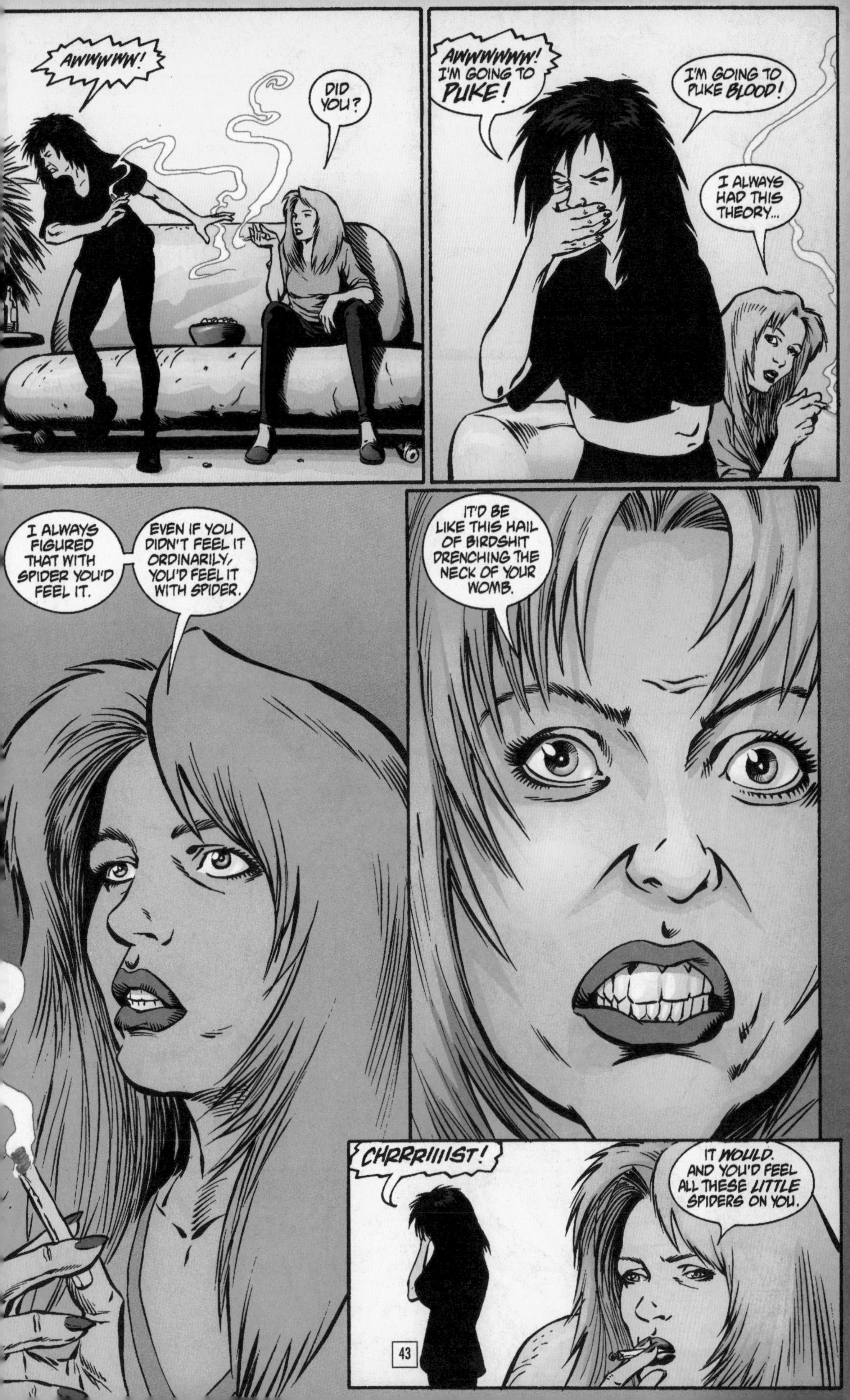
AWWWWW!
DID YOU?
AWWWWWW! I'M GOING TO PUKE!
I'M GOING TO PUKE BLOOD!
I ALWAYS HAD THIS THEORY...
I ALWAYS FIGURED THAT WITH SPIDER YOU'D FEEL IT.
EVEN IF YOU DIDN'T FEEL IT ORDINARILY, YOU'D FEEL IT WITH SPIDER.
IT'D BE LIKE THIS HAIL OF BIRDSHIT DRENCHING THE NECK OF YOUR WOMB.
CHRRRIIIIST!
IT WOULD. AND YOU'D FEEL ALL THESE LITTLE SPIDERS ON YOU.

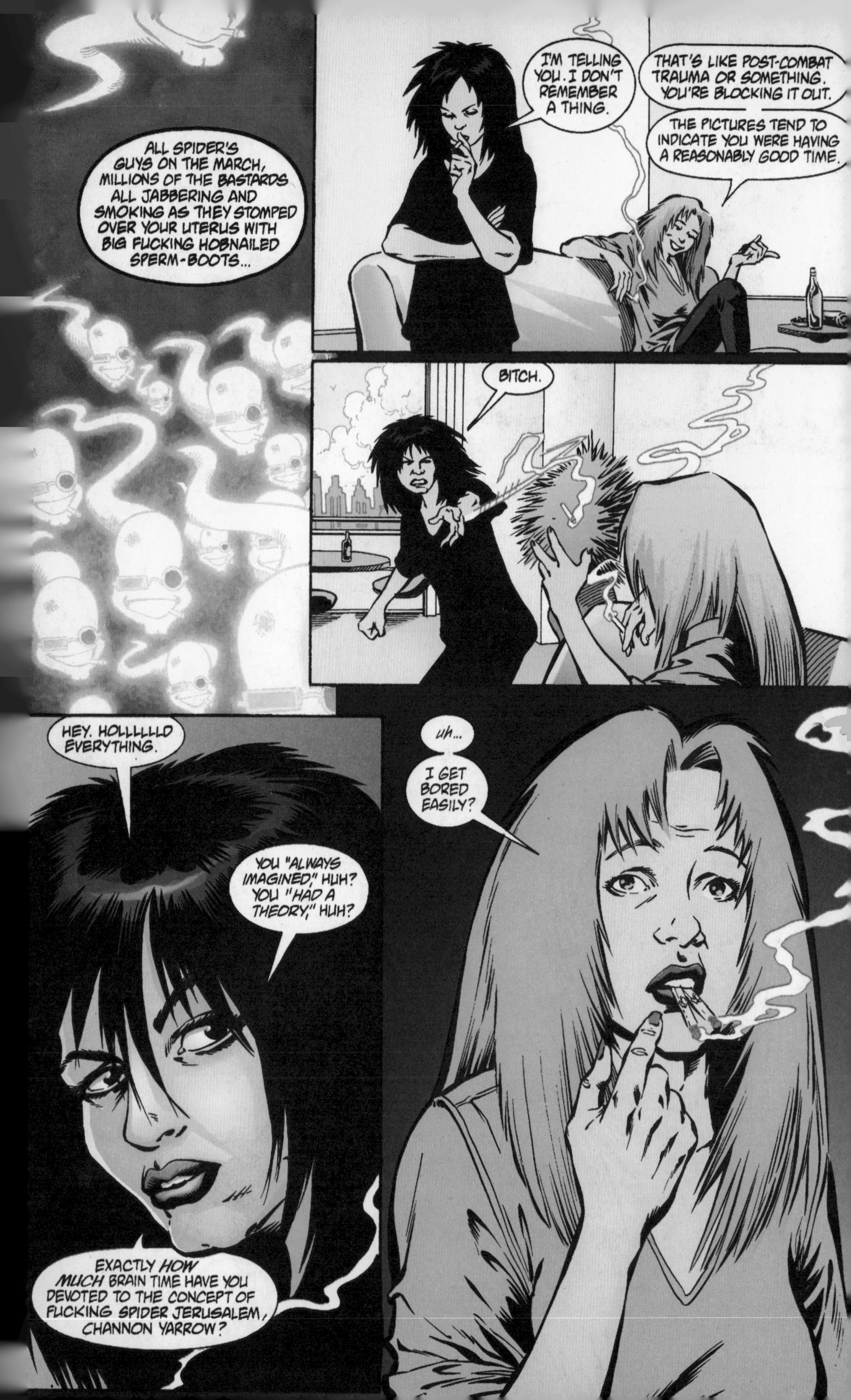
ALL SPIDER'S GUYS ON THE MARCH, MILLIONS OF THE BASTARDS ALL JABBERING AND SMOKING AS THEY STOMPED OVER YOUR UTERUS WITH BIG FUCKING HOBNAILED SPERM-BOOTS...
I'M TELLING YOU. I DON'T REMEMBER A THING.
THAT'S LIKE POST-COMBAT TRAUMA OR SOMETHING. YOU'RE BLOCKING IT OUT.
THE PICTURES TEND TO INDICATE YOU WERE HAVING A REASONABLY GOOD TIME.
BITCH.
HEY. HOLLLLLLD EVERYTHING.
YOU "ALWAYS IMAGINED," HUH? YOU "HAD A THEORY," HUH?
EXACTLY *HOW MUCH* BRAIN TIME HAVE YOU DEVOTED TO THE CONCEPT OF FUCKING SPIDER JERUSALEM, CHANNON YARROW?
uh...
I GET BORED EASILY?

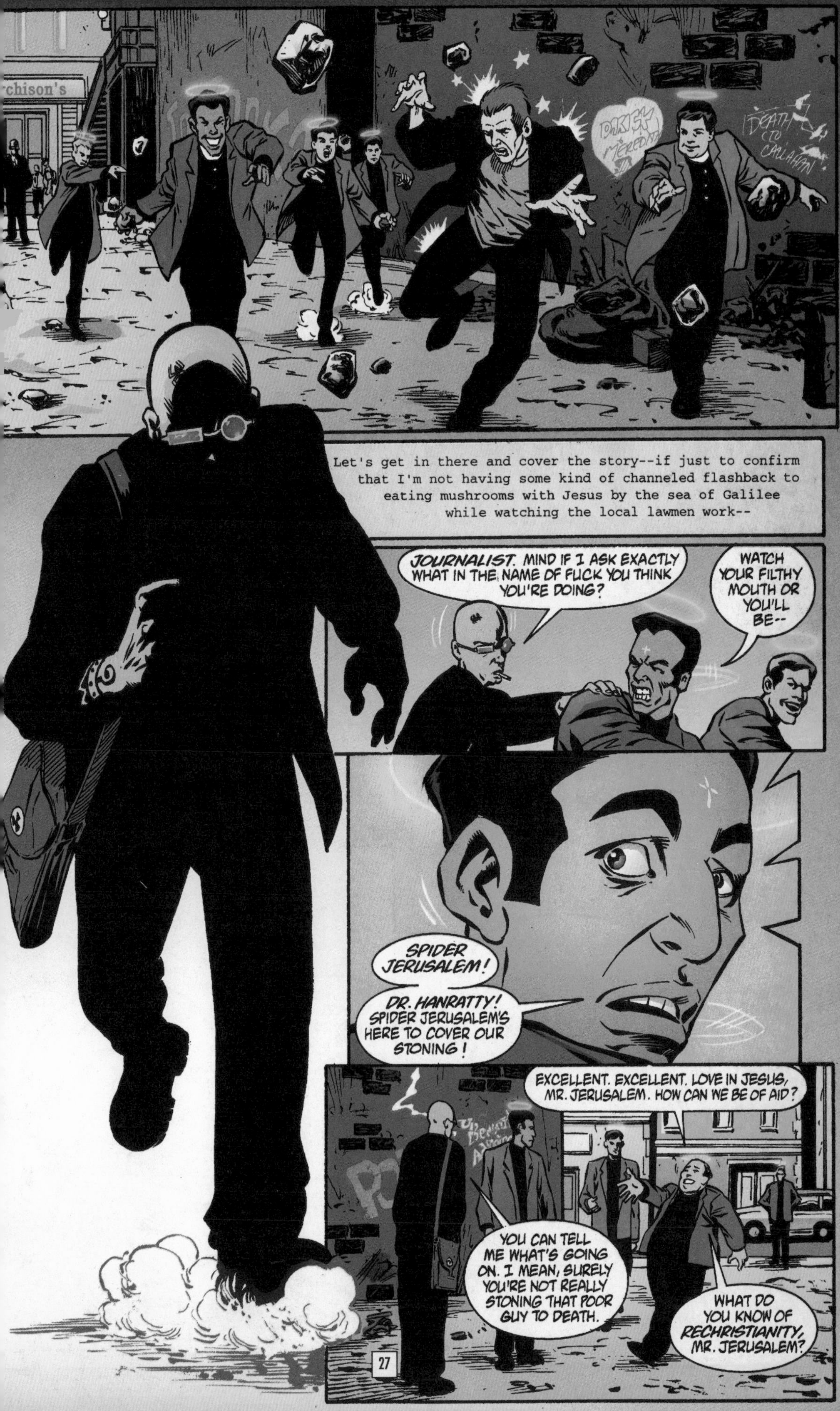

rchison's
DAREK & MEREDITH
DEATH TO CALLAHAN
Let's get in there and cover the story--if just to confirm that I'm not having some kind of channeled flashback to eating mushrooms with Jesus by the sea of Galilee while watching the local lawmen work--
JOURNALIST. MIND IF I ASK EXACTLY WHAT IN THE NAME OF FUCK YOU THINK YOU'RE DOING?
WATCH YOUR FILTHY MOUTH OR YOU'LL BE--
SPIDER JERUSALEM!
DR. HANRATTY! SPIDER JERUSALEM'S HERE TO COVER OUR STONING!
EXCELLENT. EXCELLENT. LOVE IN JESUS, MR. JERUSALEM. HOW CAN WE BE OF AID?
YOU CAN TELL ME WHAT'S GOING ON. I MEAN, SURELY YOU'RE NOT REALLY STONING THAT POOR GUY TO DEATH.
WHAT DO YOU KNOW OF RECHRISTIANITY, MR. JERUSALEM?

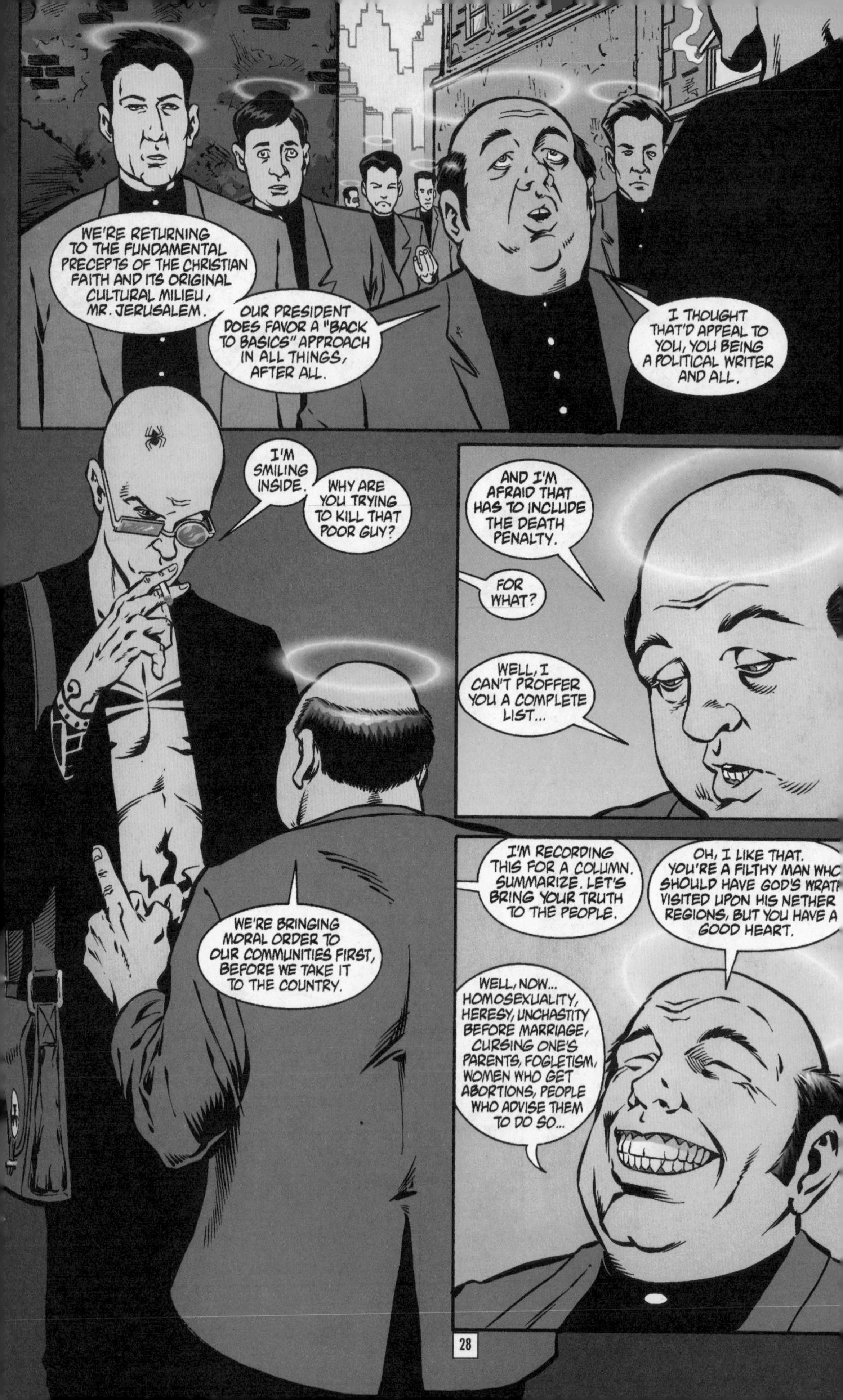
WE'RE RETURNING TO THE FUNDAMENTAL PRECEPTS OF THE CHRISTIAN FAITH AND ITS ORIGINAL CULTURAL MILIEU, MR. JERUSALEM.
OUR PRESIDENT DOES FAVOR A "BACK TO BASICS" APPROACH IN ALL THINGS, AFTER ALL.
I THOUGHT THAT'D APPEAL TO YOU, YOU BEING A POLITICAL WRITER AND ALL.
I'M SMILING INSIDE.
WHY ARE YOU TRYING TO KILL THAT POOR GUY?
WE'RE BRINGING MORAL ORDER TO OUR COMMUNITIES FIRST, BEFORE WE TAKE IT TO THE COUNTRY.
AND I'M AFRAID THAT HAS TO INCLUDE THE DEATH PENALTY.
FOR WHAT?
WELL, I CAN'T PROFFER YOU A COMPLETE LIST...
I'M RECORDING THIS FOR A COLUMN. SUMMARIZE. LET'S BRING YOUR TRUTH TO THE PEOPLE.
OH, I LIKE THAT. YOU'RE A FILTHY MAN WHO SHOULD HAVE GOD'S WRATH VISITED UPON HIS NETHER REGIONS, BUT YOU HAVE A GOOD HEART.
WELL, NOW... HOMOSEXUALITY, HERESY, UNCHASTITY BEFORE MARRIAGE, CURSING ONE'S PARENTS, FOGLETISM, WOMEN WHO GET ABORTIONS, PEOPLE WHO ADVISE THEM TO DO SO...

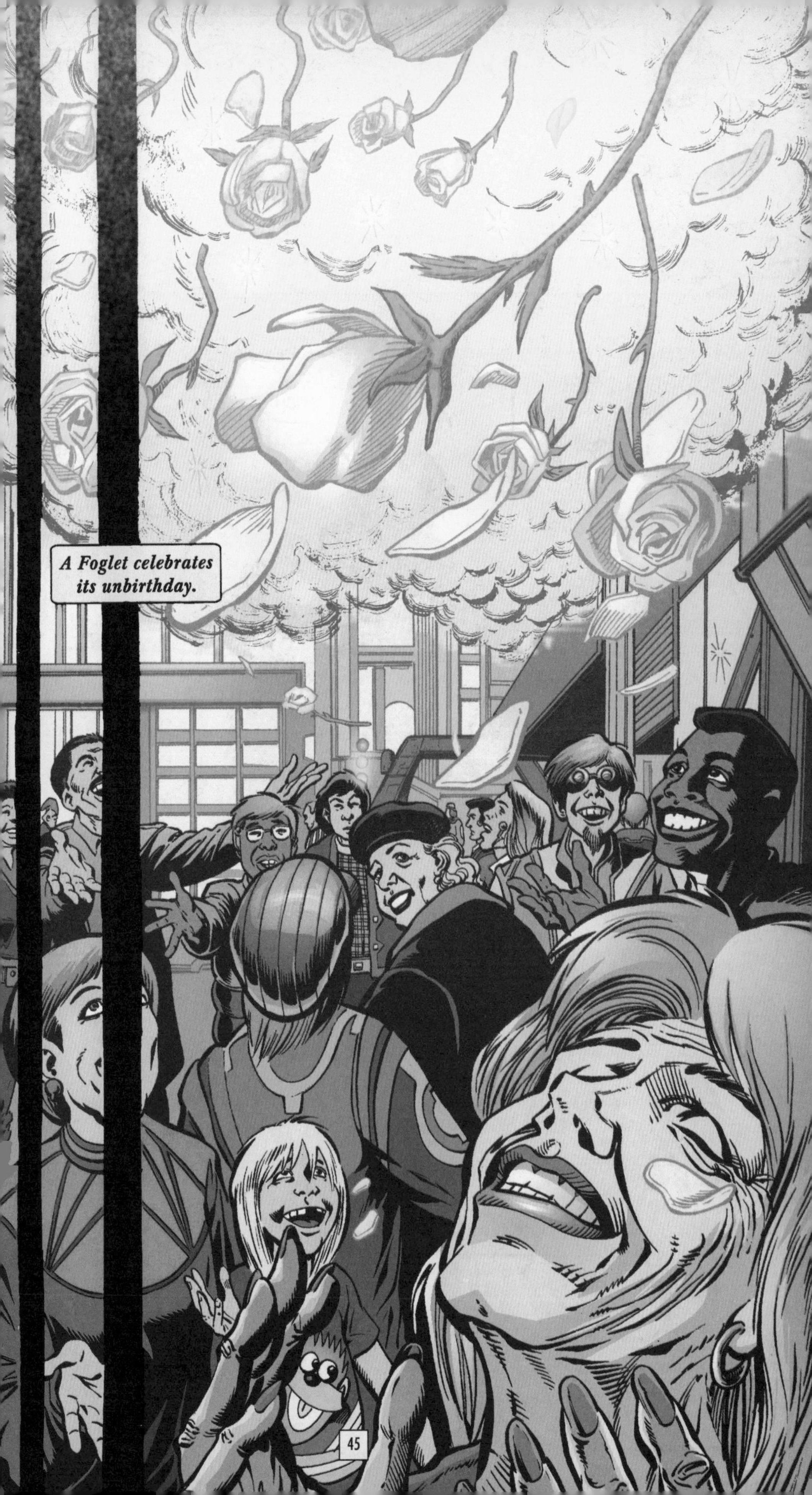
A Foglet celebrates its unbirthday.

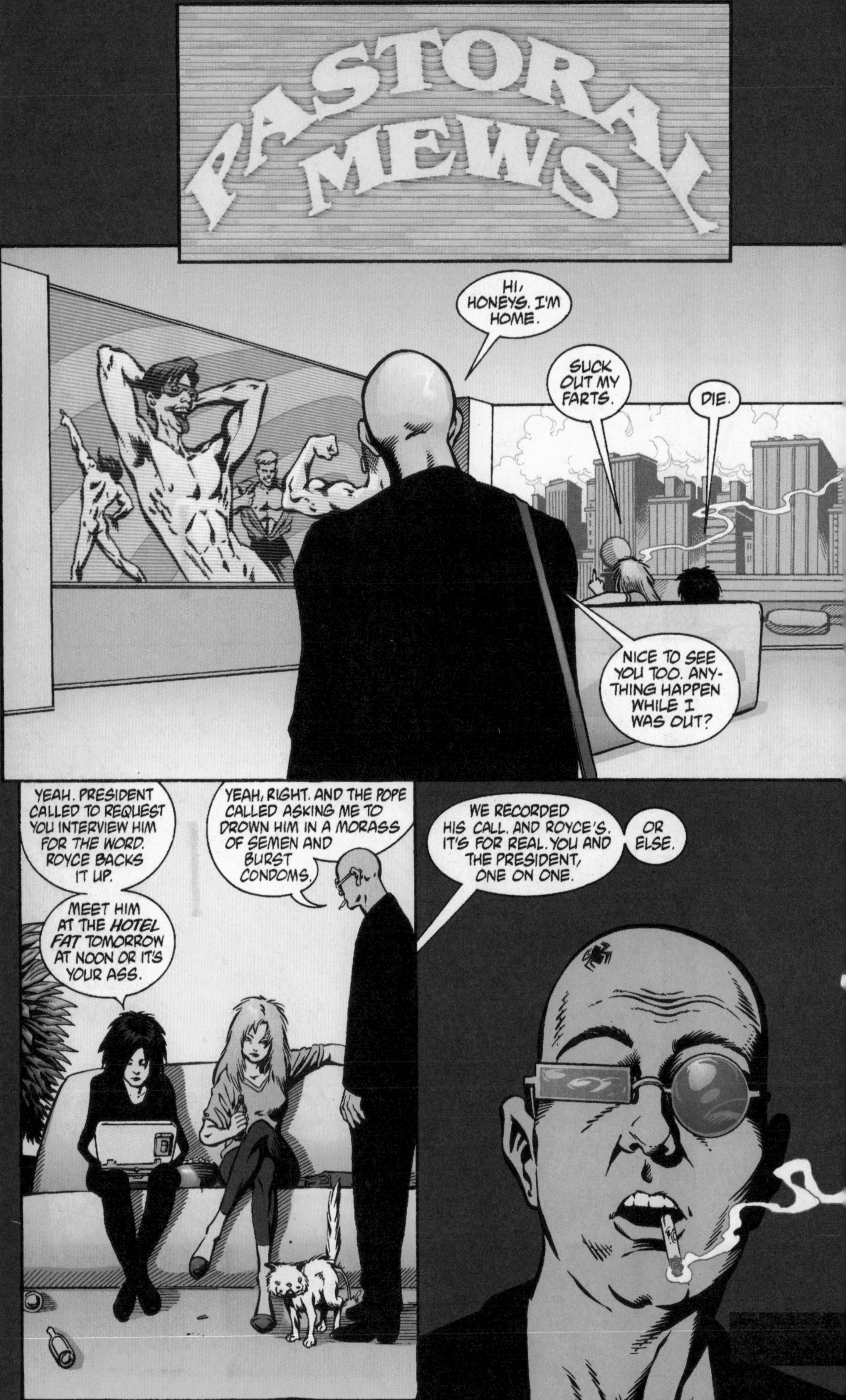
PASTORAL MEWS
HI, HONEYS. I'M HOME.
SUCK OUT MY FARTS.
DIE.
NICE TO SEE YOU TOO. ANYTHING HAPPEN WHILE I WAS OUT?
YEAH. PRESIDENT CALLED TO REQUEST YOU INTERVIEW HIM FOR THE WORD. ROYCE BACKS IT UP.
MEET HIM AT THE *HOTEL FAT* TOMORROW AT NOON OR IT'S YOUR ASS.
YEAH, RIGHT. AND THE POPE CALLED ASKING ME TO DROWN HIM IN A MORASS OF SEMEN AND BURST CONDOMS.
WE RECORDED HIS CALL. AND ROYCE'S. IT'S FOR REAL. YOU AND THE PRESIDENT, ONE ON ONE.
OR ELSE.

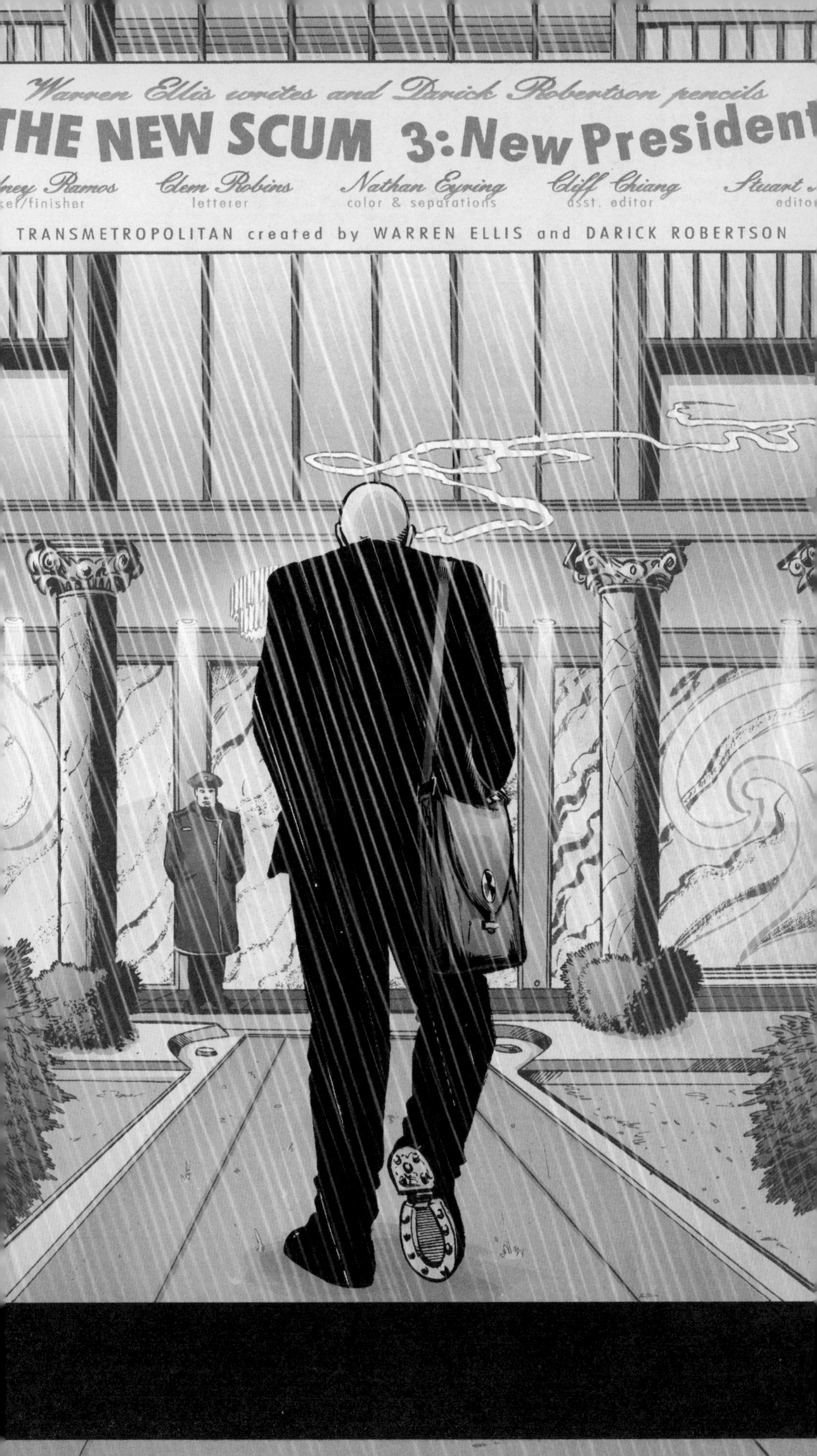
Warren Ellis writes and Darick Robertson pencils
THE NEW SCUM 3: New Presiden
ney Ramos
cer/finisher
Clem Robins
letterer
Nathan Eyring
color & separations
Cliff Chiang
asst. editor
Stuart
edito
TRANSMETROPOLITAN created by WARREN ELLIS and DARICK ROBERTSON

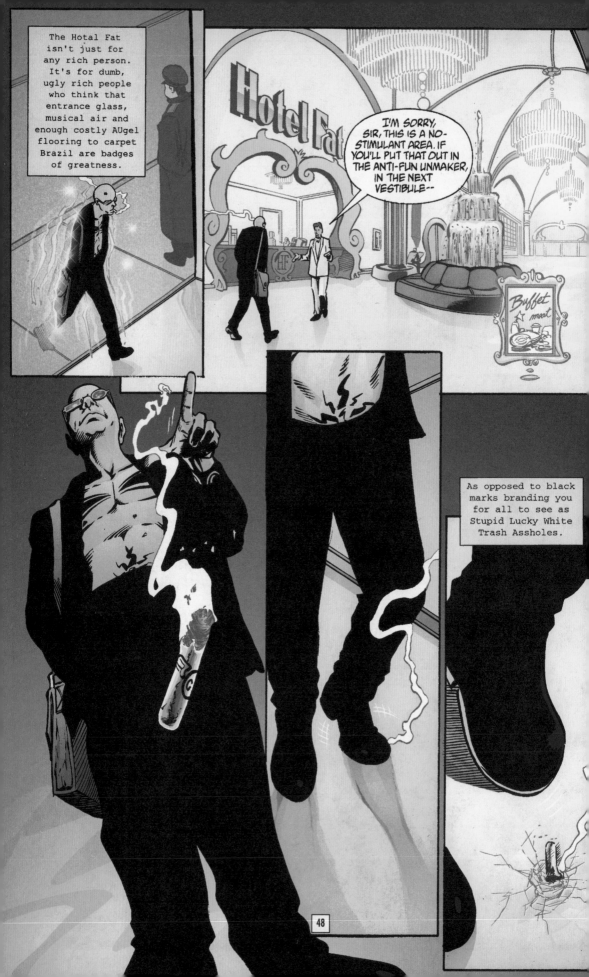

The Hotal Fat isn't just for any rich person. It's for dumb, ugly rich people who think that entrance glass, musical air and enough costly AUgel flooring to carpet Brazil are badges of greatness.

I'M SORRY, SIR, THIS IS A NO-STIMULANT AREA. IF YOU'LL PUT THAT OUT IN THE ANTI-FUN UNMAKER, IN THE NEXT VESTIBULE--

Buffet meat

As opposed to black marks branding you for all to see as Stupid Lucky White Trash Assholes.

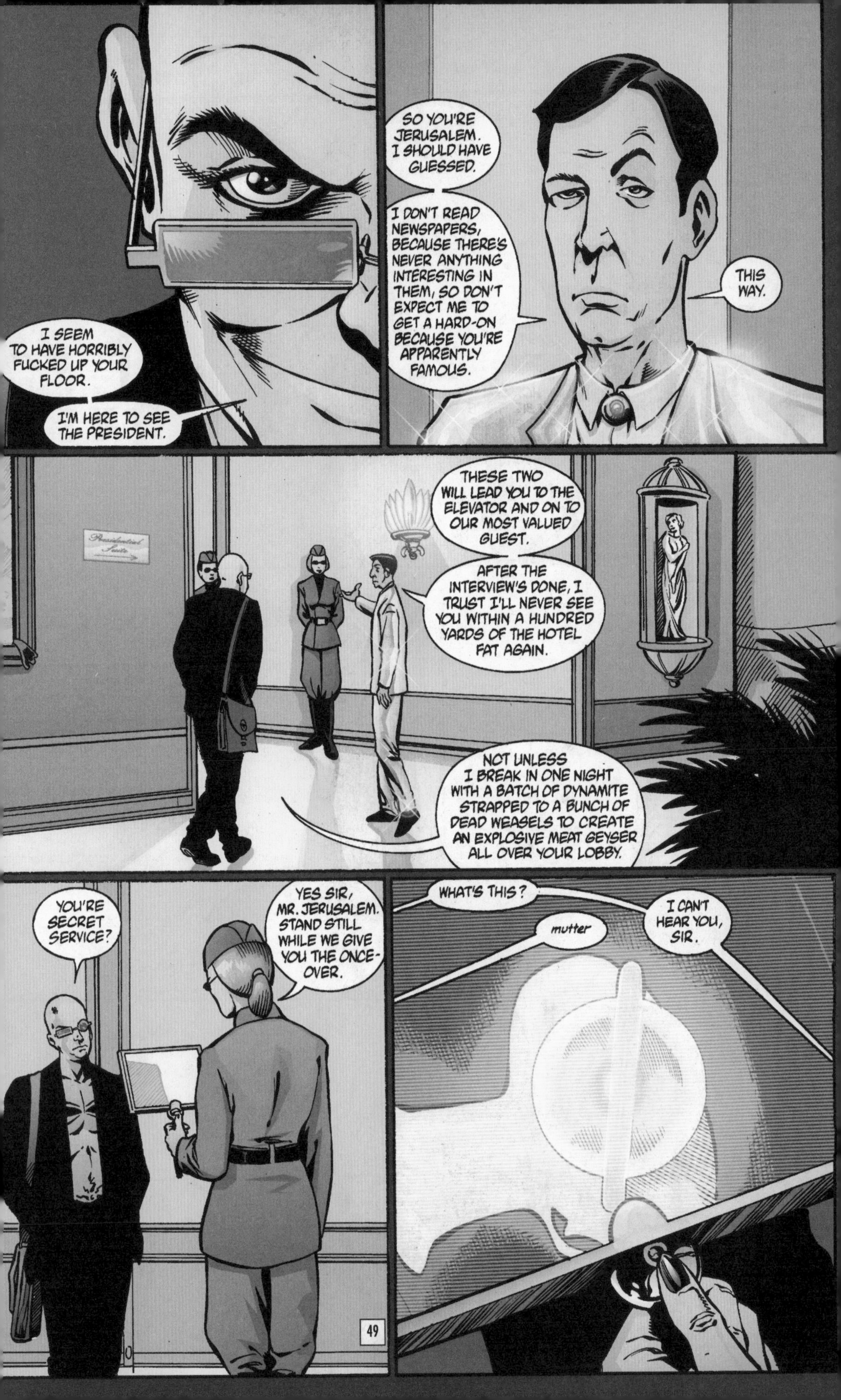
I SEEM TO HAVE HORRIBLY FUCKED UP YOUR FLOOR.
I'M HERE TO SEE THE PRESIDENT.
SO YOU'RE JERUSALEM. I SHOULD HAVE GUESSED.
I DON'T READ NEWSPAPERS, BECAUSE THERE'S NEVER ANYTHING INTERESTING IN THEM, SO DON'T EXPECT ME TO GET A HARD-ON BECAUSE YOU'RE APPARENTLY FAMOUS.
THIS WAY.
THESE TWO WILL LEAD YOU TO THE ELEVATOR AND ON TO OUR MOST VALUED GUEST.
AFTER THE INTERVIEW'S DONE, I TRUST I'LL NEVER SEE YOU WITHIN A HUNDRED YARDS OF THE HOTEL FAT AGAIN.
NOT UNLESS I BREAK IN ONE NIGHT WITH A BATCH OF DYNAMITE STRAPPED TO A BUNCH OF DEAD WEASELS TO CREATE AN EXPLOSIVE MEAT GEYSER ALL OVER YOUR LOBBY.
YOU'RE SECRET SERVICE?
YES SIR, MR. JERUSALEM. STAND STILL WHILE WE GIVE YOU THE ONCE-OVER.
WHAT'S THIS?
mutter
I CAN'T HEAR YOU, SIR.
49

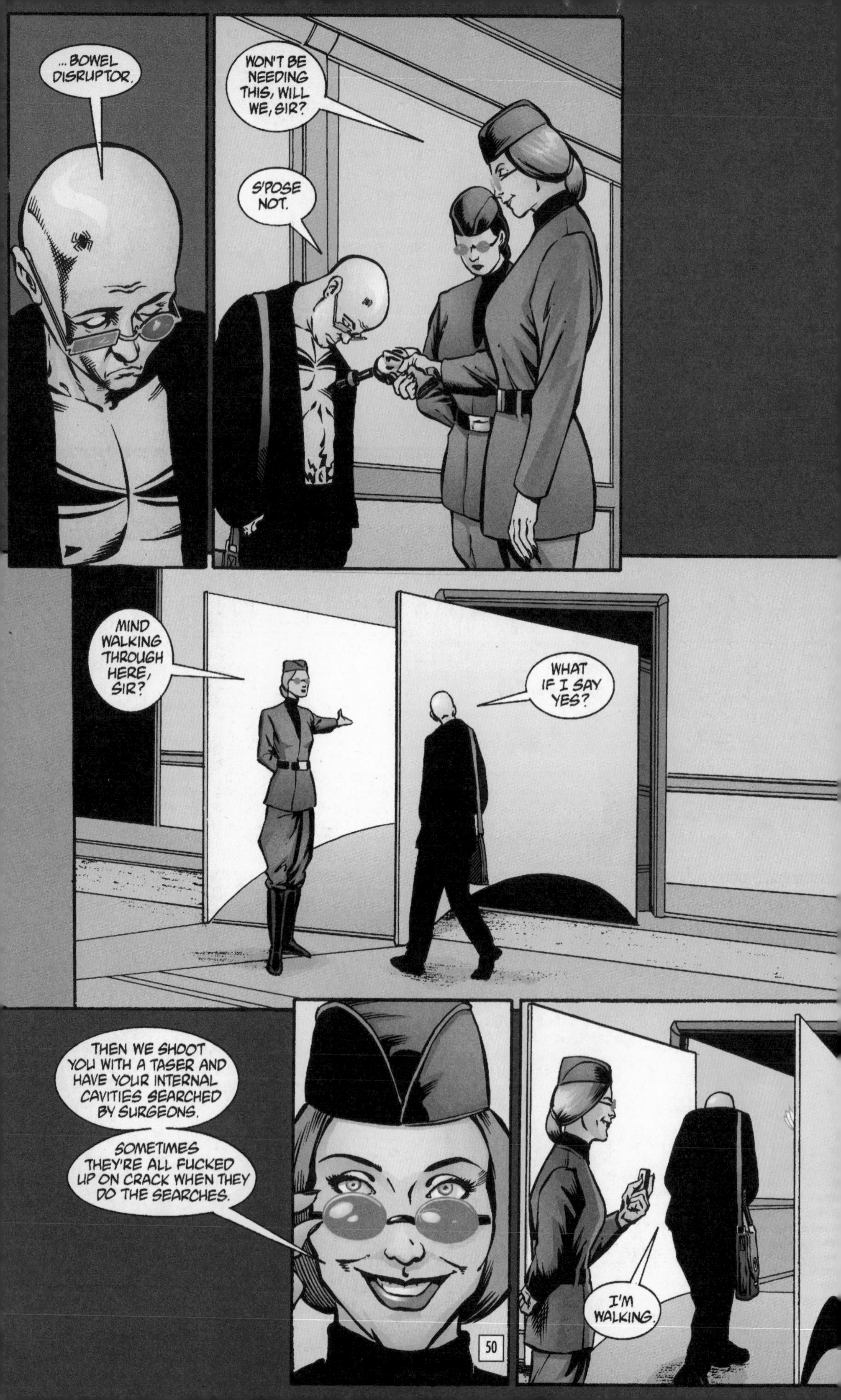
...BOWEL DISRUPTOR.
WON'T BE NEEDING THIS, WILL WE, SIR?
S'POSE NOT.
MIND WALKING THROUGH HERE, SIR?
WHAT IF I SAY YES?
THEN WE SHOOT YOU WITH A TASER AND HAVE YOUR INTERNAL CAVITIES SEARCHED BY SURGEONS.
SOMETIMES THEY'RE ALL FUCKED UP ON CRACK WHEN THEY DO THE SEARCHES.
I'M WALKING.

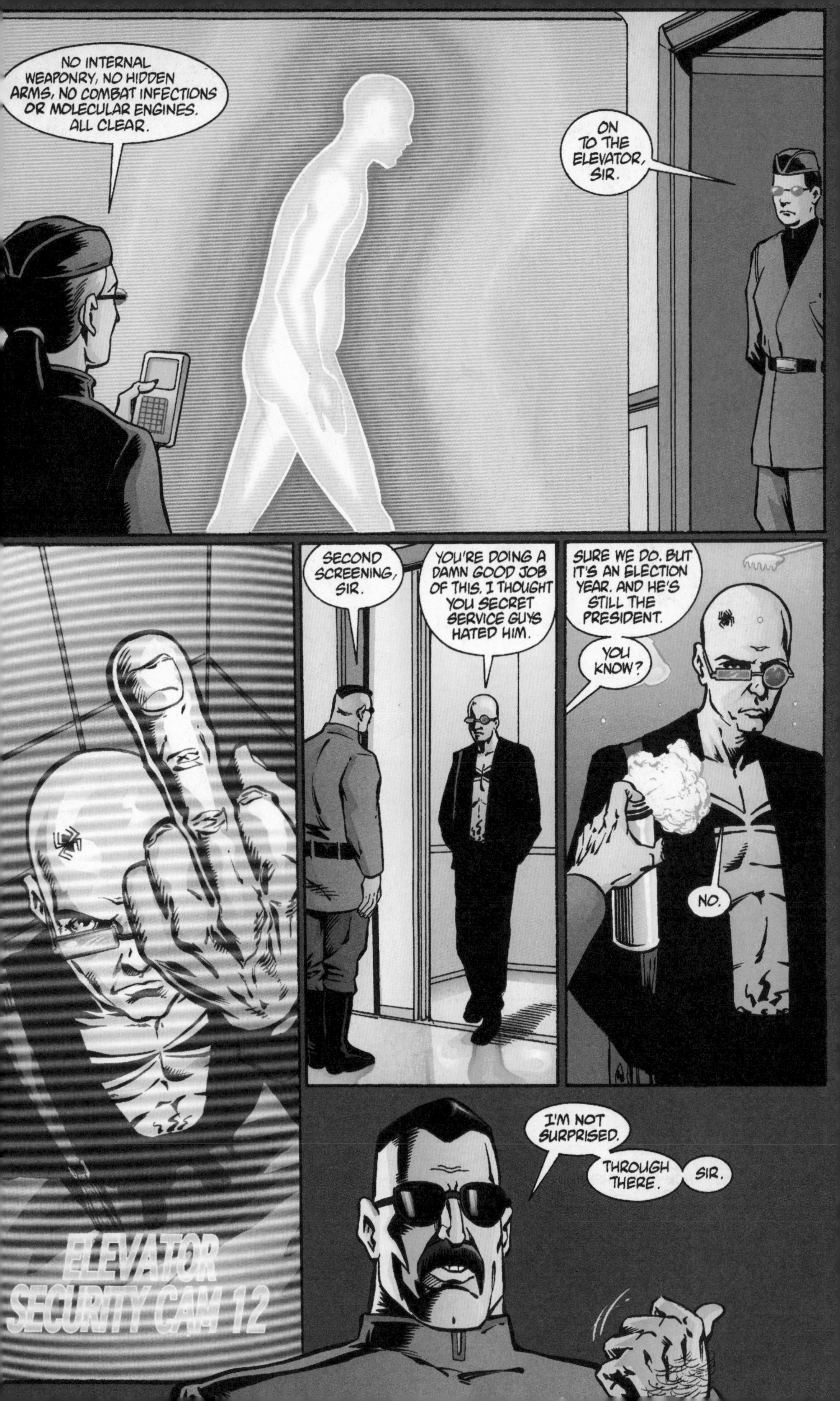

NO INTERNAL WEAPONRY, NO HIDDEN ARMS, NO COMBAT INFECTIONS OR MOLECULAR ENGINES. ALL CLEAR.
ON TO THE ELEVATOR, SIR.
ELEVATOR SECURITY CAM 12
SECOND SCREENING, SIR.
YOU'RE DOING A DAMN GOOD JOB OF THIS. I THOUGHT YOU SECRET SERVICE GUYS HATED HIM.
SURE WE DO. BUT IT'S AN ELECTION YEAR. AND HE'S STILL THE PRESIDENT.
YOU KNOW?
NO.
I'M NOT SURPRISED.
THROUGH THERE.
SIR.

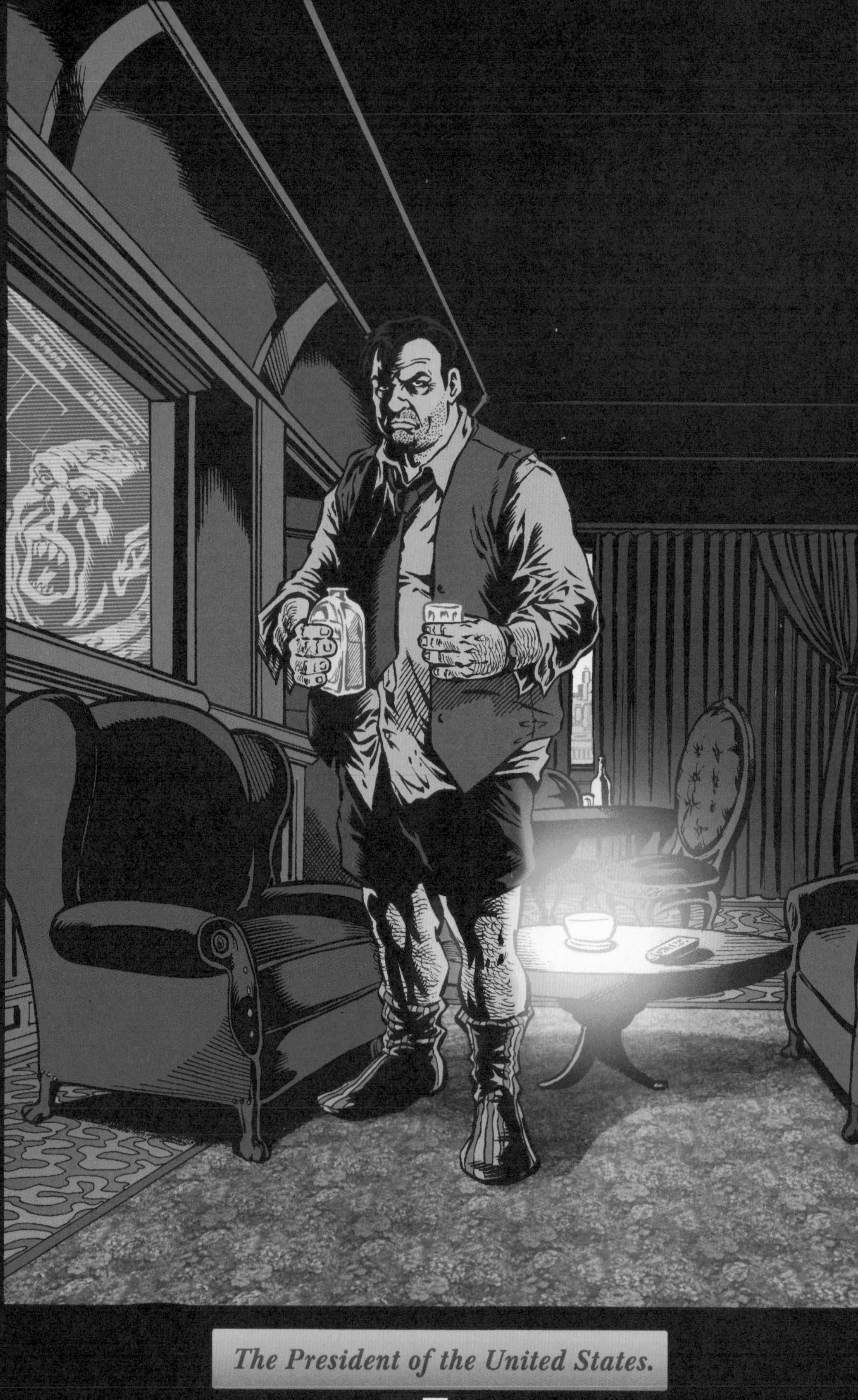
The President of the United States.

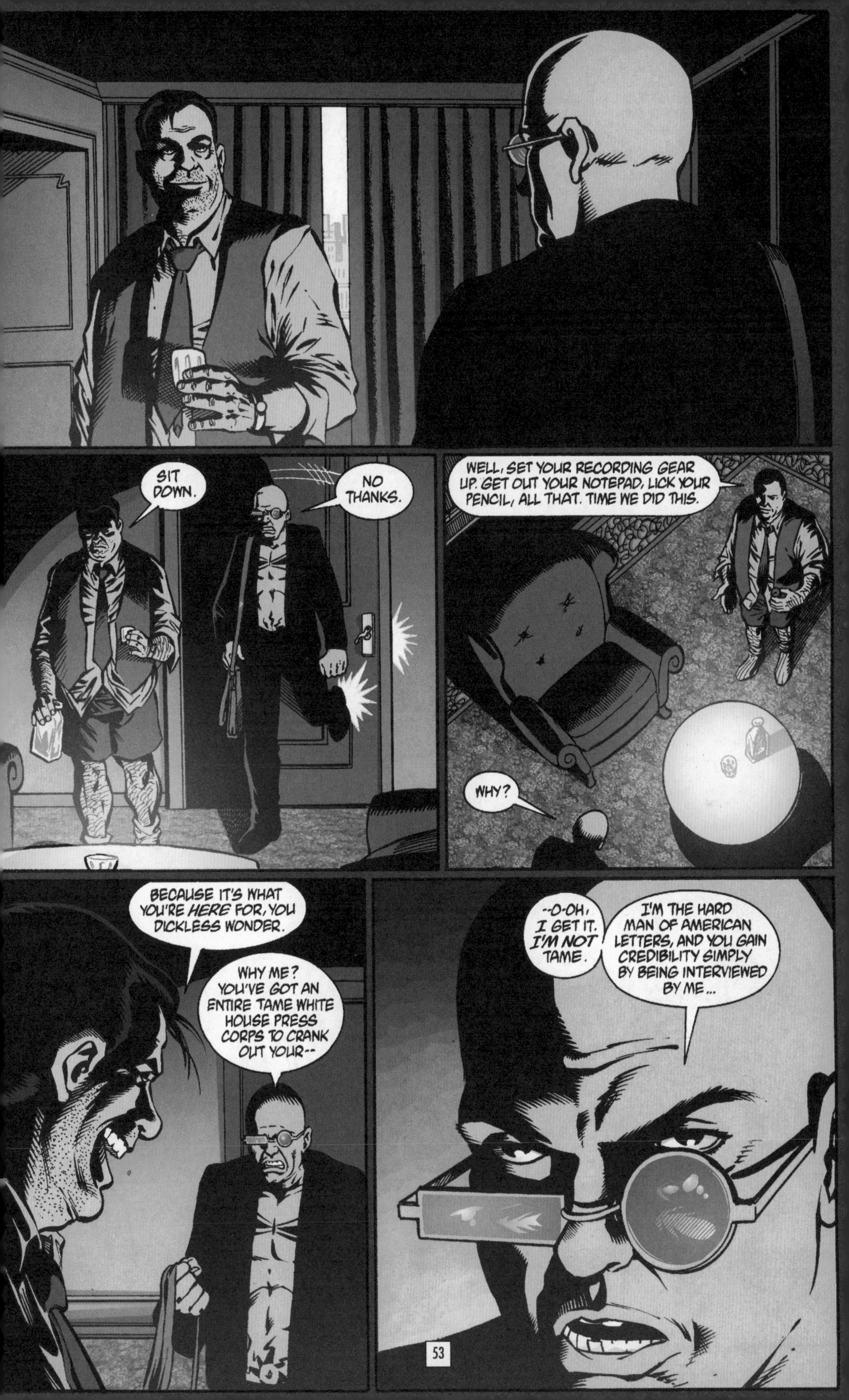
SIT DOWN.
NO THANKS.
WELL, SET YOUR RECORDING GEAR UP. GET OUT YOUR NOTEPAD, LICK YOUR PENCIL, ALL THAT. TIME WE DID THIS.
WHY?
BECAUSE IT'S WHAT YOU'RE *HERE* FOR, YOU DICKLESS WONDER.
WHY ME? YOU'VE GOT AN ENTIRE TAME WHITE HOUSE PRESS CORPS TO CRANK OUT YOUR--
--O-OH, I GET IT. *I'M NOT* TAME.
I'M THE HARD MAN OF AMERICAN LETTERS, AND YOU GAIN CREDIBILITY SIMPLY BY BEING INTERVIEWED BY ME...

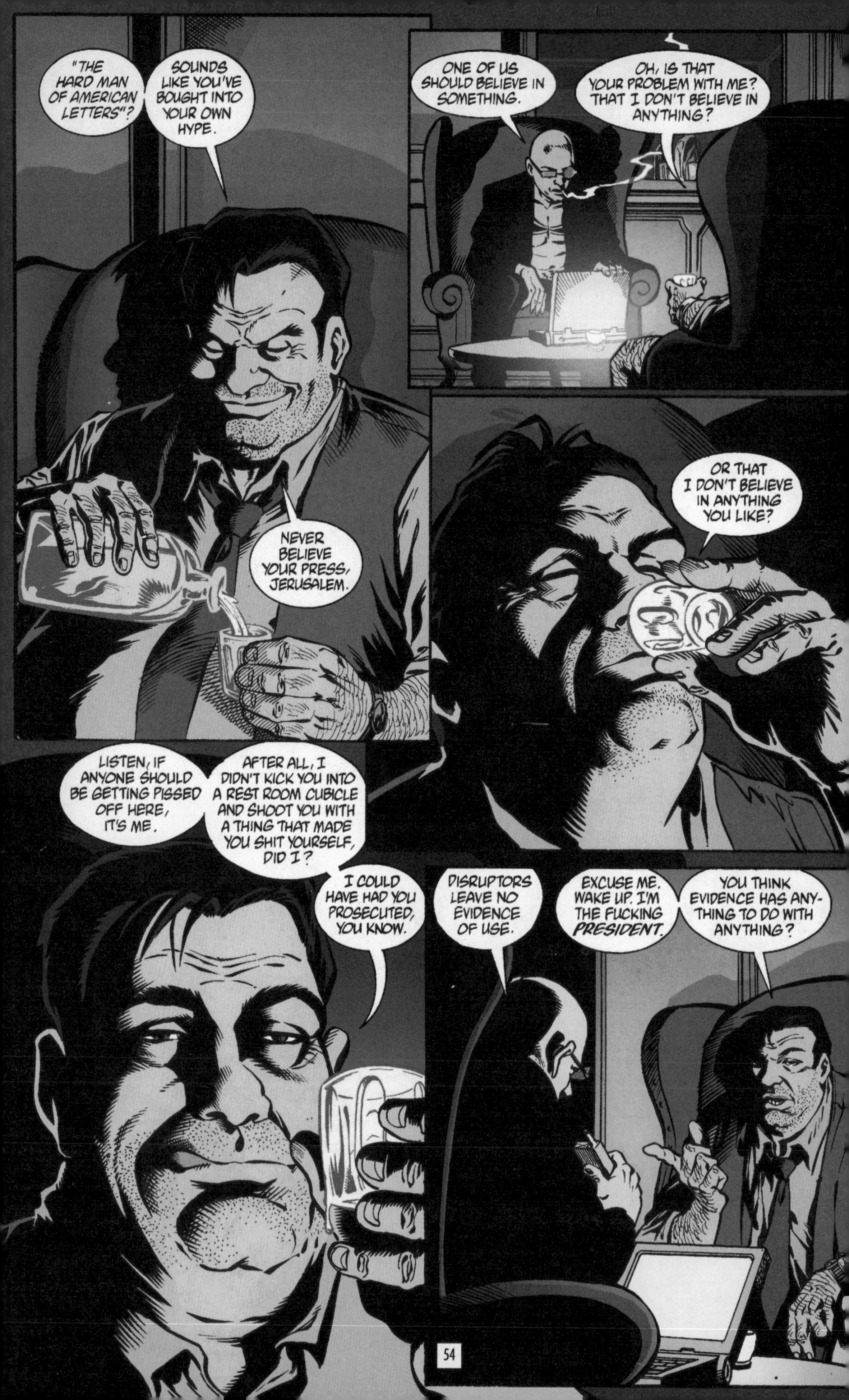
"THE HARD MAN OF AMERICAN LETTERS"?
SOUNDS LIKE YOU'VE BOUGHT INTO YOUR OWN HYPE.
NEVER BELIEVE YOUR PRESS, JERUSALEM.
ONE OF US SHOULD BELIEVE IN SOMETHING.
OH, IS THAT YOUR PROBLEM WITH ME? THAT I DON'T BELIEVE IN ANYTHING?
OR THAT I DON'T BELIEVE IN ANYTHING YOU LIKE?
LISTEN, IF ANYONE SHOULD BE GETTING PISSED OFF HERE, IT'S ME.
AFTER ALL, I DIDN'T KICK YOU INTO A REST ROOM CUBICLE AND SHOOT YOU WITH A THING THAT MADE YOU SHIT YOURSELF, DID I?
I COULD HAVE HAD YOU PROSECUTED, YOU KNOW.
DISRUPTORS LEAVE NO EVIDENCE OF USE.
EXCUSE ME. WAKE UP. I'M THE FUCKING *PRESIDENT*.
YOU THINK EVIDENCE HAS ANYTHING TO DO WITH ANYTHING?

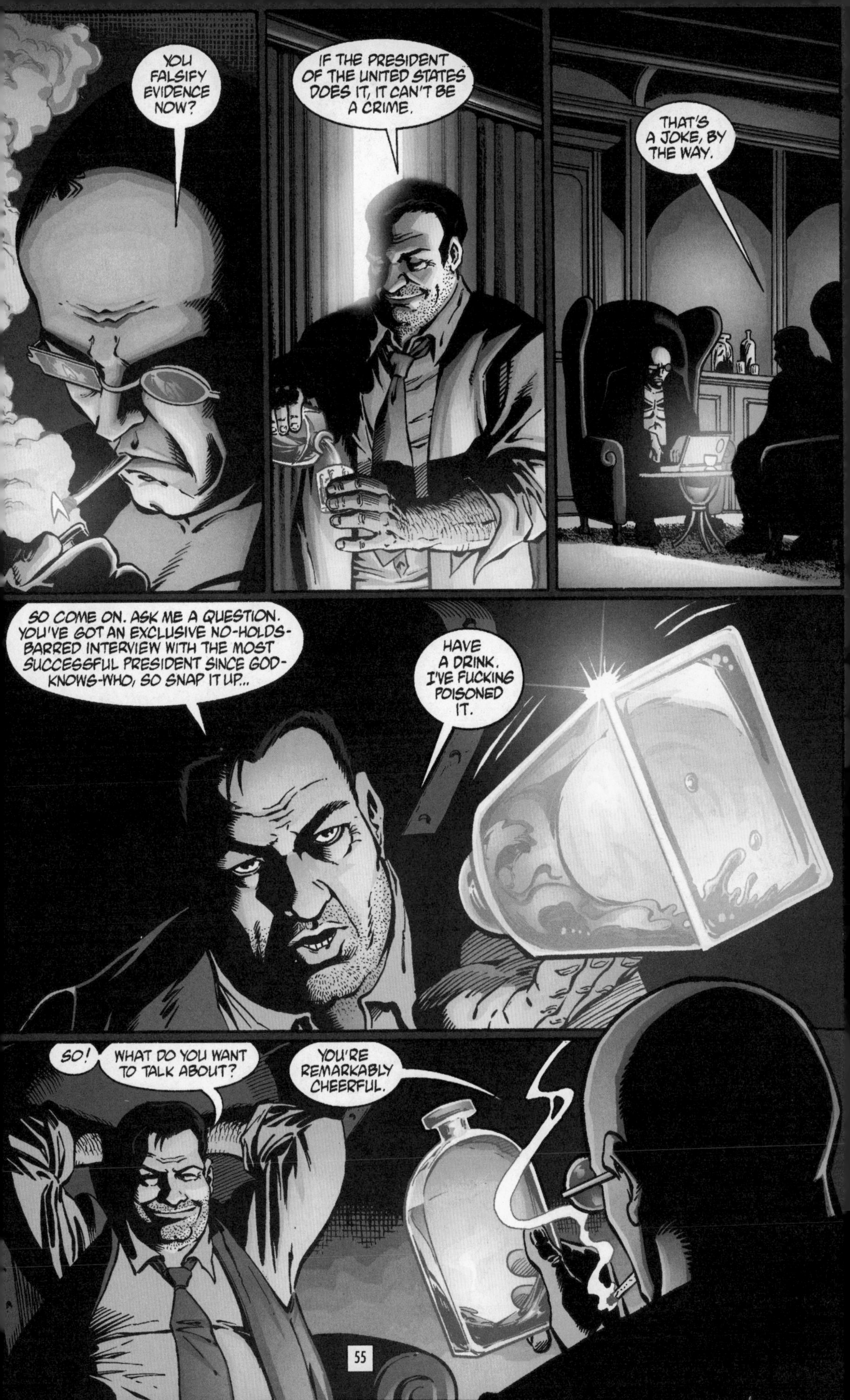
YOU FALSIFY EVIDENCE NOW?
IF THE PRESIDENT OF THE UNITED STATES DOES IT, IT CAN'T BE A CRIME.
THAT'S A JOKE, BY THE WAY.
SO COME ON. ASK ME A QUESTION. YOU'VE GOT AN EXCLUSIVE NO-HOLDS-BARRED INTERVIEW WITH THE MOST SUCCESSFUL PRESIDENT SINCE GOD-KNOWS-WHO, SO SNAP IT UP...
HAVE A DRINK. I'VE FUCKING POISONED IT.
SO!
WHAT DO YOU WANT TO TALK ABOUT?
YOU'RE REMARKABLY CHEERFUL.

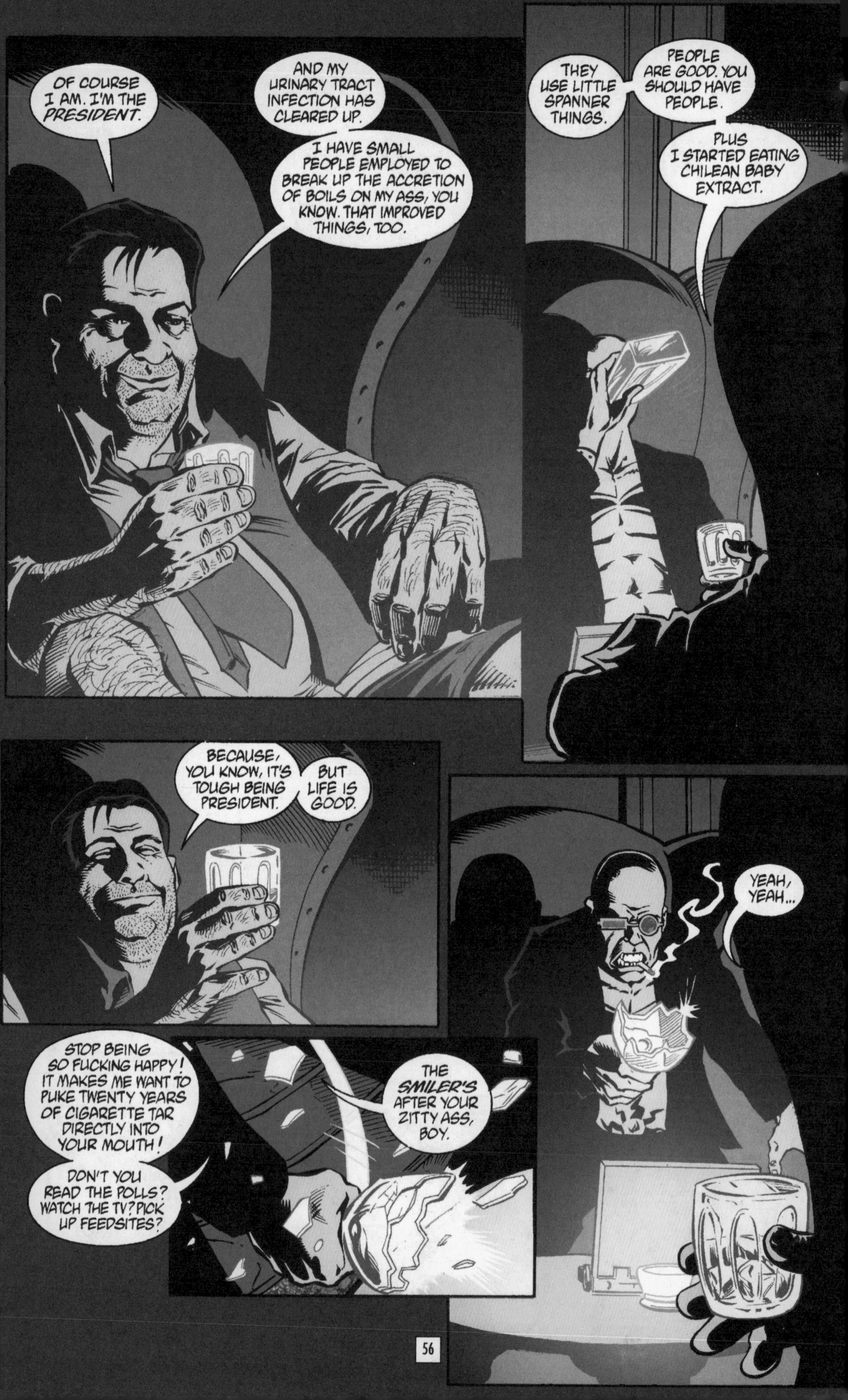

OF COURSE I AM. I'M THE *PRESIDENT*.
AND MY URINARY TRACT INFECTION HAS CLEARED UP.
I HAVE SMALL PEOPLE EMPLOYED TO BREAK UP THE ACCRETION OF BOILS ON MY ASS, YOU KNOW. THAT IMPROVED THINGS, TOO.
THEY USE LITTLE SPANNER THINGS.
PEOPLE ARE GOOD. YOU SHOULD HAVE PEOPLE.
PLUS I STARTED EATING CHILEAN BABY EXTRACT.
BECAUSE, YOU KNOW, IT'S TOUGH BEING PRESIDENT.
BUT LIFE IS GOOD.
YEAH, YEAH...
STOP BEING SO FUCKING HAPPY! IT MAKES ME WANT TO PUKE TWENTY YEARS OF CIGARETTE TAR DIRECTLY INTO YOUR MOUTH!
DON'T YOU READ THE POLLS? WATCH THE TV? PICK UP FEEDSITES?
THE *SMILER'S* AFTER YOUR ZITTY ASS, BOY.

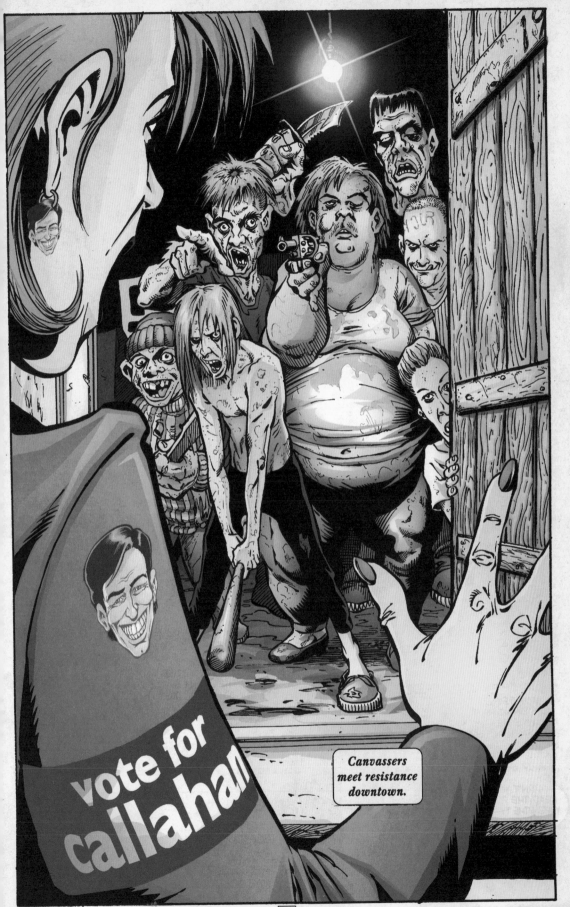

vote for callahan

Canvassers meet resistance downtown.

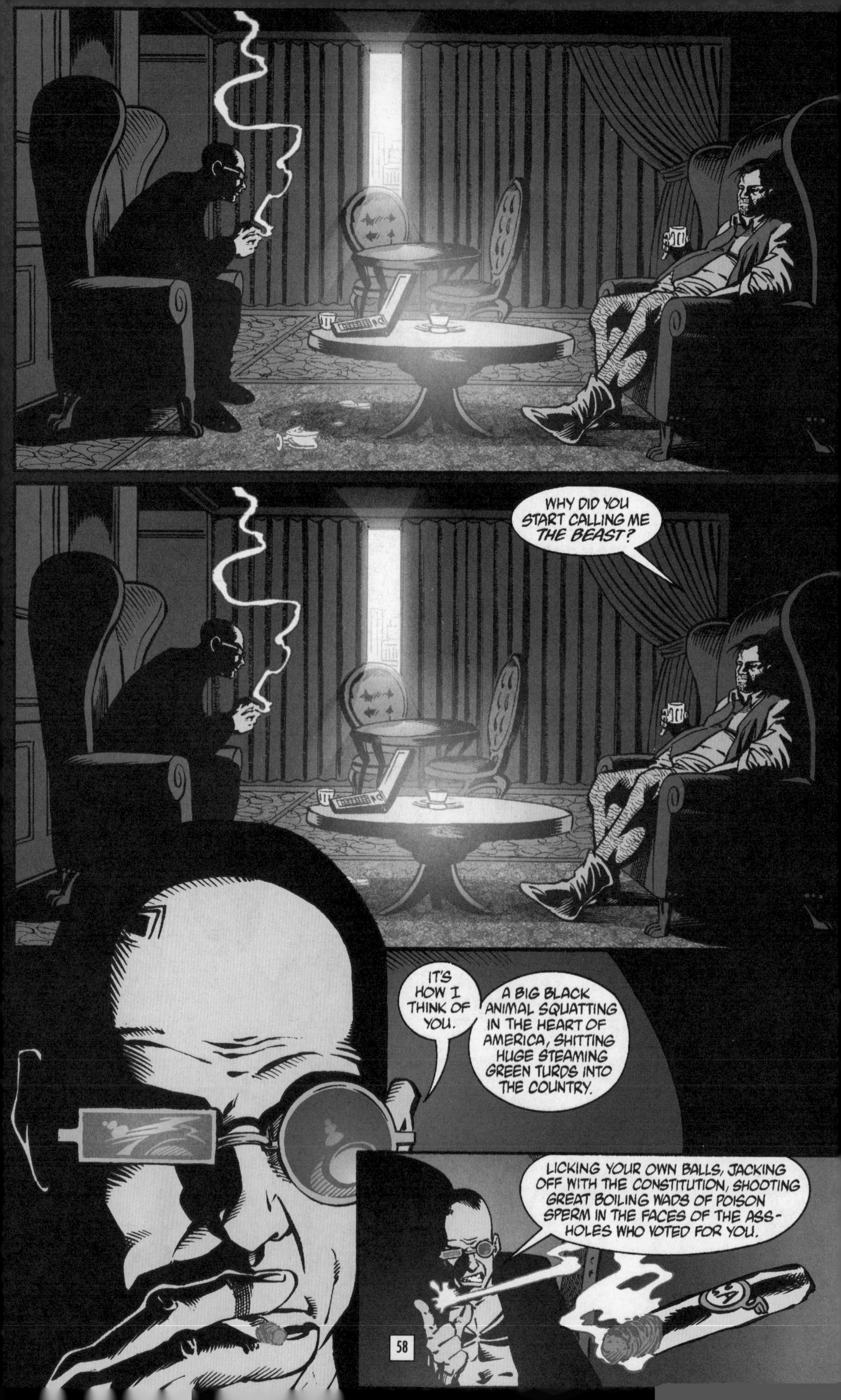
WHY DID YOU START CALLING ME *THE BEAST*?
IT'S HOW I THINK OF YOU.
A BIG BLACK ANIMAL SQUATTING IN THE HEART OF AMERICA, SHITTING HUGE STEAMING GREEN TURDS INTO THE COUNTRY.
LICKING YOUR OWN BALLS, JACKING OFF WITH THE CONSTITUTION, SHOOTING GREAT BOILING WADS OF POISON SPERM IN THE FACES OF THE ASS-HOLES WHO VOTED FOR YOU.

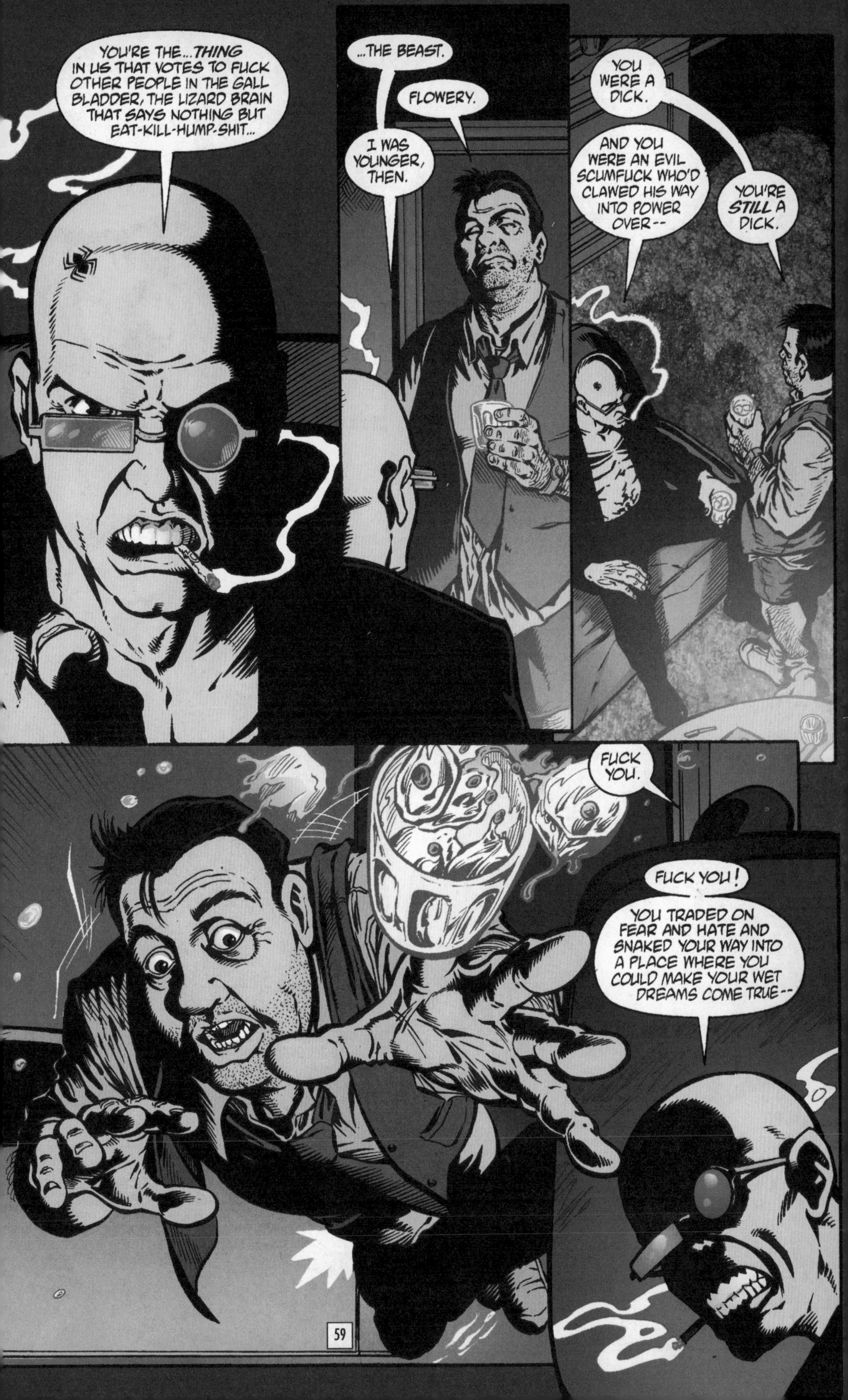
YOU'RE THE... *THING* IN US THAT VOTES TO FUCK OTHER PEOPLE IN THE GALL BLADDER, THE LIZARD BRAIN THAT SAYS NOTHING BUT EAT-KILL-HUMP-SHIT...
...THE BEAST.
FLOWERY.
I WAS YOUNGER, THEN.
YOU WERE A DICK.
AND YOU WERE AN EVIL SCUMFUCK WHO'D CLAWED HIS WAY INTO POWER OVER--
YOU'RE *STILL* A DICK.
FUCK YOU.
FUCK YOU!
YOU TRADED ON FEAR AND HATE AND SNAKED YOUR WAY INTO A PLACE WHERE YOU COULD MAKE YOUR WET DREAMS COME TRUE--

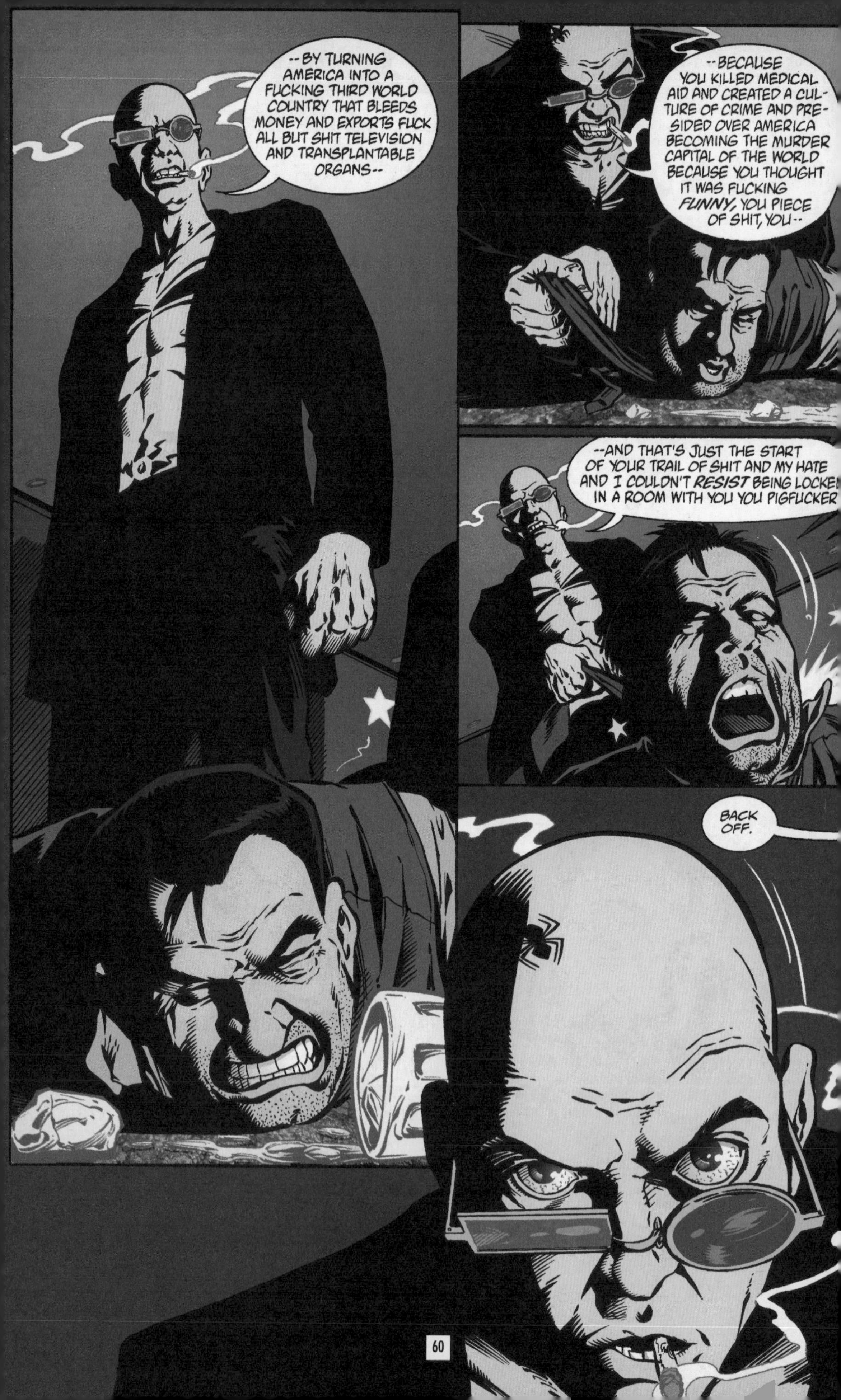

--BY TURNING AMERICA INTO A FUCKING THIRD WORLD COUNTRY THAT BLEEDS MONEY AND EXPORTS FUCK ALL BUT SHIT TELEVISION AND TRANSPLANTABLE ORGANS--
--BECAUSE YOU KILLED MEDICAL AID AND CREATED A CUL-TURE OF CRIME AND PRE-SIDED OVER AMERICA BECOMING THE MURDER CAPITAL OF THE WORLD BECAUSE YOU THOUGHT IT WAS FUCKING *FUNNY*, YOU PIECE OF SHIT, YOU--
--AND THAT'S JUST THE START OF YOUR TRAIL OF SHIT AND MY HATE AND I COULDN'T *RESIST* BEING LOCKE IN A ROOM WITH YOU YOU PIGFUCKER
BACK OFF.

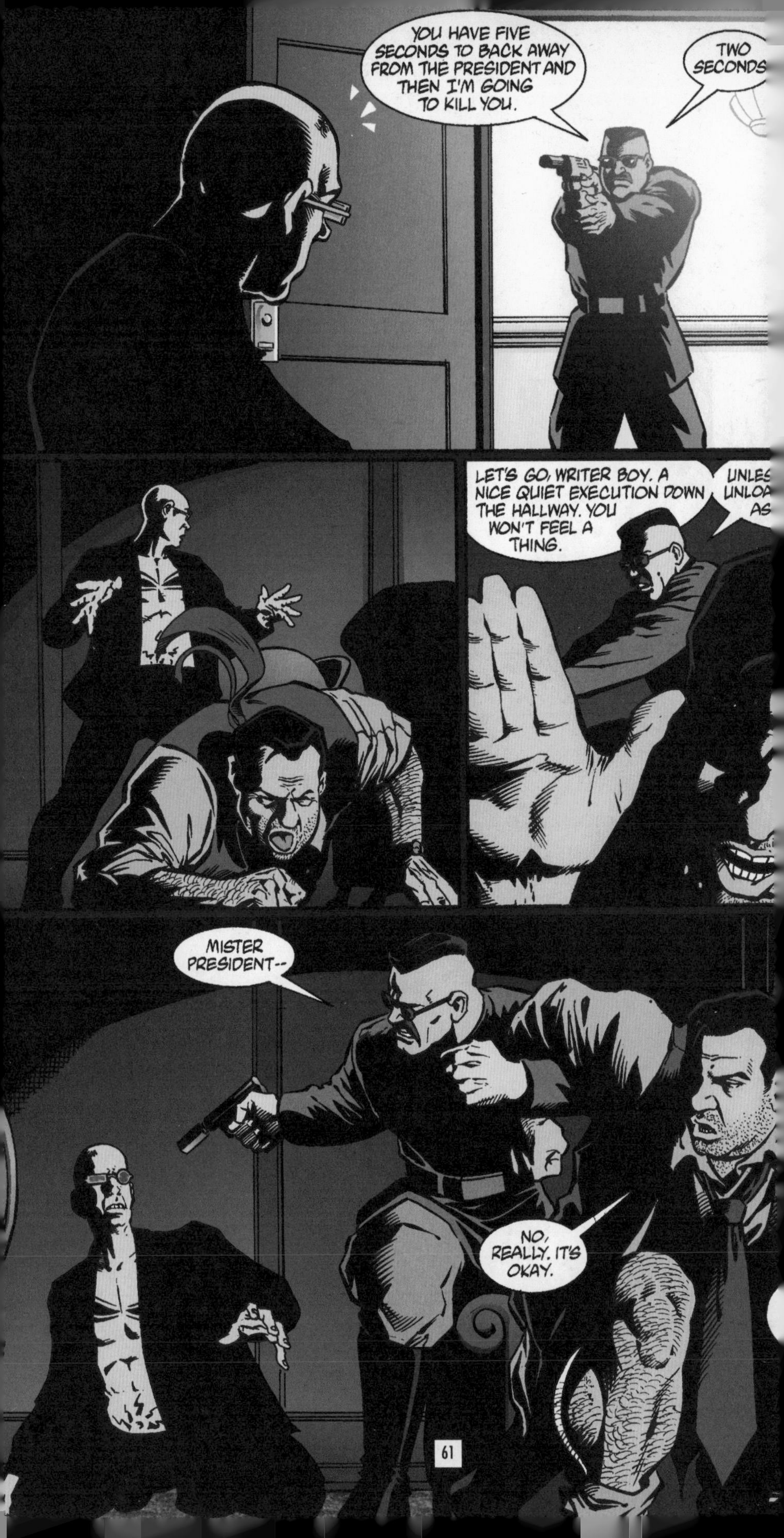
YOU HAVE FIVE SECONDS TO BACK AWAY FROM THE PRESIDENT AND THEN I'M GOING TO KILL YOU.
TWO SECONDS
LET'S GO, WRITER BOY. A NICE QUIET EXECUTION DOWN THE HALLWAY. YOU WON'T FEEL A THING.
MISTER PRESIDENT--
NO, REALLY. IT'S OKAY.

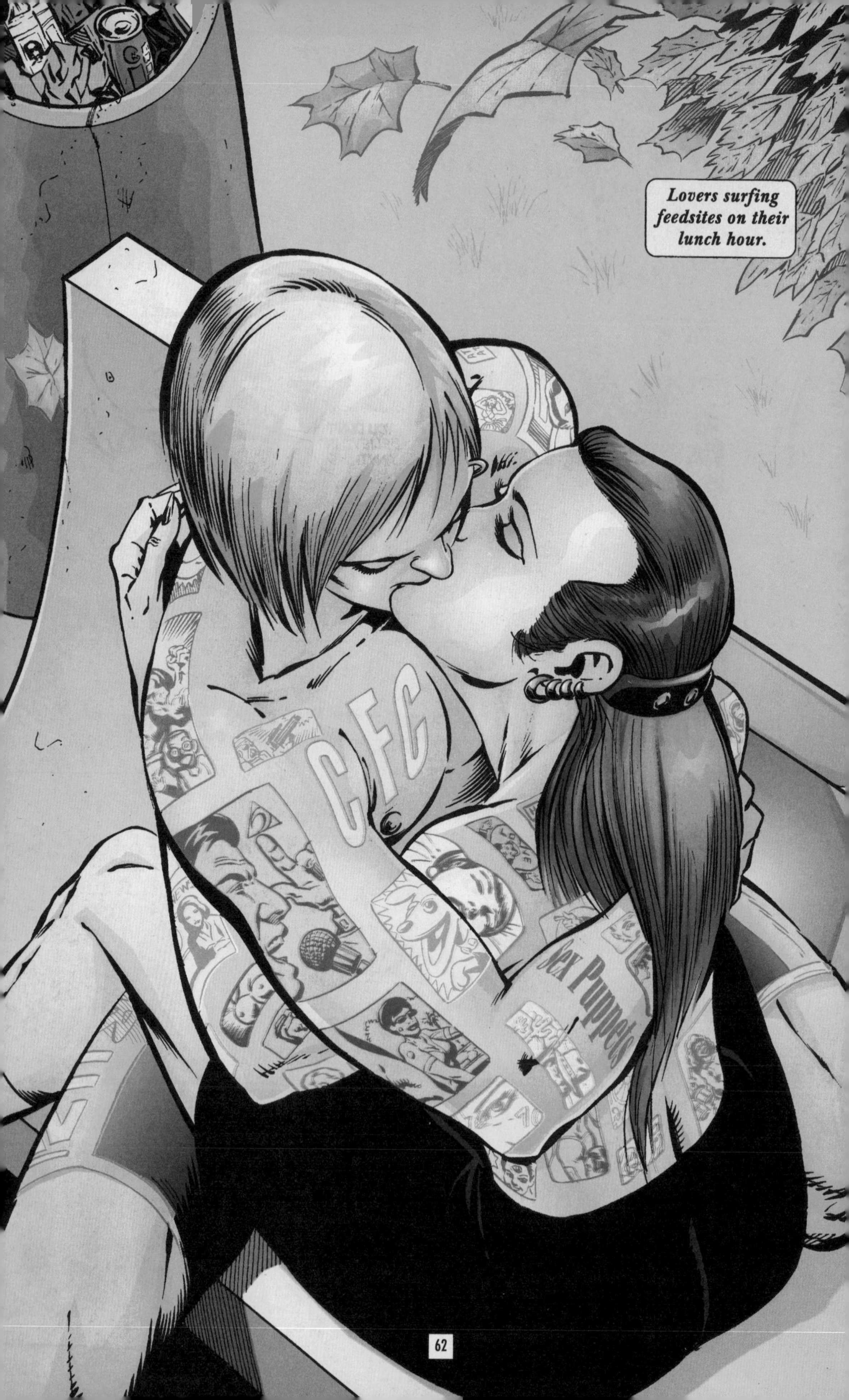
Lovers surfing feedsites on their lunch hour.
CFC
Sex Puppets

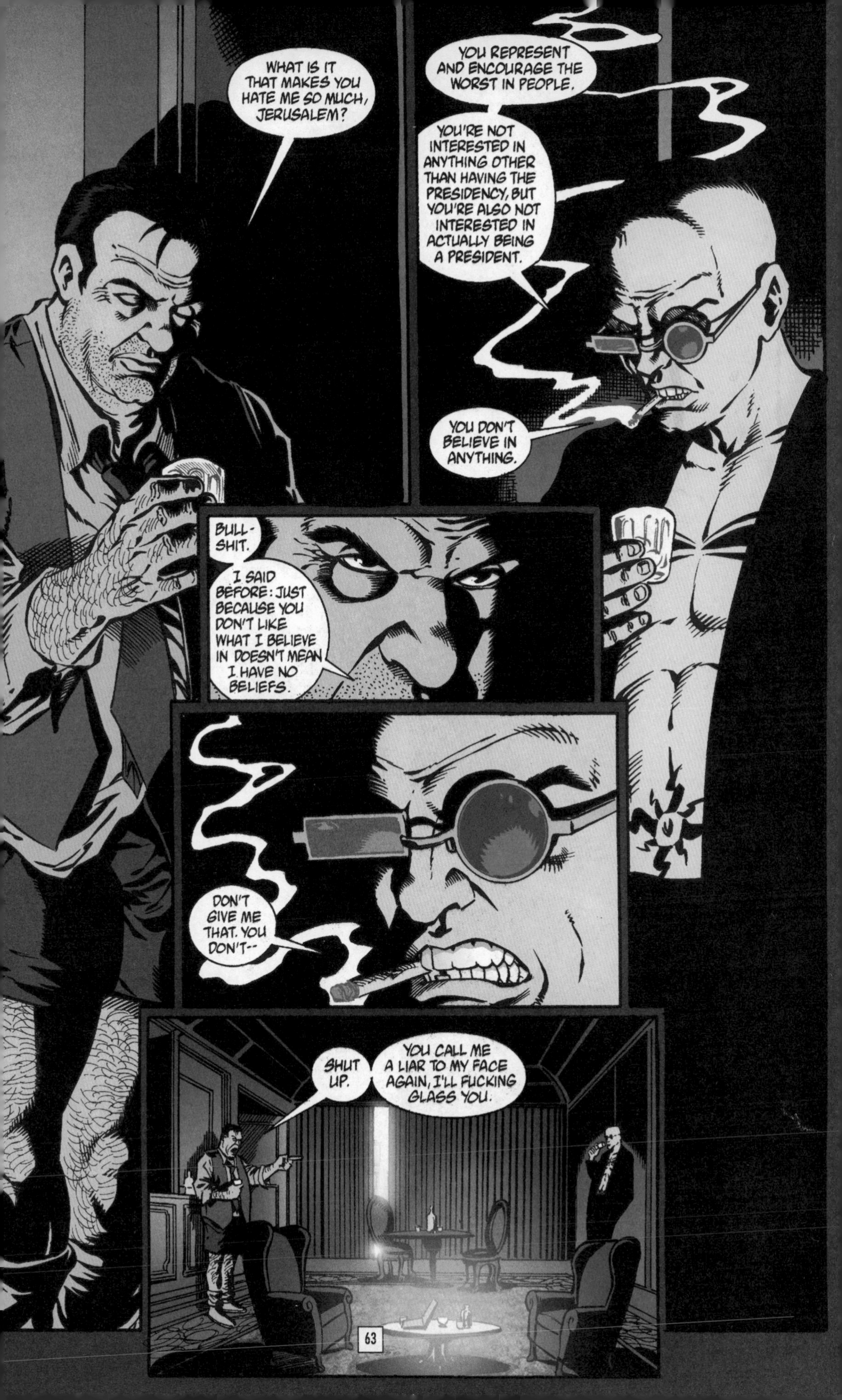
WHAT IS IT THAT MAKES YOU HATE ME SO MUCH, JERUSALEM?
YOU REPRESENT AND ENCOURAGE THE WORST IN PEOPLE.
YOU'RE NOT INTERESTED IN ANYTHING OTHER THAN HAVING THE PRESIDENCY, BUT YOU'RE ALSO NOT INTERESTED IN ACTUALLY BEING A PRESIDENT.
YOU DON'T BELIEVE IN ANYTHING.
BULL-SHIT.
I SAID BEFORE: JUST BECAUSE YOU DON'T LIKE WHAT I BELIEVE IN DOESN'T MEAN I HAVE NO BELIEFS.
DON'T GIVE ME THAT. YOU DON'T--
SHUT UP.
YOU CALL ME A LIAR TO MY FACE AGAIN, I'LL FUCKING GLASS YOU.

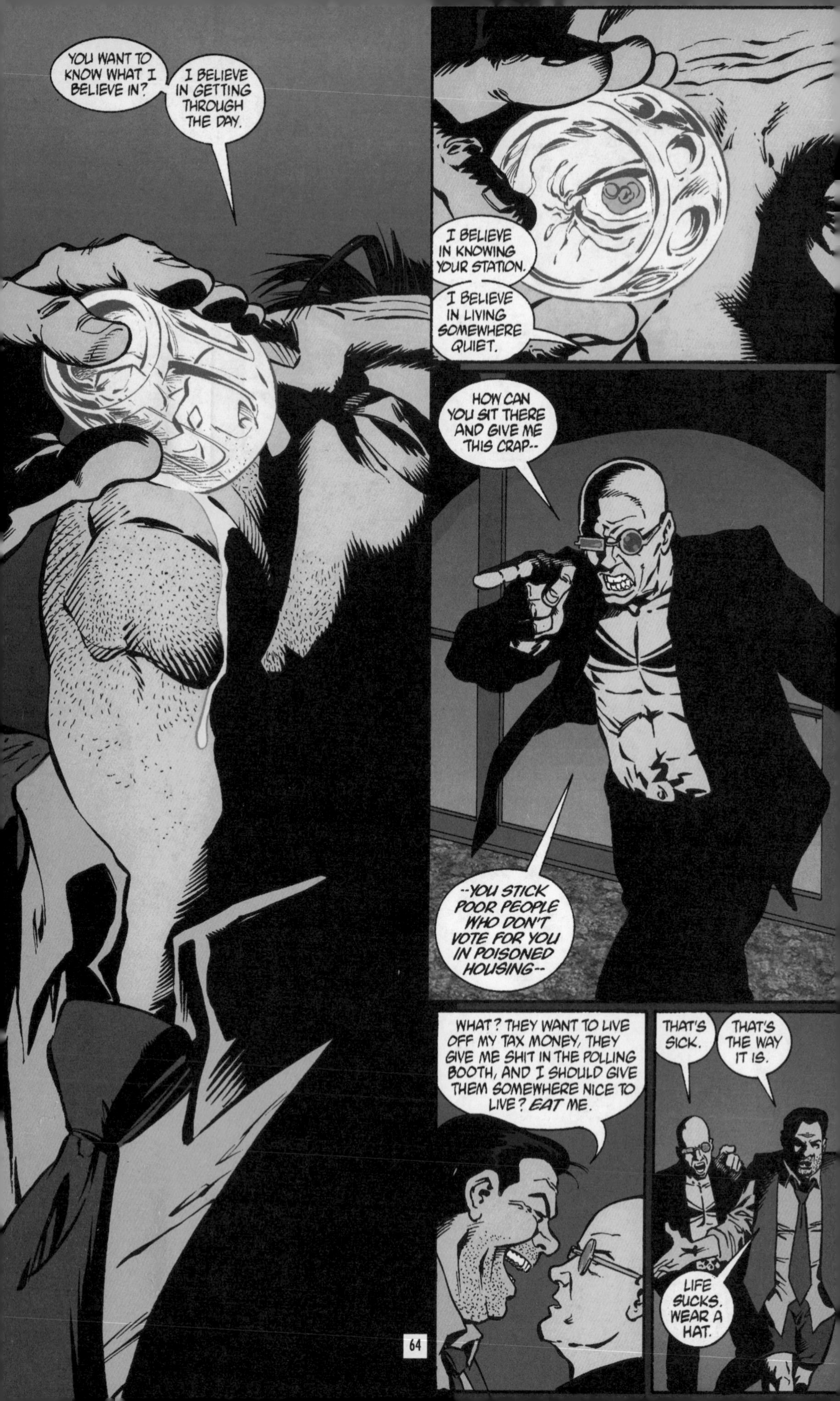
YOU WANT TO KNOW WHAT I BELIEVE IN?
I BELIEVE IN GETTING THROUGH THE DAY.
I BELIEVE IN KNOWING YOUR STATION.
I BELIEVE IN LIVING SOMEWHERE QUIET.
HOW CAN YOU SIT THERE AND GIVE ME THIS CRAP--
--YOU STICK POOR PEOPLE WHO DON'T VOTE FOR YOU IN POISONED HOUSING--
WHAT? THEY WANT TO LIVE OFF MY TAX MONEY, THEY GIVE ME SHIT IN THE POLLING BOOTH, AND I SHOULD GIVE THEM SOMEWHERE NICE TO LIVE? EAT ME.
THAT'S SICK.
THAT'S THE WAY IT IS.
LIFE SUCKS. WEAR A HAT.

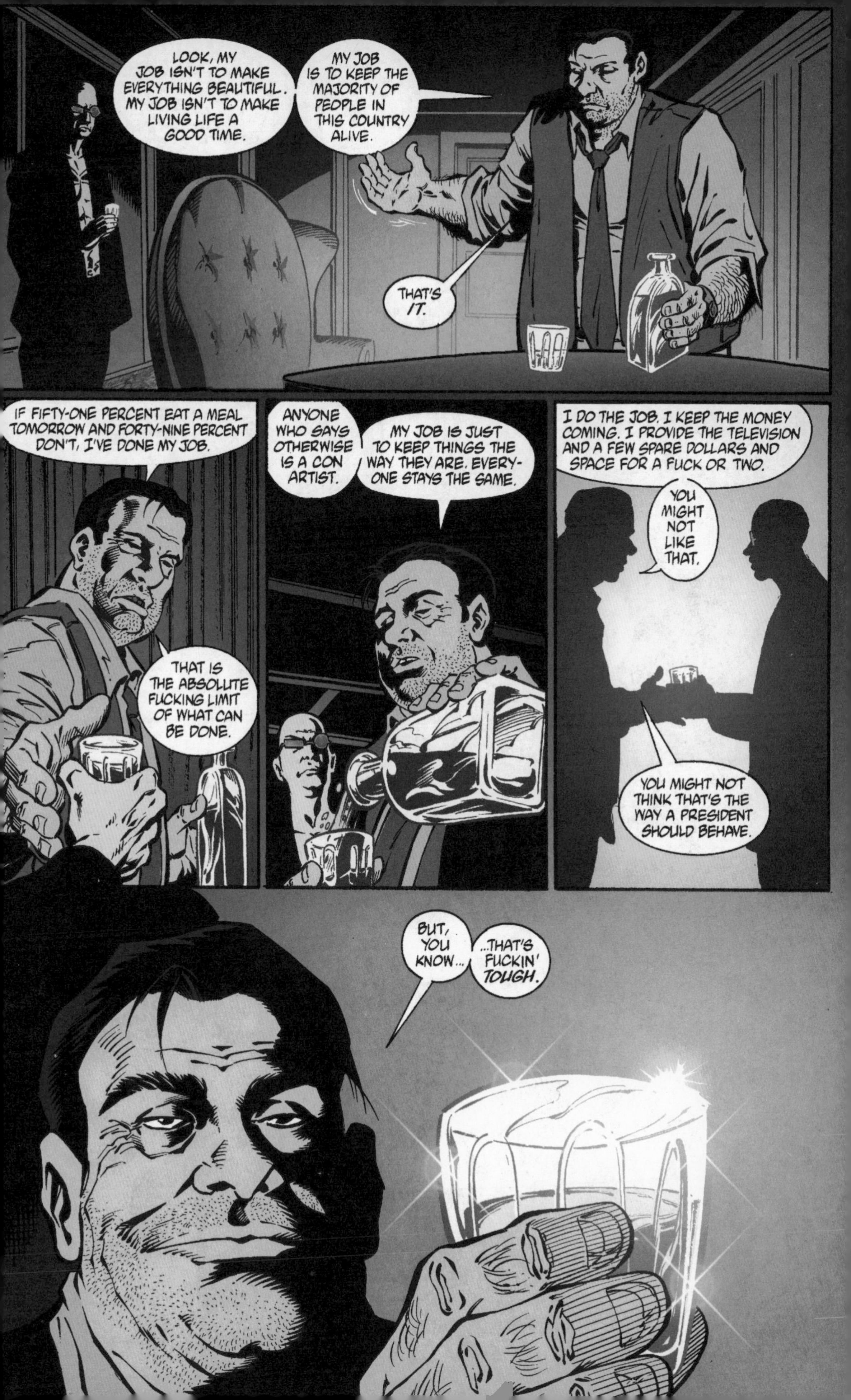
LOOK, MY JOB ISN'T TO MAKE EVERYTHING BEAUTIFUL. MY JOB ISN'T TO MAKE LIVING LIFE A GOOD TIME.
MY JOB IS TO KEEP THE MAJORITY OF PEOPLE IN THIS COUNTRY ALIVE.
THAT'S *IT*.
IF FIFTY-ONE PERCENT EAT A MEAL TOMORROW AND FORTY-NINE PERCENT DON'T, I'VE DONE MY JOB.
THAT IS THE ABSOLUTE FUCKING LIMIT OF WHAT CAN BE DONE.
ANYONE WHO SAYS OTHERWISE IS A CON ARTIST.
MY JOB IS JUST TO KEEP THINGS THE WAY THEY ARE. EVERYONE STAYS THE SAME.
I DO THE JOB. I KEEP THE MONEY COMING. I PROVIDE THE TELEVISION AND A FEW SPARE DOLLARS AND SPACE FOR A FUCK OR TWO.
YOU MIGHT NOT LIKE THAT.
YOU MIGHT NOT THINK THAT'S THE WAY A PRESIDENT SHOULD BEHAVE.
BUT, YOU KNOW...
...THAT'S FUCKIN' *TOUGH*.

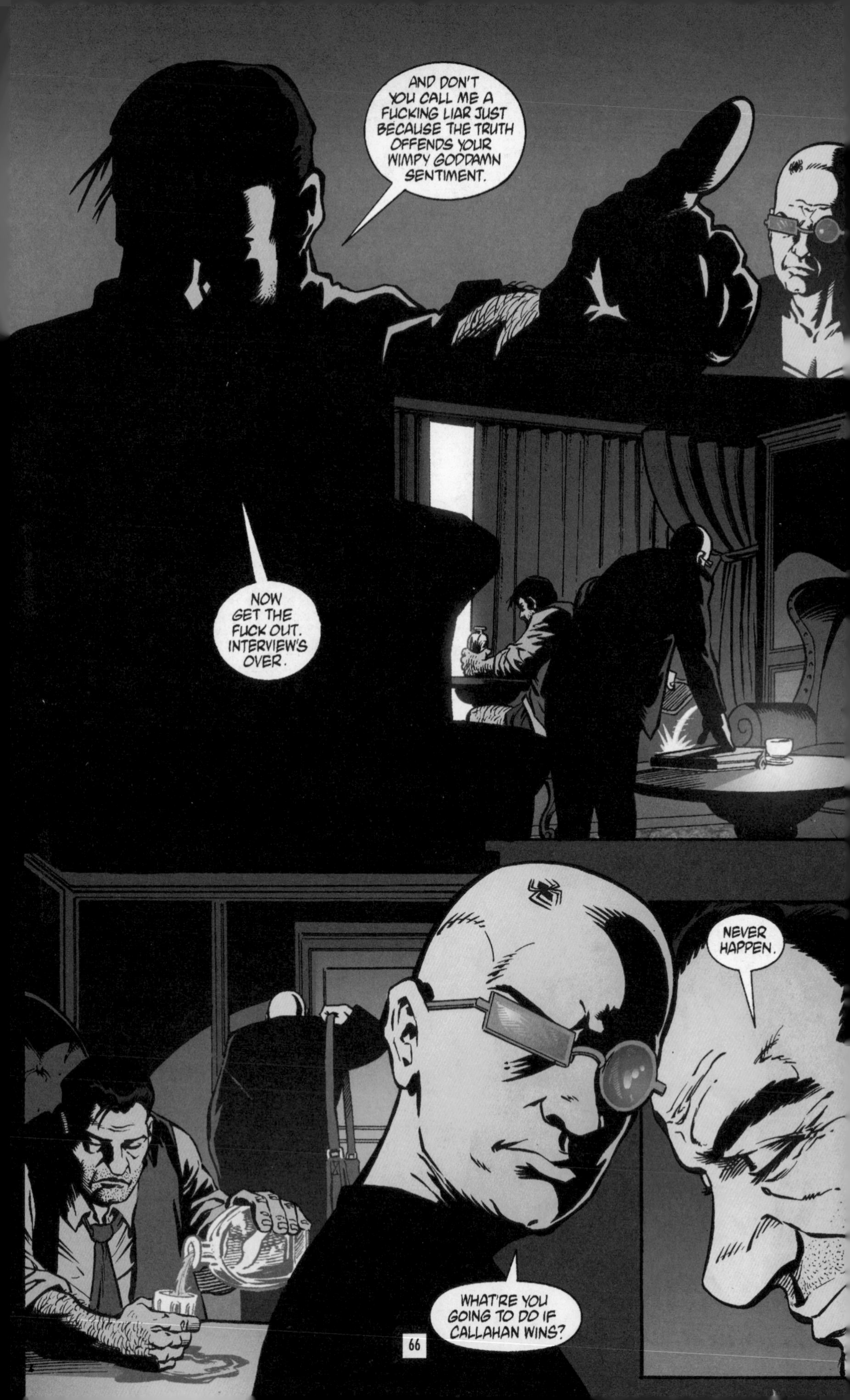
AND DON'T YOU CALL ME A FUCKING LIAR JUST BECAUSE THE TRUTH OFFENDS YOUR WIMPY GODDAMN SENTIMENT.
NOW GET THE FUCK OUT. INTERVIEW'S OVER.
WHAT'RE YOU GOING TO DO IF CALLAHAN WINS?
NEVER HAPPEN.

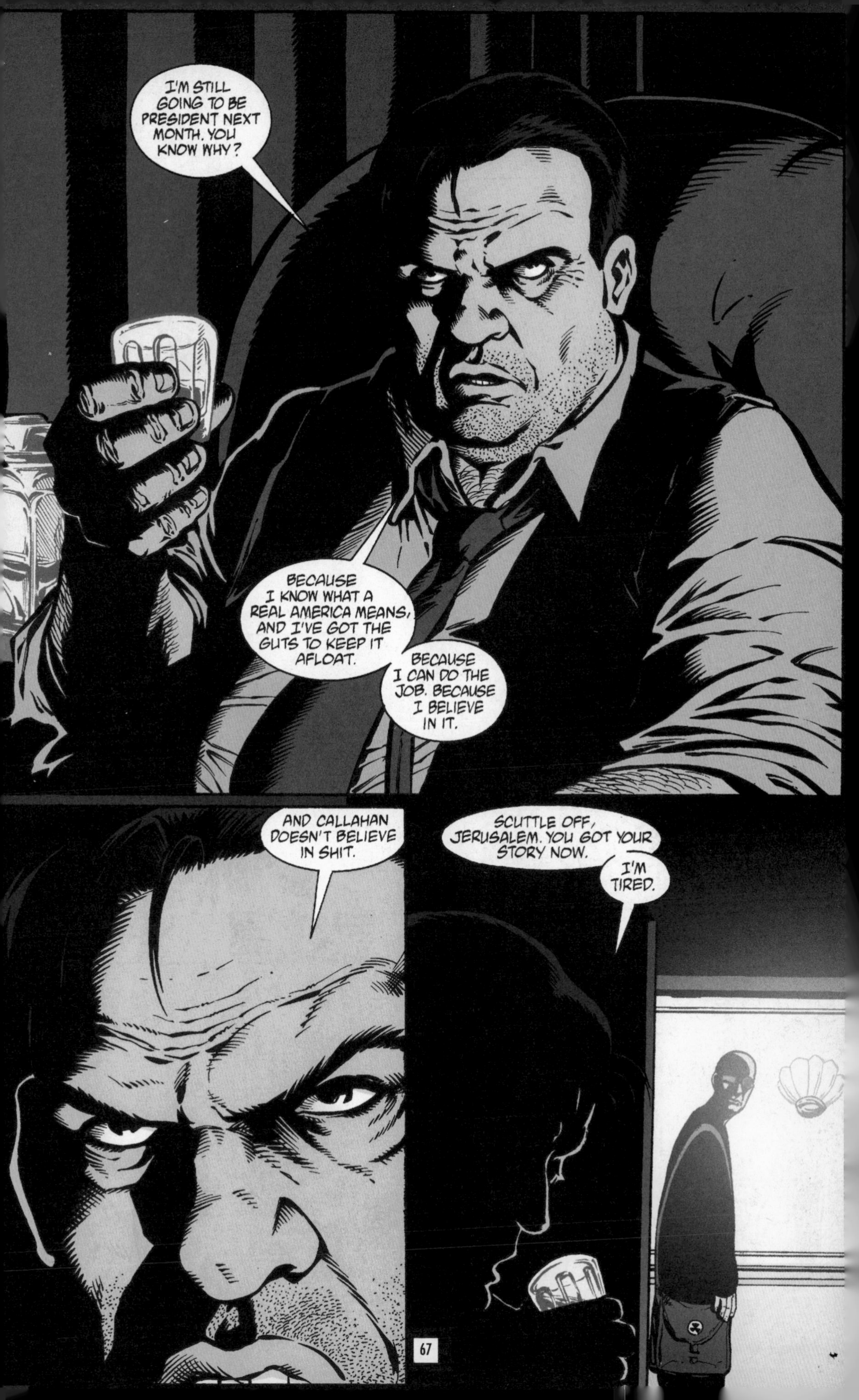
I'M STILL GOING TO BE PRESIDENT NEXT MONTH. YOU KNOW WHY?
BECAUSE I KNOW WHAT A REAL AMERICA MEANS, AND I'VE GOT THE GUTS TO KEEP IT AFLOAT.
BECAUSE I CAN DO THE JOB. BECAUSE I BELIEVE IN IT.
AND CALLAHAN DOESN'T BELIEVE IN SHIT.
SCUTTLE OFF, JERUSALEM. YOU GOT YOUR STORY NOW.
I'M TIRED.

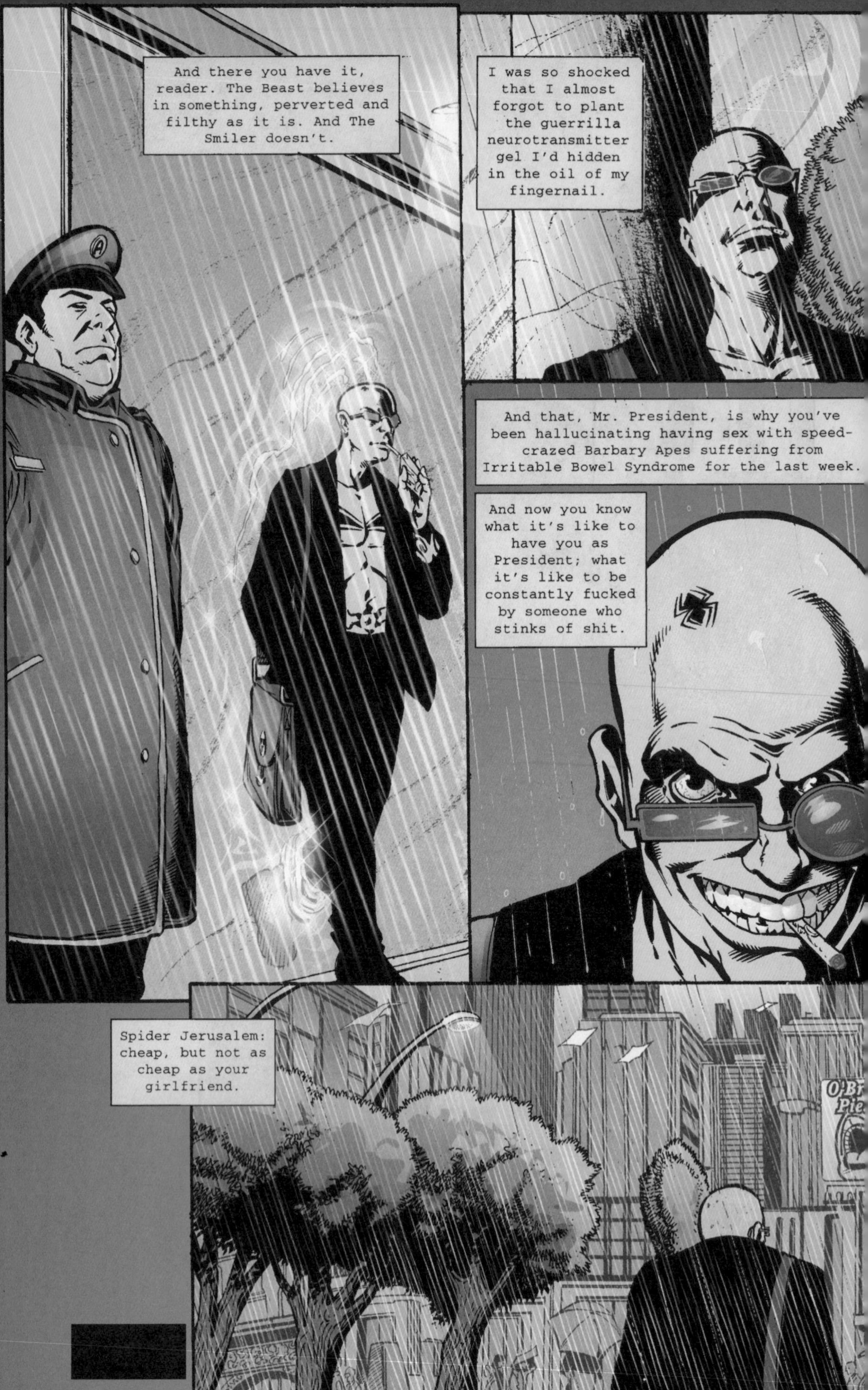
And there you have it, reader. The Beast believes in something, perverted and filthy as it is. And The Smiler doesn't.
I was so shocked that I almost forgot to plant the guerrilla neurotransmitter gel I'd hidden in the oil of my fingernail.
And that, Mr. President, is why you've been hallucinating having sex with speed-crazed Barbary Apes suffering from Irritable Bowel Syndrome for the last week.
And now you know what it's like to have you as President; what it's like to be constantly fucked by someone who stinks of shit.
Spider Jerusalem: cheap, but not as cheap as your girlfriend.

WARREN ELLIS WRITES AND DARICK ROBERTSON PENCILS

THE NEW SCUM

4: NEW STREETS

RODNEY RAMOS
INKER

CLEM ROBINS
LETTERER

NATHAN EYRING
COLOR & SEPARATIONS

GEOF DARROW
COVER

CLIFF CHIANG
ASSISTANT EDITOR

STUART MOORE
EDITOR

TRANSMETROPOLITAN
created by WARREN ELLIS
& DARICK ROBERTSON

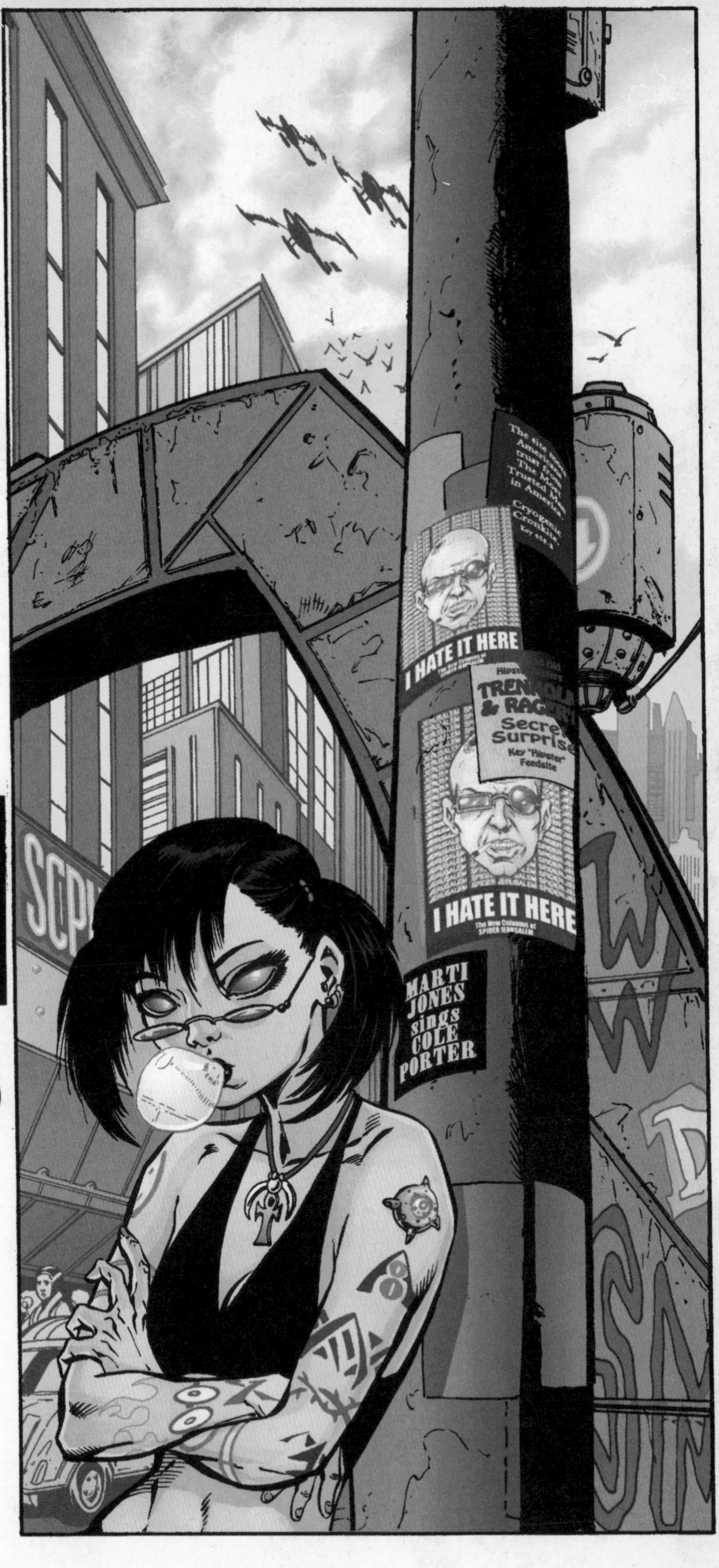
Cryogenic Cronkite.
I HATE IT HERE
Key "Hipster" Feedsite
I HATE IT HERE
The New Columns of SPIDER JERUSALEM
MARTI JONES sings COLE PORTER

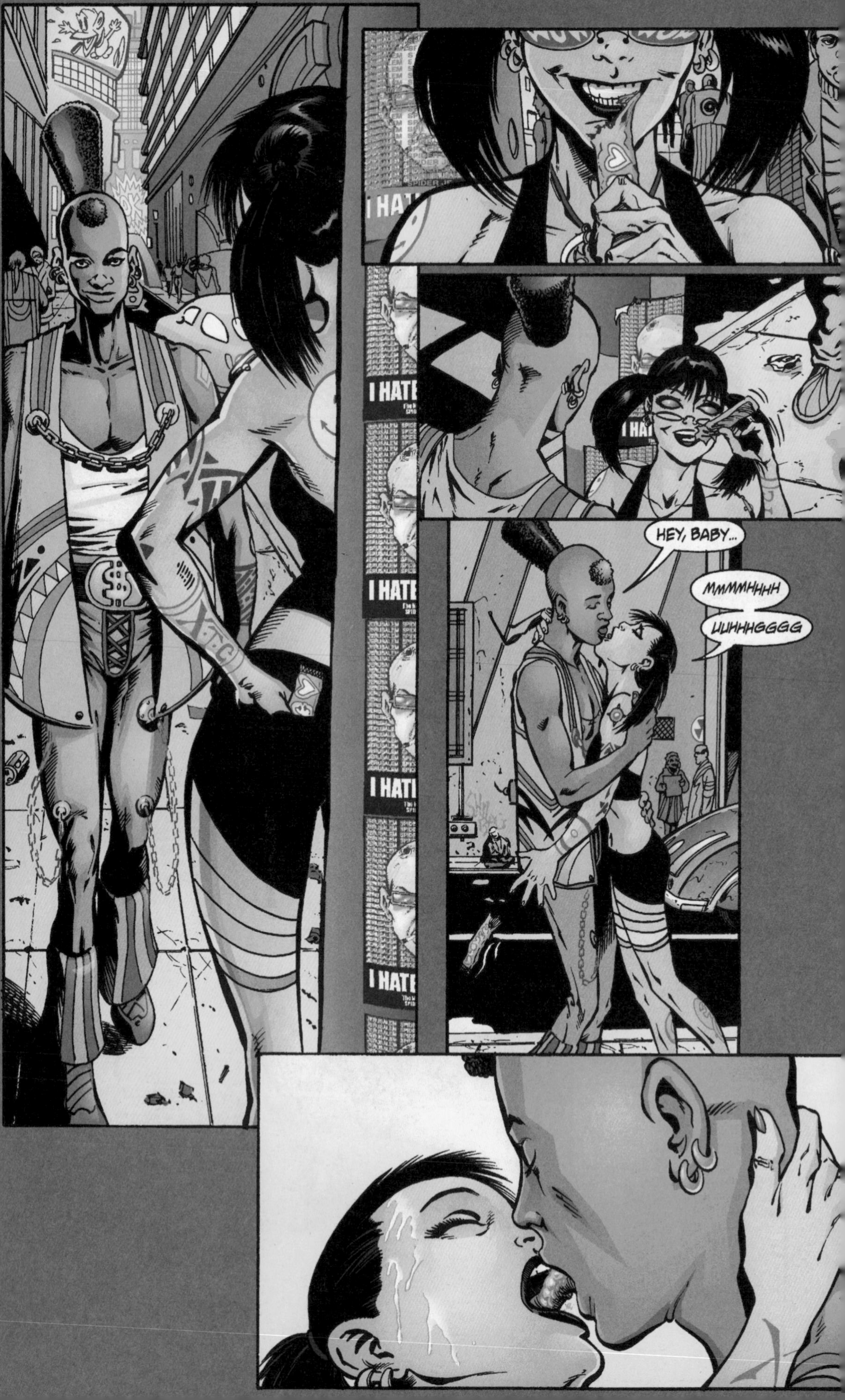
HEY, BABY...
MMMMHHHH
UUHHHGGGG

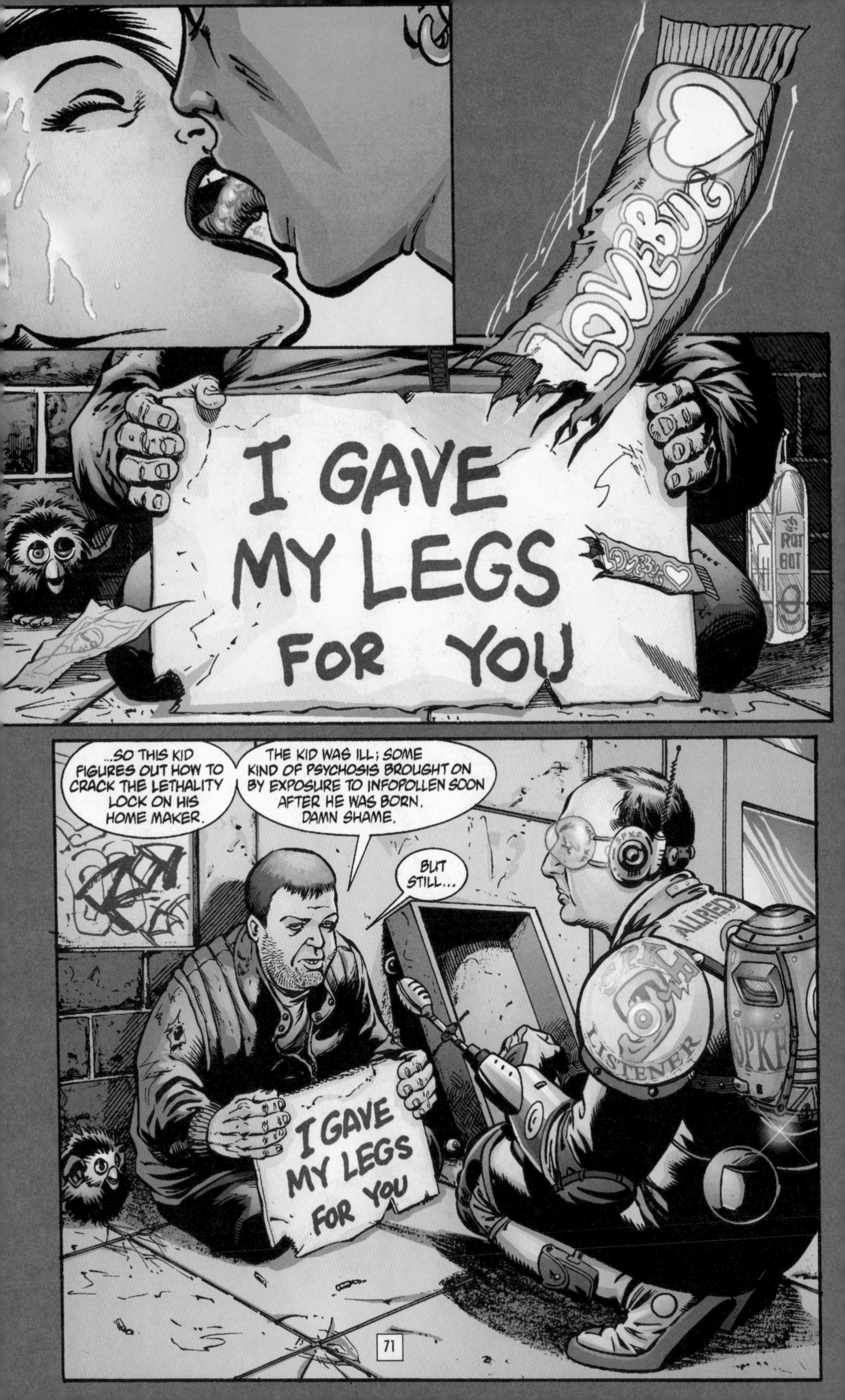
LOVEBUG™
I GAVE MY LEGS FOR YOU
LOVEBUG
ROT BOT
...SO THIS KID FIGURES OUT HOW TO CRACK THE LETHALITY LOCK ON HIS HOME MAKER.
THE KID WAS ILL; SOME KIND OF PSYCHOSIS BROUGHT ON BY EXPOSURE TO INFOPOLLEN SOON AFTER HE WAS BORN. DAMN SHAME.
BUT STILL...
I GAVE MY LEGS FOR YOU
ALLRED
SPKH
LISTENER
SPKH

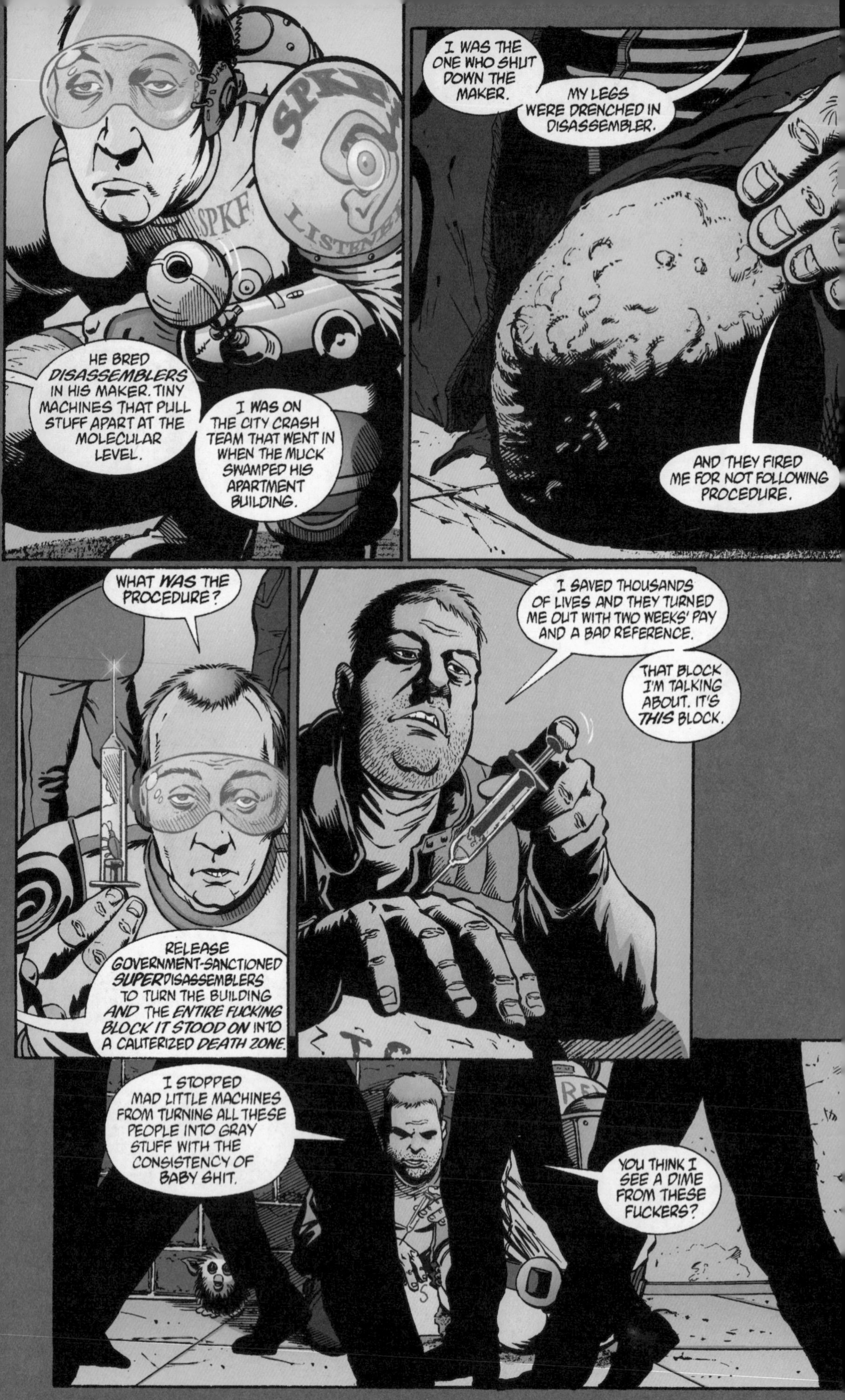
HE BRED DISASSEMBLERS IN HIS MAKER. TINY MACHINES THAT PULL STUFF APART AT THE MOLECULAR LEVEL.
I WAS ON THE CITY CRASH TEAM THAT WENT IN WHEN THE MUCK SWAMPED HIS APARTMENT BUILDING.
I WAS THE ONE WHO SHUT DOWN THE MAKER.
MY LEGS WERE DRENCHED IN DISASSEMBLER.
AND THEY FIRED ME FOR NOT FOLLOWING PROCEDURE.
WHAT WAS THE PROCEDURE?
RELEASE GOVERNMENT-SANCTIONED SUPERDISASSEMBLERS TO TURN THE BUILDING AND THE ENTIRE FUCKING BLOCK IT STOOD ON INTO A CAUTERIZED DEATH ZONE.
I SAVED THOUSANDS OF LIVES AND THEY TURNED ME OUT WITH TWO WEEKS' PAY AND A BAD REFERENCE.
THAT BLOCK I'M TALKING ABOUT. IT'S THIS BLOCK.
I STOPPED MAD LITTLE MACHINES FROM TURNING ALL THESE PEOPLE INTO GRAY STUFF WITH THE CONSISTENCY OF BABY SHIT.
YOU THINK I SEE A DIME FROM THESE FUCKERS?

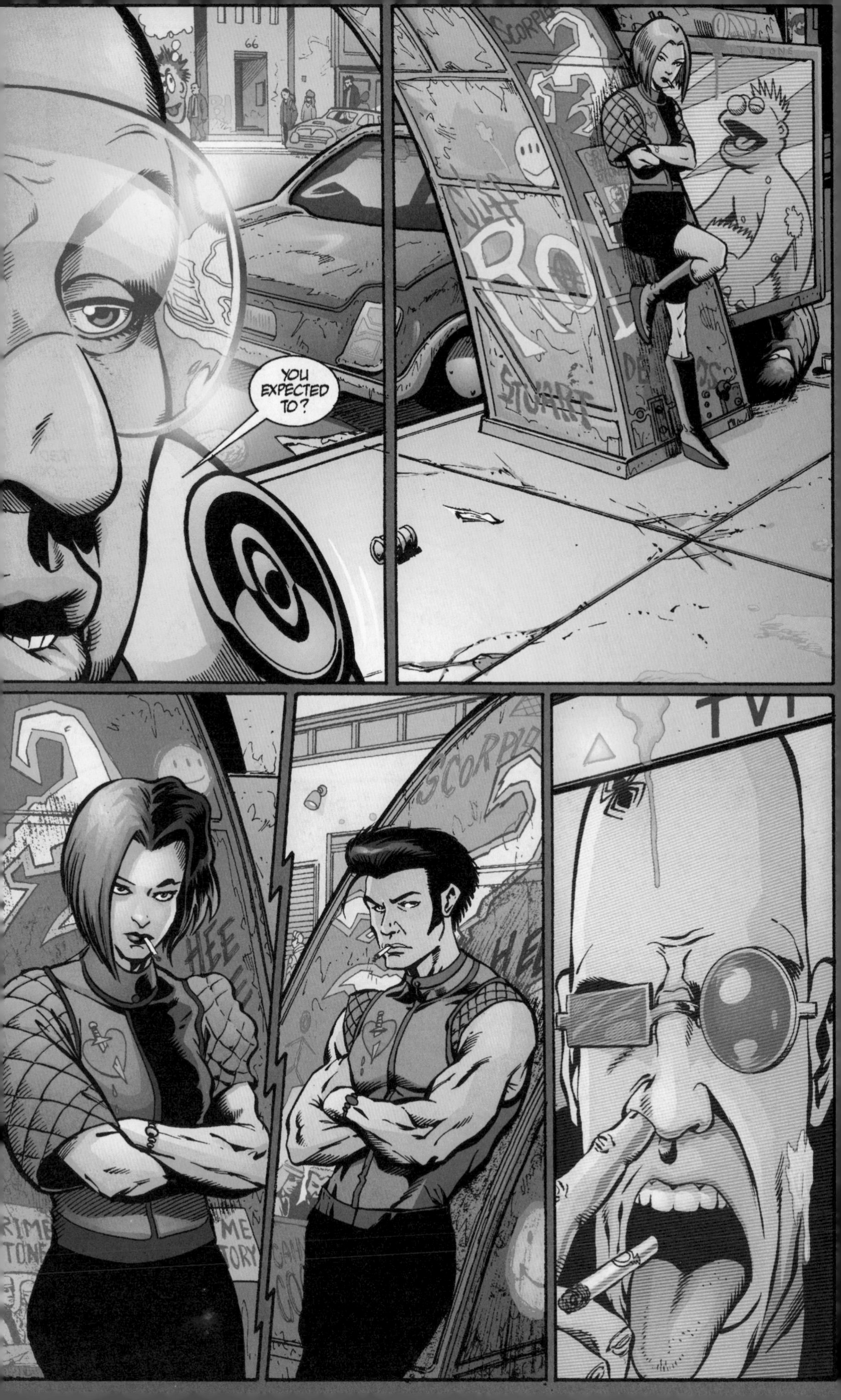
YOU EXPECTED TO?

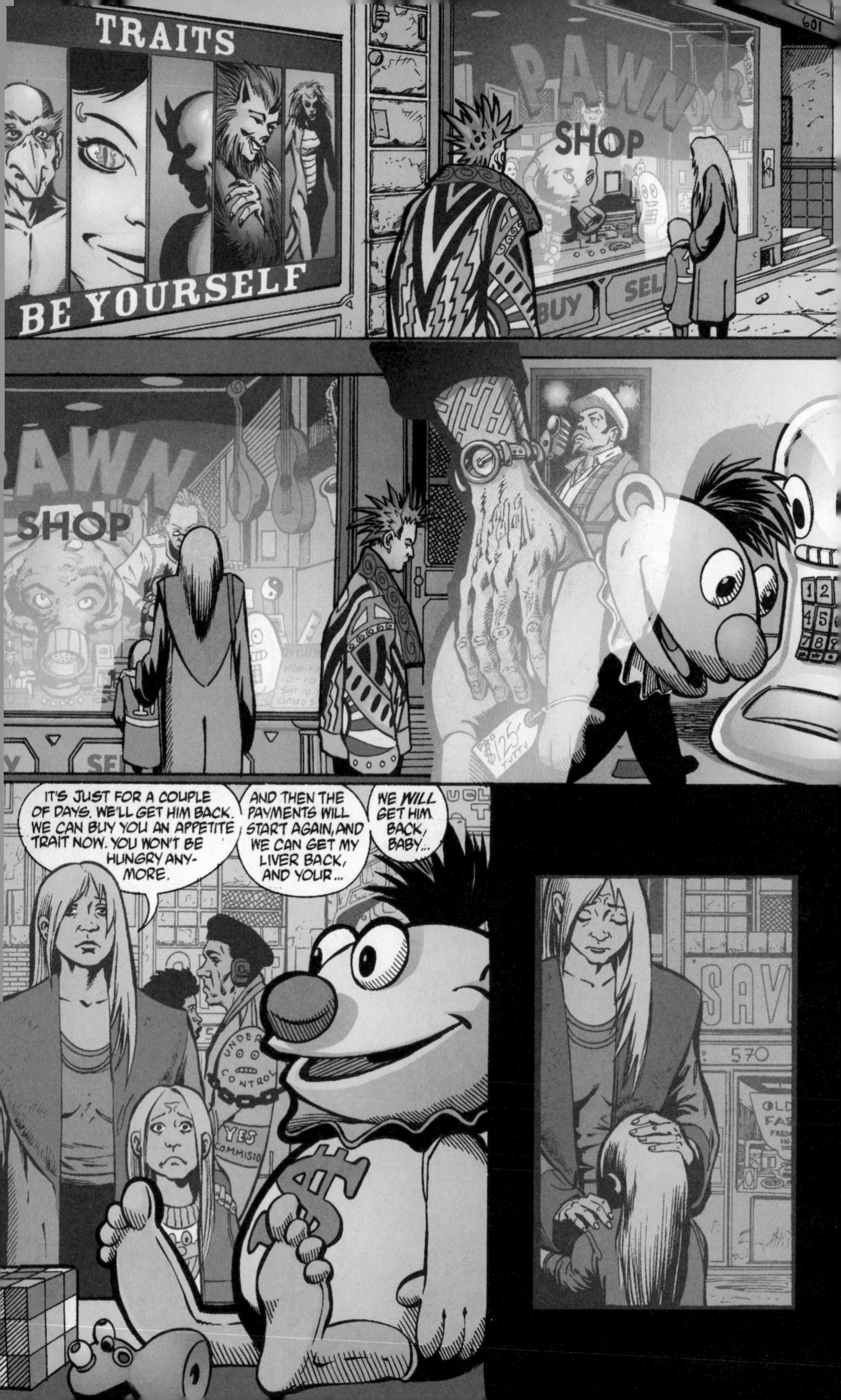

601
TRAITS
BE YOURSELF
PAWN
SHOP
BUY
SEL
PAWN
SHOP
$125
IT'S JUST FOR A COUPLE OF DAYS. WE'LL GET HIM BACK. WE CAN BUY YOU AN APPETITE TRAIT NOW. YOU WON'T BE HUNGRY ANY-MORE.
AND THEN THE PAYMENTS WILL START AGAIN, AND WE CAN GET MY LIVER BACK, AND YOUR...
WE WILL GET HIM BACK, BABY...
UNDER CONTROL
YES COMMISSION
SAV
570

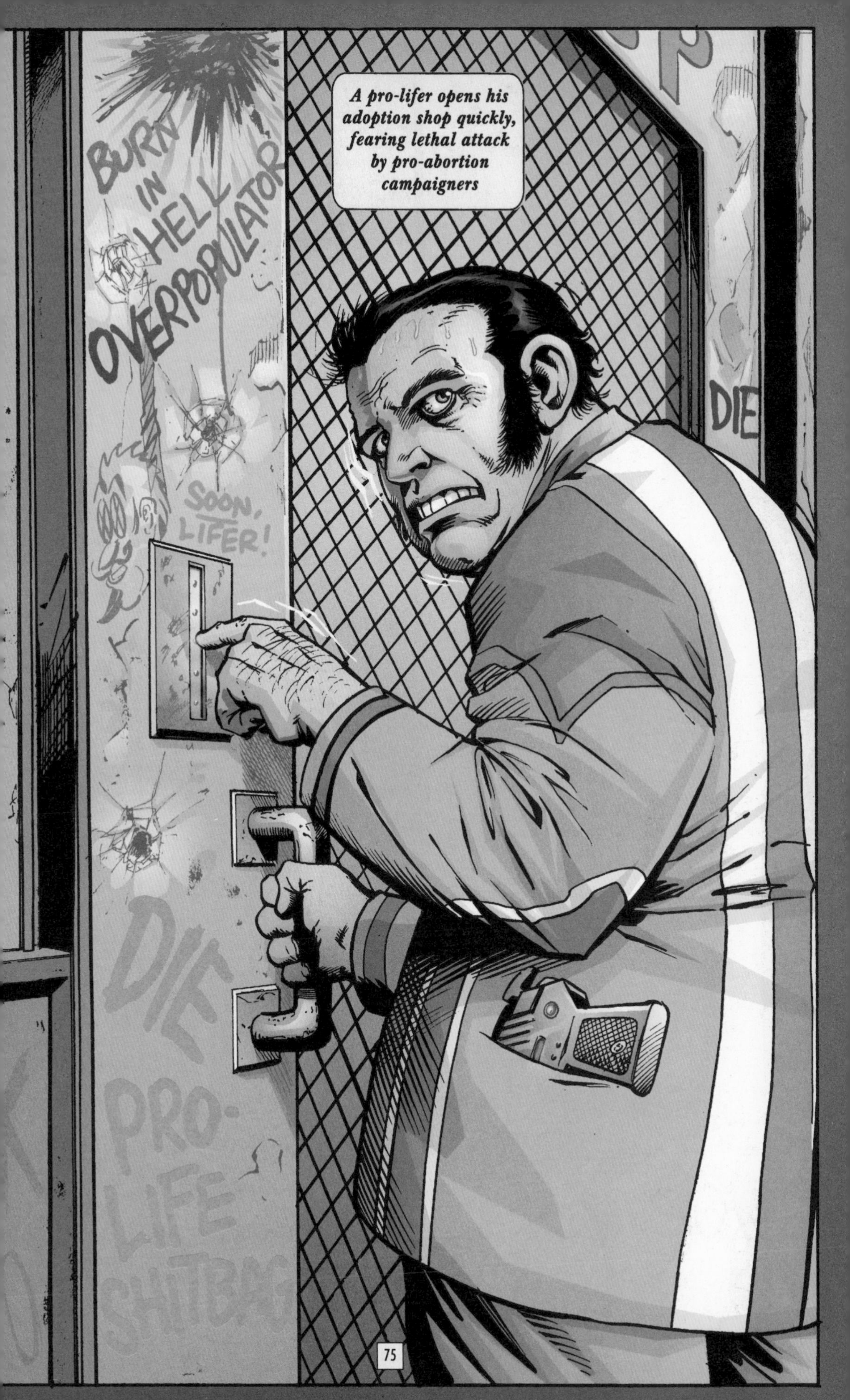
A pro-lifer opens his adoption shop quickly, fearing lethal attack by pro-abortion campaigners
BURN IN HELL OVERPOPULATOR
SOON, LIFER!
DIE
DIE
PRO-LIFE

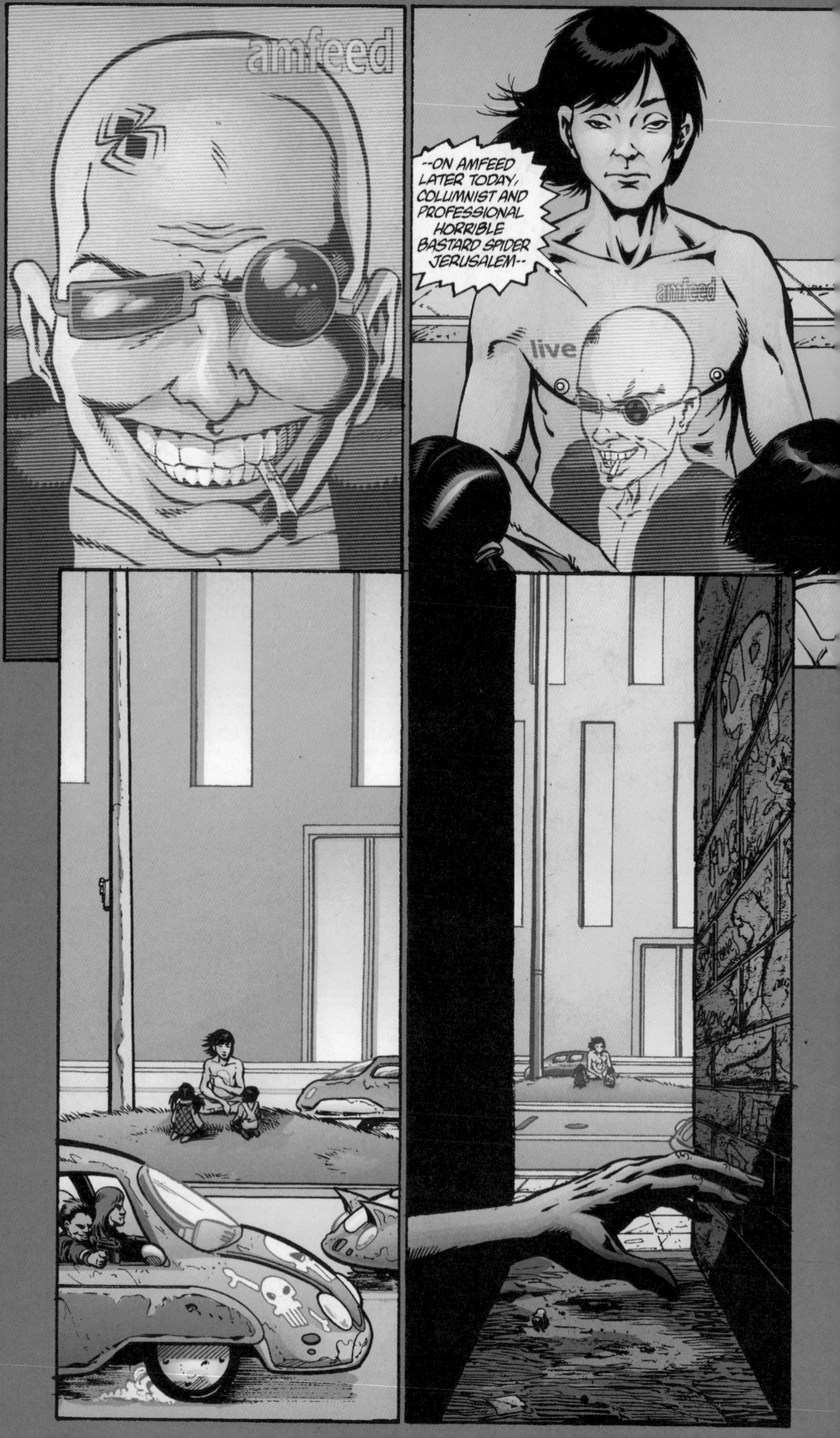
amfeed
--ON AMFEED LATER TODAY, COLUMNIST AND PROFESSIONAL HORRIBLE BASTARD SPIDER JERUSALEM--
amfeed
live

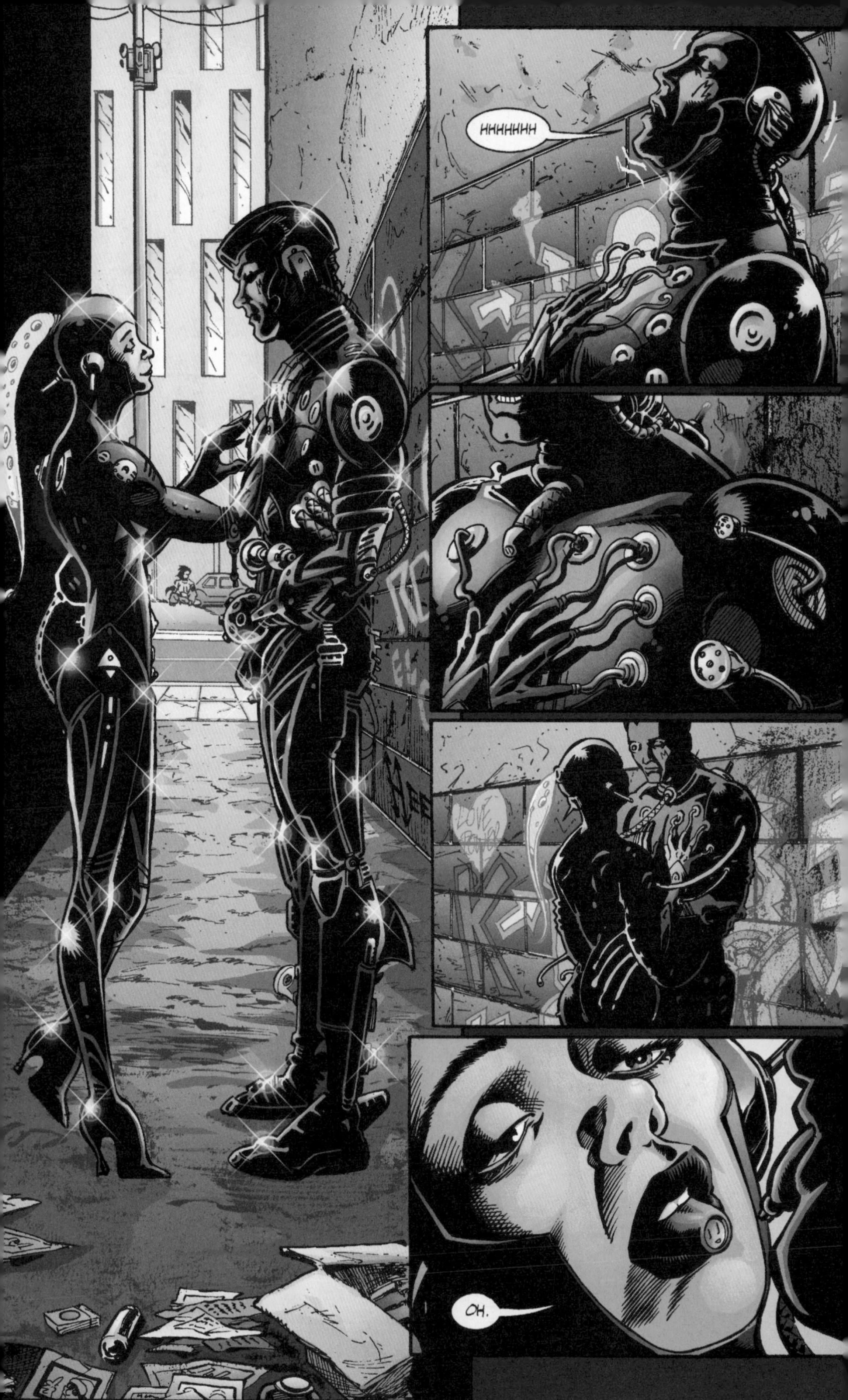
HHHHHHH
OH.

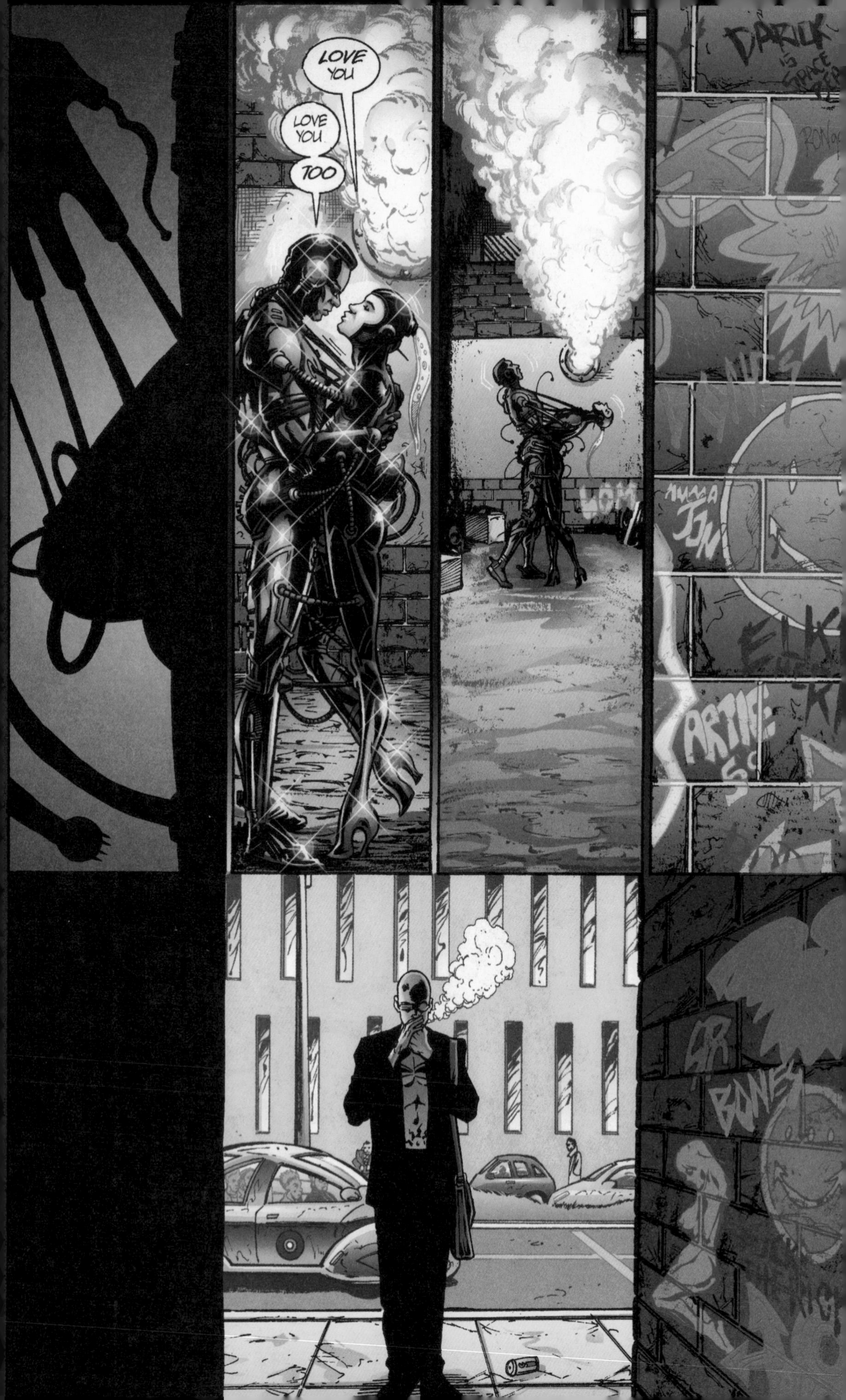
LOVE YOU
LOVE YOU
TOO

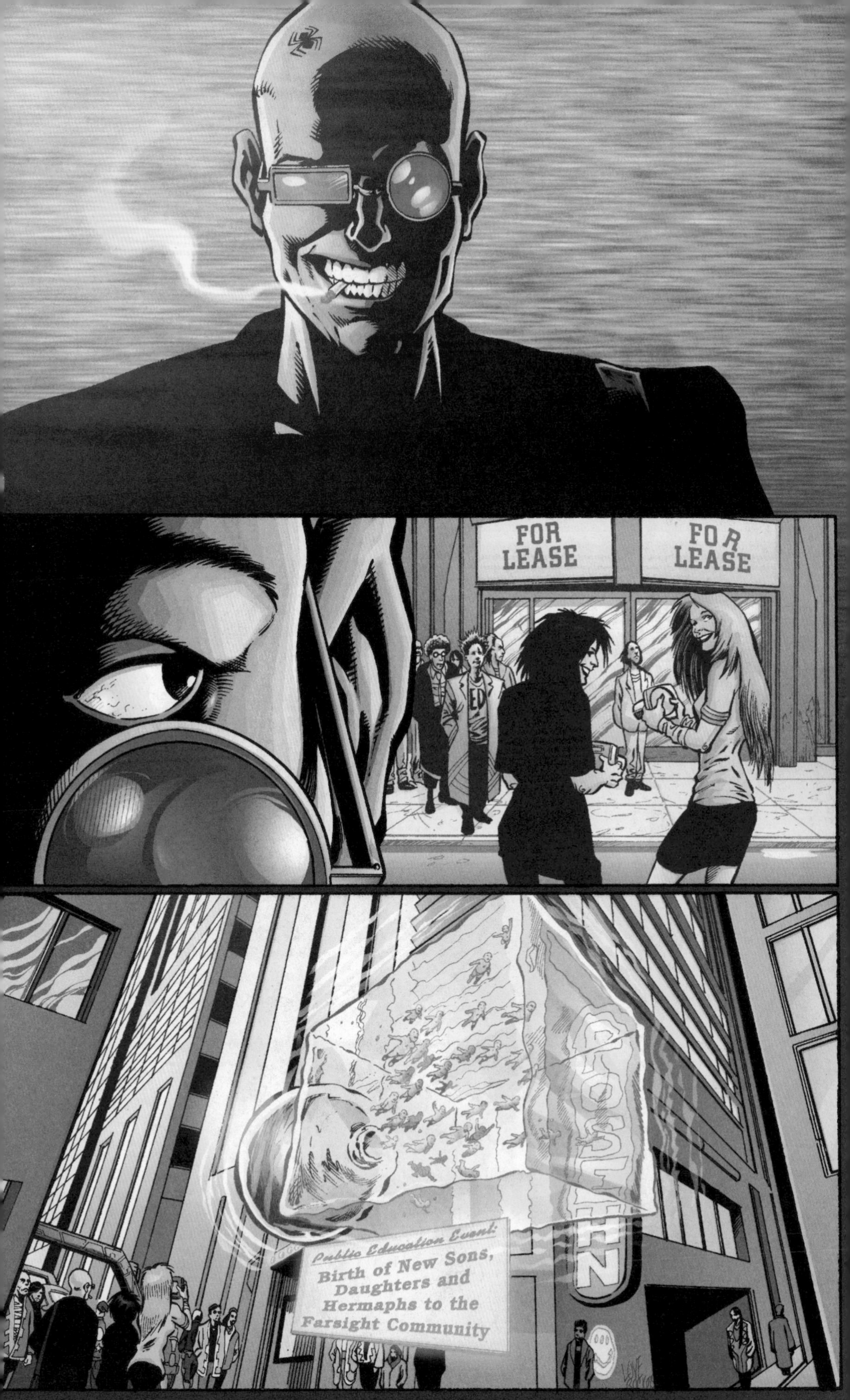
FOR LEASE
FOR LEASE
Public Education Event:
Birth of New Sons, Daughters and Hermaphs to the Farsight Community

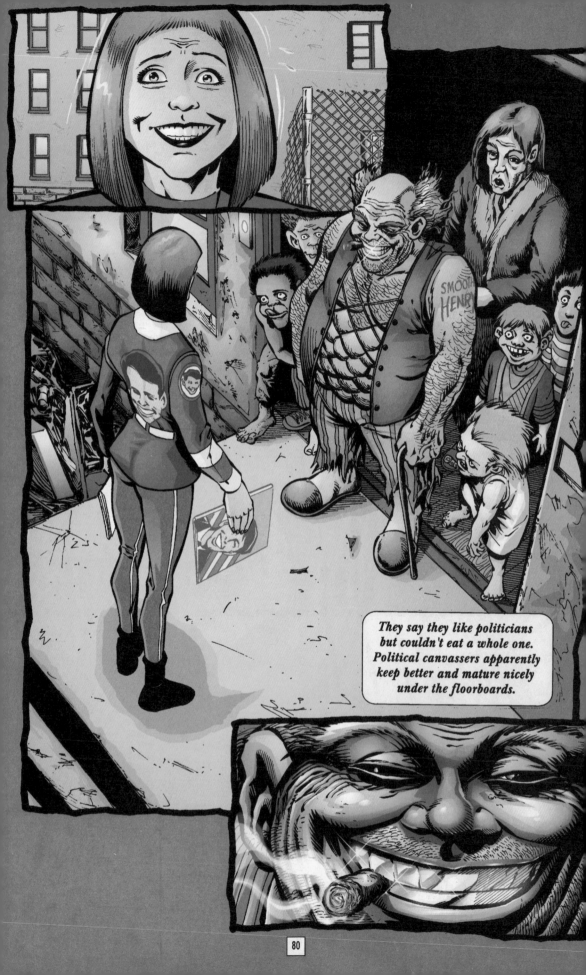

They say they like politicians but couldn't eat a whole one. Political canvassers apparently keep better and mature nicely under the floorboards.

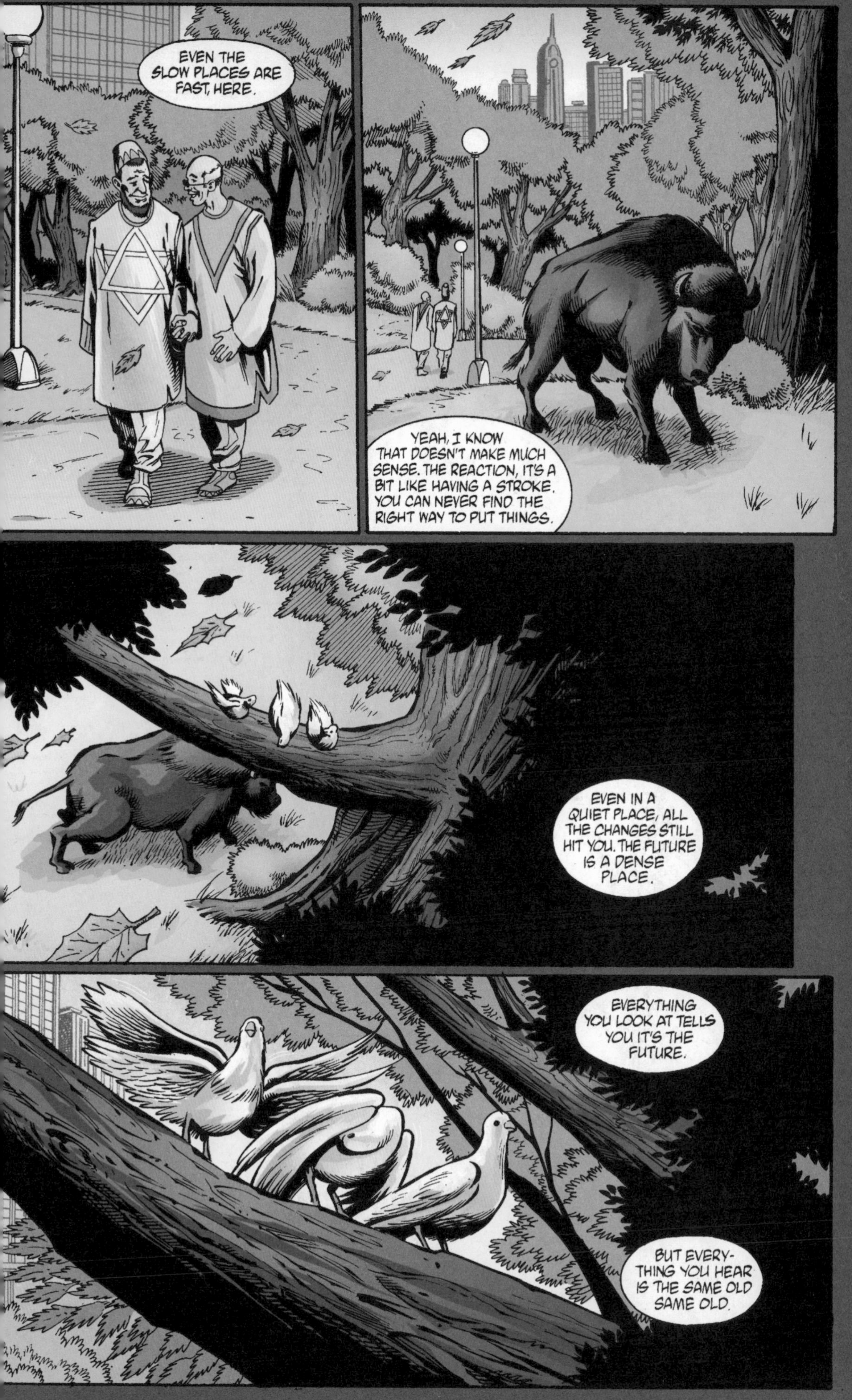
EVEN THE SLOW PLACES ARE FAST, HERE.
YEAH, I KNOW THAT DOESN'T MAKE MUCH SENSE. THE REACTION, IT'S A BIT LIKE HAVING A STROKE. YOU CAN NEVER FIND THE RIGHT WAY TO PUT THINGS.
EVEN IN A QUIET PLACE, ALL THE CHANGES STILL HIT YOU. THE FUTURE IS A DENSE PLACE.
EVERYTHING YOU LOOK AT TELLS YOU IT'S THE FUTURE.
BUT EVERY-THING YOU HEAR IS THE SAME OLD SAME OLD.

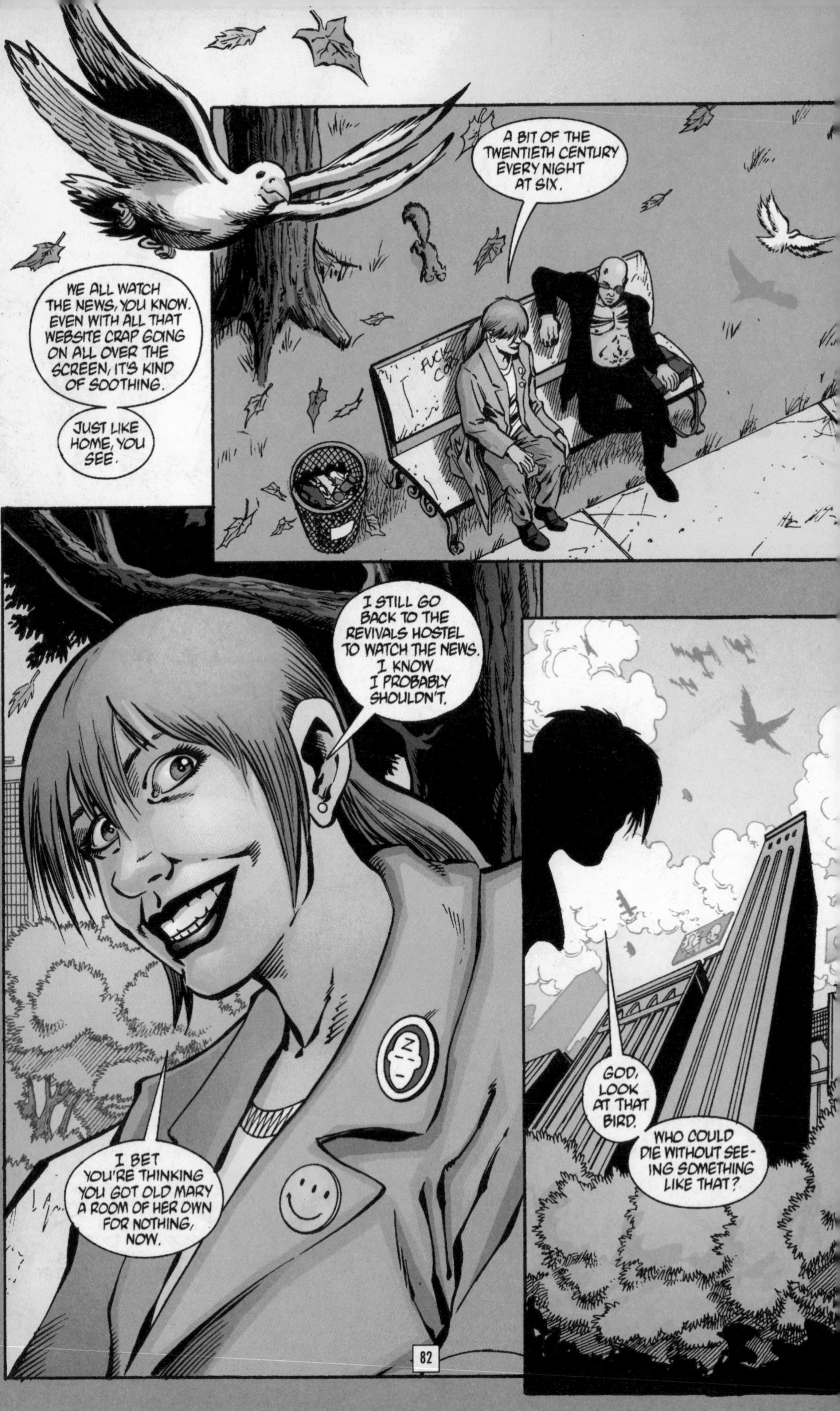
WE ALL WATCH THE NEWS, YOU KNOW. EVEN WITH ALL THAT WEBSITE CRAP GOING ON ALL OVER THE SCREEN, IT'S KIND OF SOOTHING.
JUST LIKE HOME, YOU SEE.
A BIT OF THE TWENTIETH CENTURY EVERY NIGHT AT SIX.
I STILL GO BACK TO THE REVIVALS HOSTEL TO WATCH THE NEWS. I KNOW I PROBABLY SHOULDN'T.
I BET YOU'RE THINKING YOU GOT OLD MARY A ROOM OF HER OWN FOR NOTHING, NOW.
GOD, LOOK AT THAT BIRD.
WHO COULD DIE WITHOUT SEEING SOMETHING LIKE THAT?

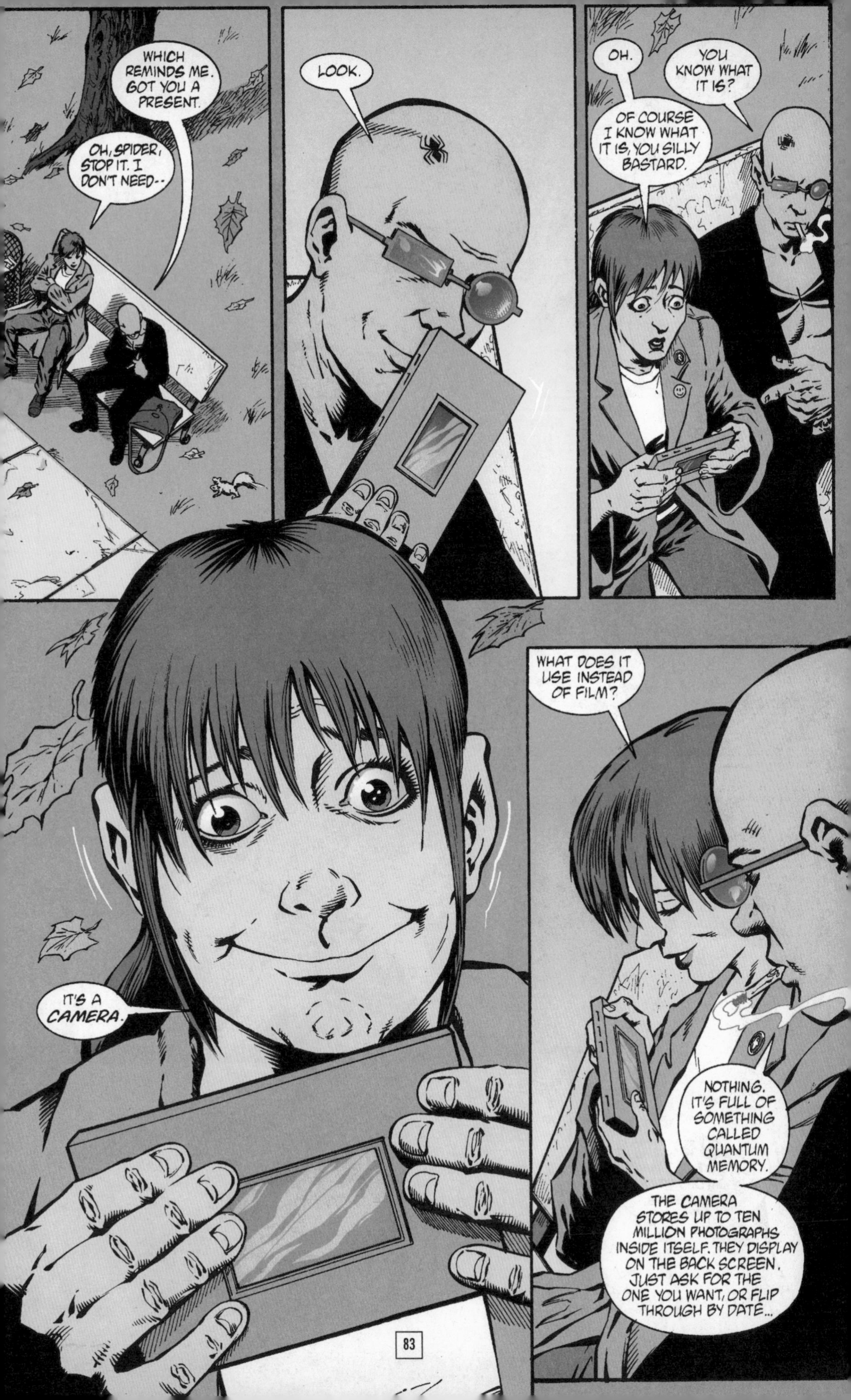
WHICH REMINDS ME. GOT YOU A PRESENT.
OH, SPIDER, STOP IT. I DON'T NEED--
LOOK.
OH.
YOU KNOW WHAT IT IS?
OF COURSE I KNOW WHAT IT IS, YOU SILLY BASTARD.
IT'S A CAMERA.
WHAT DOES IT USE INSTEAD OF FILM?
NOTHING. IT'S FULL OF SOMETHING CALLED QUANTUM MEMORY.
THE CAMERA STORES UP TO TEN MILLION PHOTOGRAPHS INSIDE ITSELF. THEY DISPLAY ON THE BACK SCREEN. JUST ASK FOR THE ONE YOU WANT, OR FLIP THROUGH BY DATE...

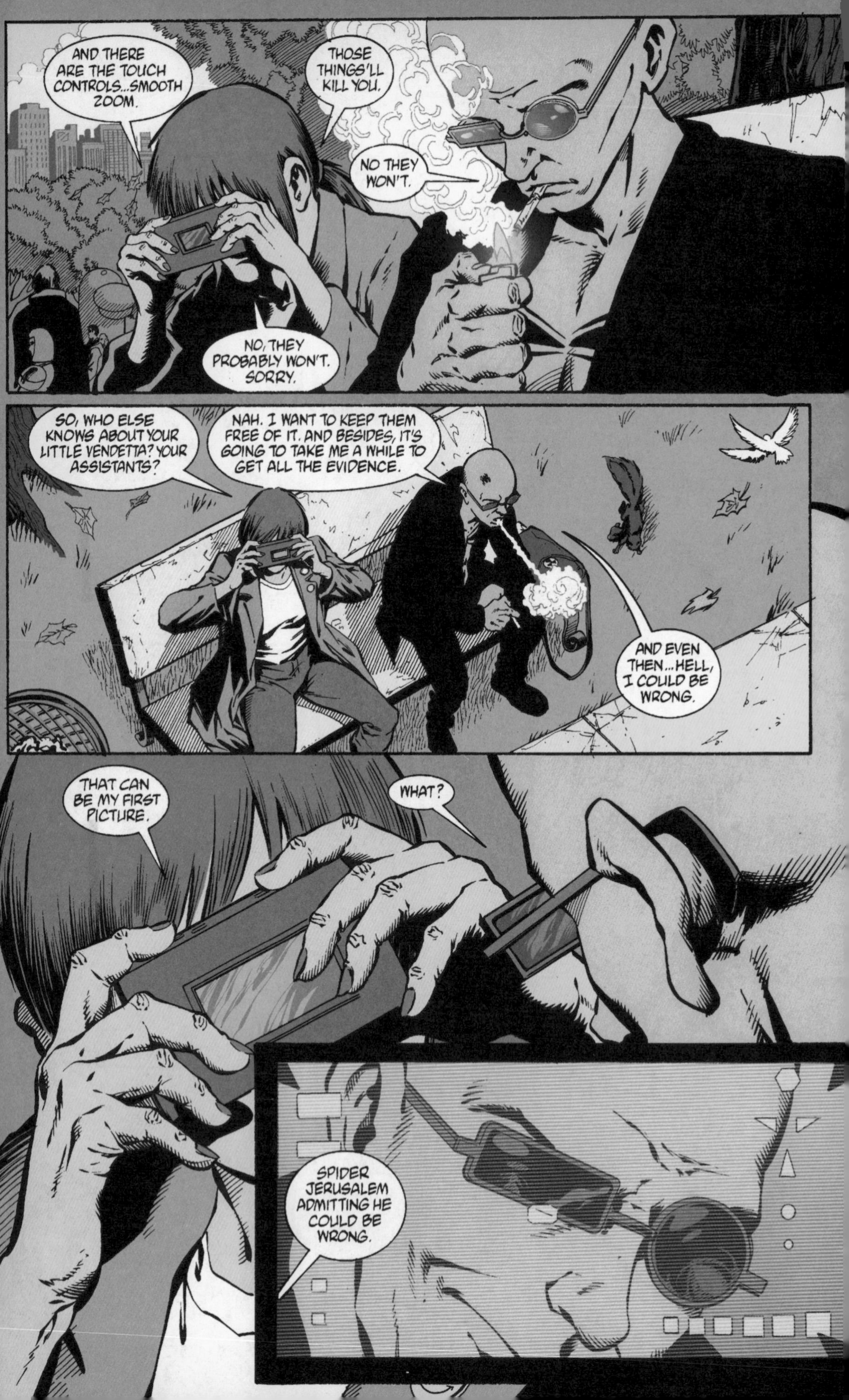
AND THERE ARE THE TOUCH CONTROLS...SMOOTH ZOOM.
THOSE THINGS'LL KILL YOU.
NO THEY WON'T.
NO, THEY PROBABLY WON'T. SORRY.
SO, WHO ELSE KNOWS ABOUT YOUR LITTLE VENDETTA? YOUR ASSISTANTS?
NAH. I WANT TO KEEP THEM FREE OF IT. AND BESIDES, IT'S GOING TO TAKE ME A WHILE TO GET ALL THE EVIDENCE.
AND EVEN THEN...HELL, I COULD BE WRONG.
THAT CAN BE MY FIRST PICTURE.
WHAT?
SPIDER JERUSALEM ADMITTING HE COULD BE WRONG.

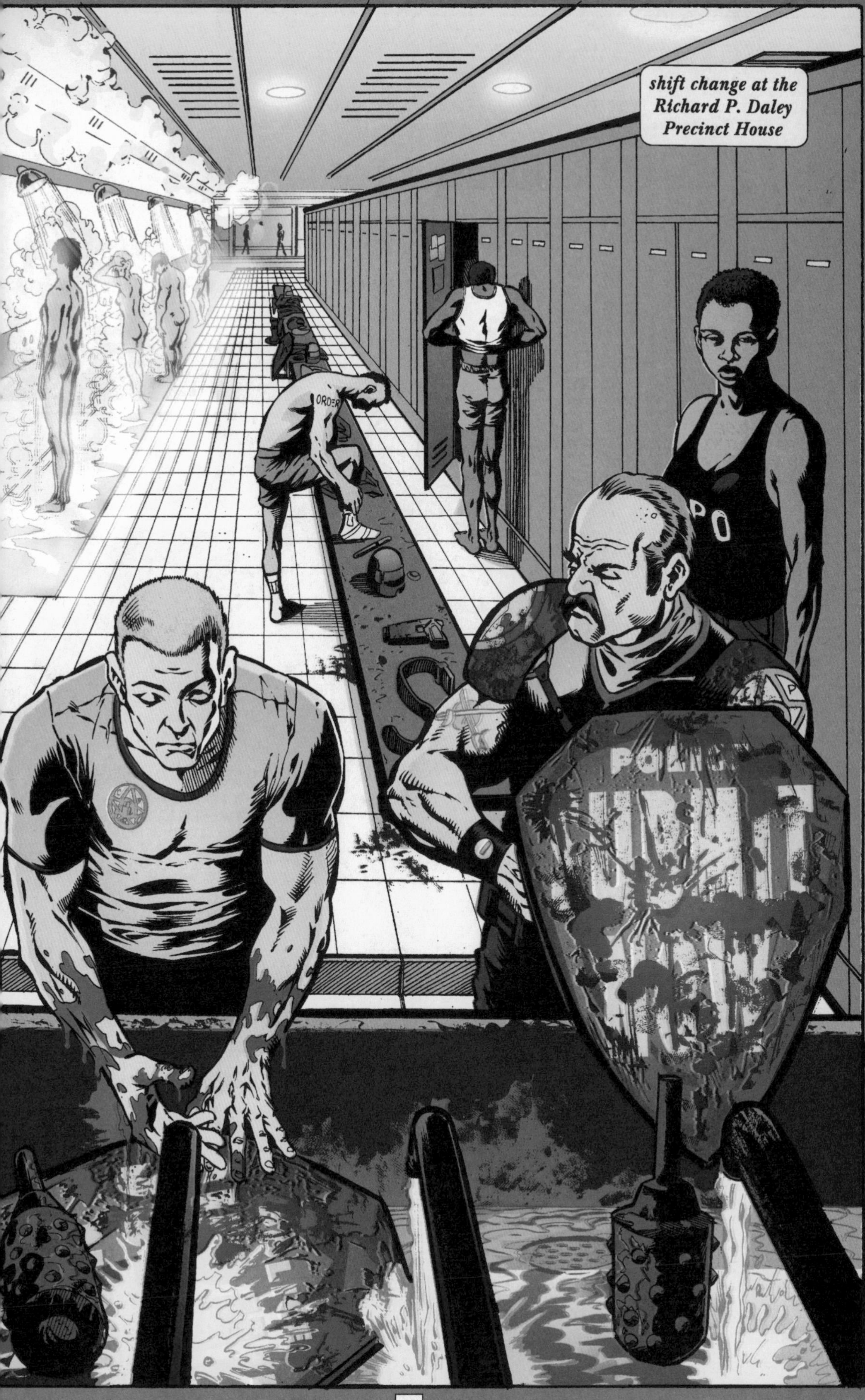
shift change at the
Richard P. Daley
Precinct House
ORDER
PO

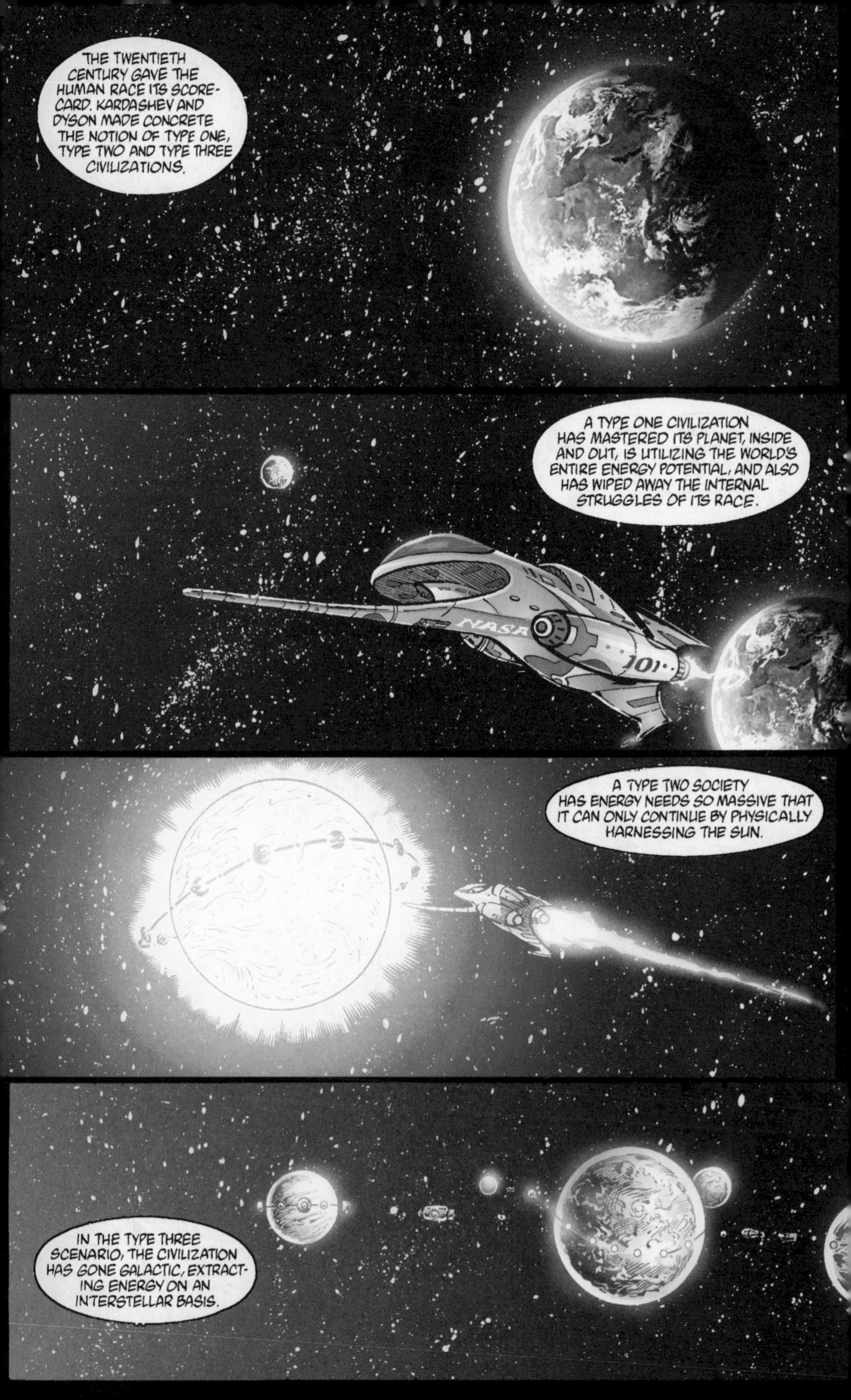
THE TWENTIETH CENTURY GAVE THE HUMAN RACE ITS SCORE-CARD. KARDASHEV AND DYSON MADE CONCRETE THE NOTION OF TYPE ONE, TYPE TWO AND TYPE THREE CIVILIZATIONS.
A TYPE ONE CIVILIZATION HAS MASTERED ITS PLANET, INSIDE AND OUT, IS UTILIZING THE WORLD'S ENTIRE ENERGY POTENTIAL, AND ALSO HAS WIPED AWAY THE INTERNAL STRUGGLES OF ITS RACE.
NASA
101
A TYPE TWO SOCIETY HAS ENERGY NEEDS SO MASSIVE THAT IT CAN ONLY CONTINUE BY PHYSICALLY HARNESSING THE SUN.
IN THE TYPE THREE SCENARIO, THE CIVILIZATION HAS GONE GALACTIC, EXTRACT-ING ENERGY ON AN INTERSTELLAR BASIS.

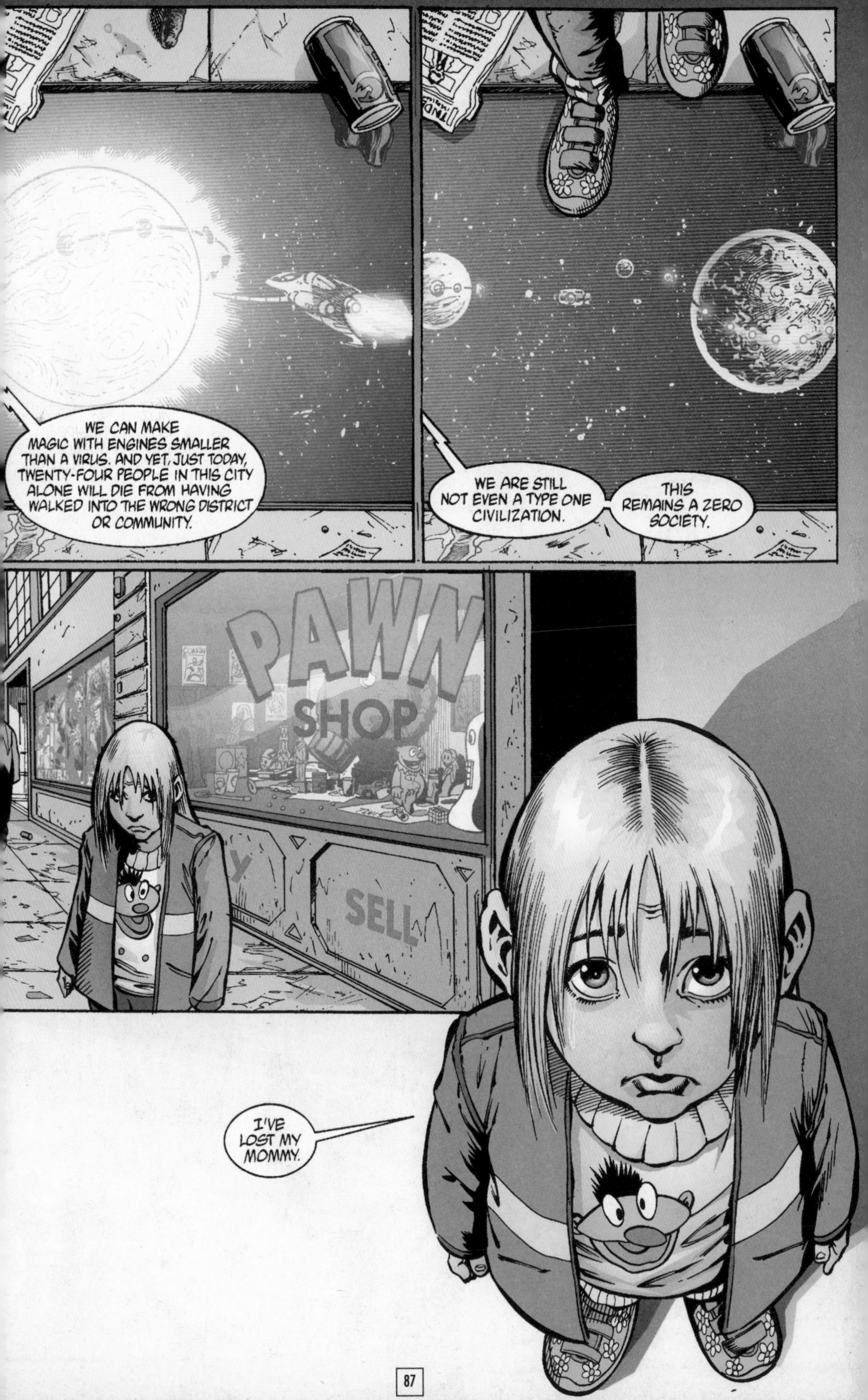
WE CAN MAKE MAGIC WITH ENGINES SMALLER THAN A VIRUS. AND YET, JUST TODAY, TWENTY-FOUR PEOPLE IN THIS CITY ALONE WILL DIE FROM HAVING WALKED INTO THE WRONG DISTRICT OR COMMUNITY.
WE ARE STILL NOT EVEN A TYPE ONE CIVILIZATION.
THIS REMAINS A ZERO SOCIETY.
PAWN
SHOP
SELL
I'VE LOST MY MOMMY.

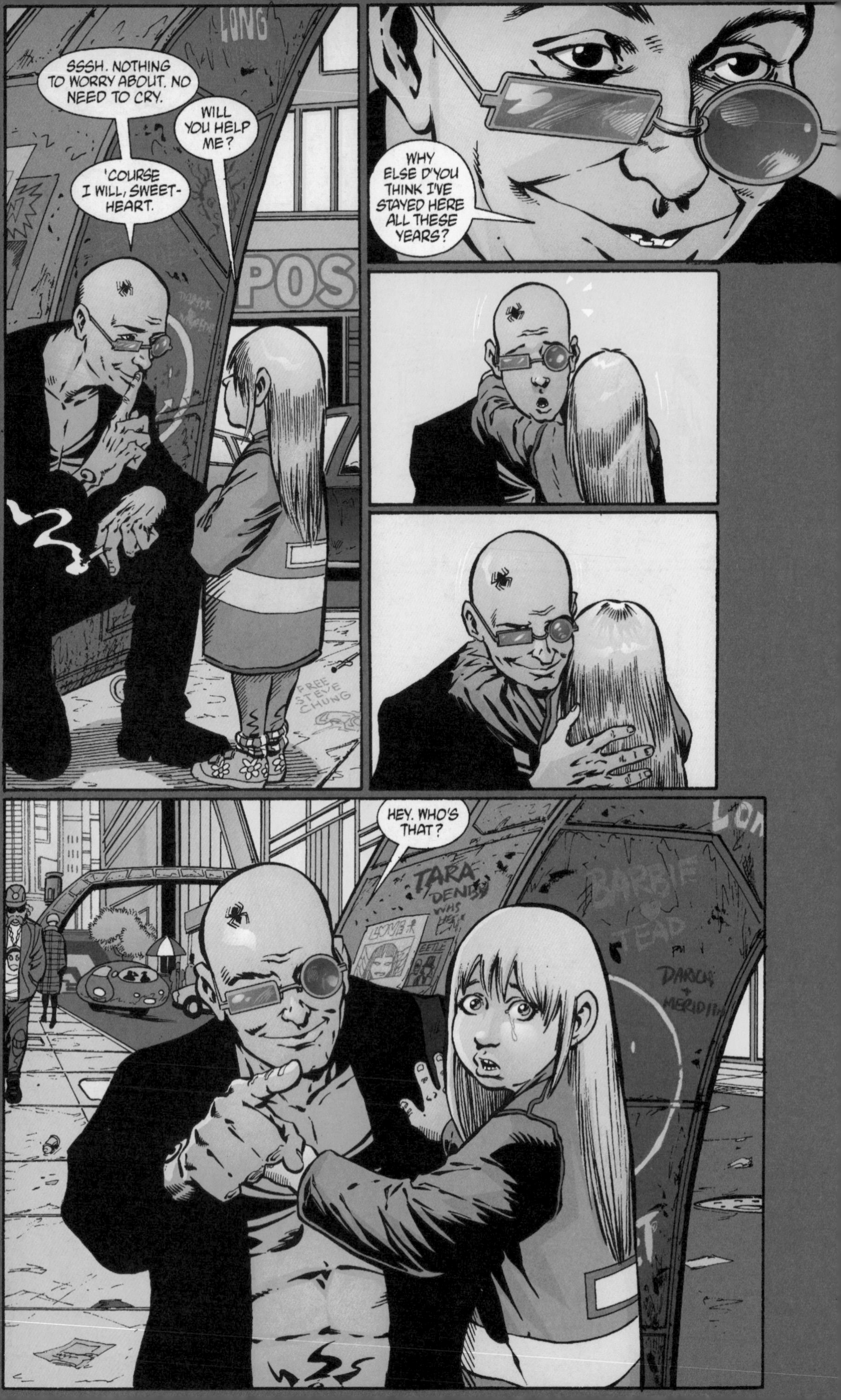
SSSH. NOTHING TO WORRY ABOUT. NO NEED TO CRY.
WILL YOU HELP ME?
'COURSE I WILL, SWEET-HEART.
WHY ELSE D'YOU THINK I'VE STAYED HERE ALL THESE YEARS?
HEY. WHO'S THAT?

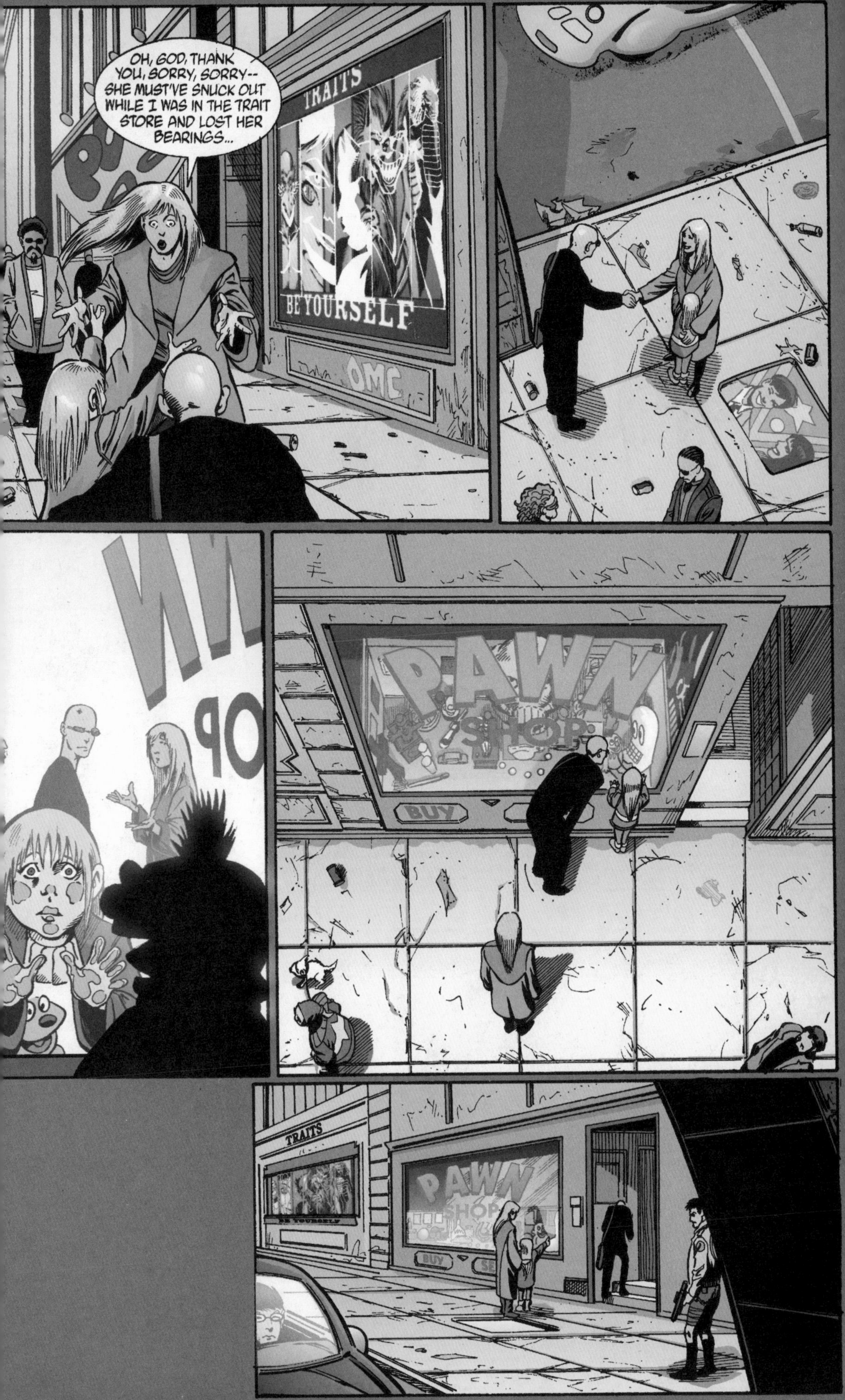
OH, GOD, THANK YOU, SORRY, SORRY-- SHE MUST'VE SNUCK OUT WHILE I WAS IN THE TRAIT STORE AND LOST HER BEARINGS...
TRAITS
BE YOURSELF
OMC
PAWN SHOP
BUY
TRAITS
PAWN SHOP
BUY

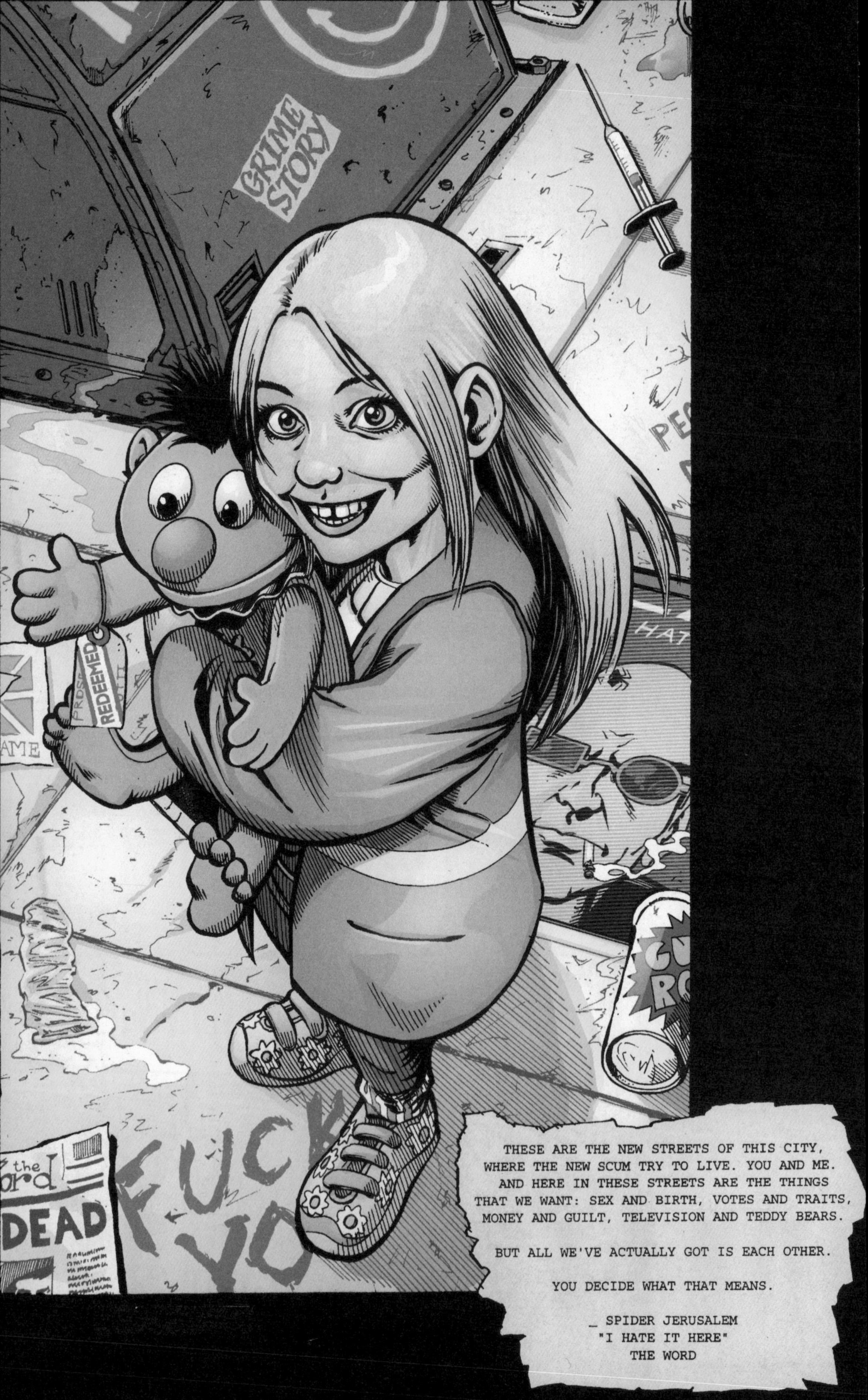
GRIME STORY
REDEEMED
DEAD
FUCK
THESE ARE THE NEW STREETS OF THIS CITY, WHERE THE NEW SCUM TRY TO LIVE. YOU AND ME. AND HERE IN THESE STREETS ARE THE THINGS THAT WE WANT: SEX AND BIRTH, VOTES AND TRAITS, MONEY AND GUILT, TELEVISION AND TEDDY BEARS.
BUT ALL WE'VE ACTUALLY GOT IS EACH OTHER.
YOU DECIDE WHAT THAT MEANS.
_ SPIDER JERUSALEM
"I HATE IT HERE"
THE WORD

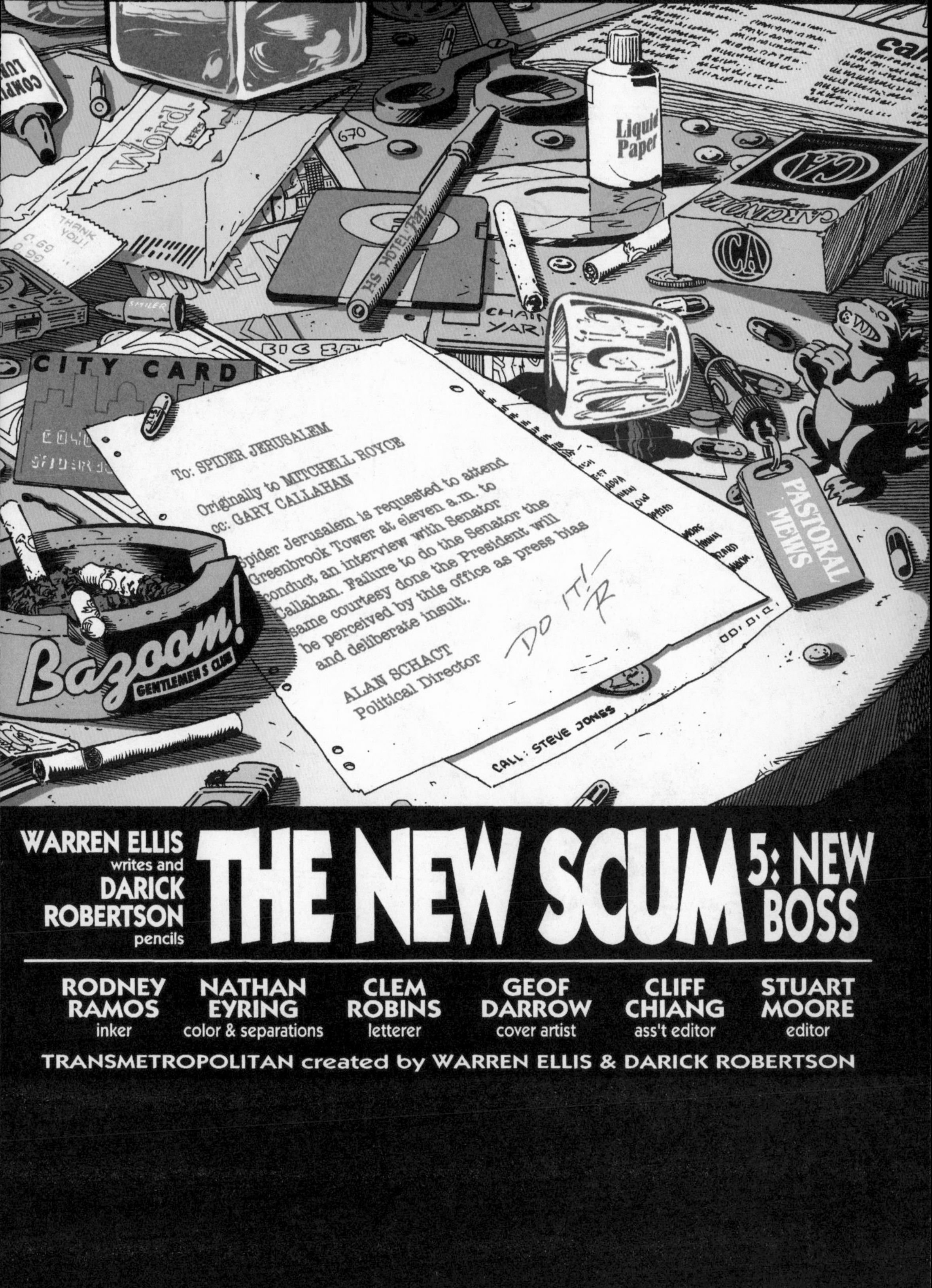
Liquid Paper
Word
THANK YOU!
CITY CARD
CARCINOMA
CA
PASTORAL MEWS
Bazoom!
GENTLEMEN'S CLUB
To: SPIDER JERUSALEM
Originally to MITCHELL ROYCE
cc: GARY CALLAHAN
Spider Jerusalem is requested to attend Greenbrook Tower at eleven a.m. to conduct an interview with Senator Callahan. Failure to do the Senator the same courtesy done the President will be perceived by this office as press bias and deliberate insult.
ALAN SCHACT
Political Director
DO IT! R
CALL: STEVE JONES

WARREN ELLIS writes and **DARICK ROBERTSON** pencils

THE NEW SCUM

5: NEW BOSS

RODNEY RAMOS inker
NATHAN EYRING color & separations
CLEM ROBINS letterer
GEOF DARROW cover artist
CLIFF CHIANG ass't editor
STUART MOORE editor

TRANSMETROPOLITAN created by WARREN ELLIS & DARICK ROBERTSON

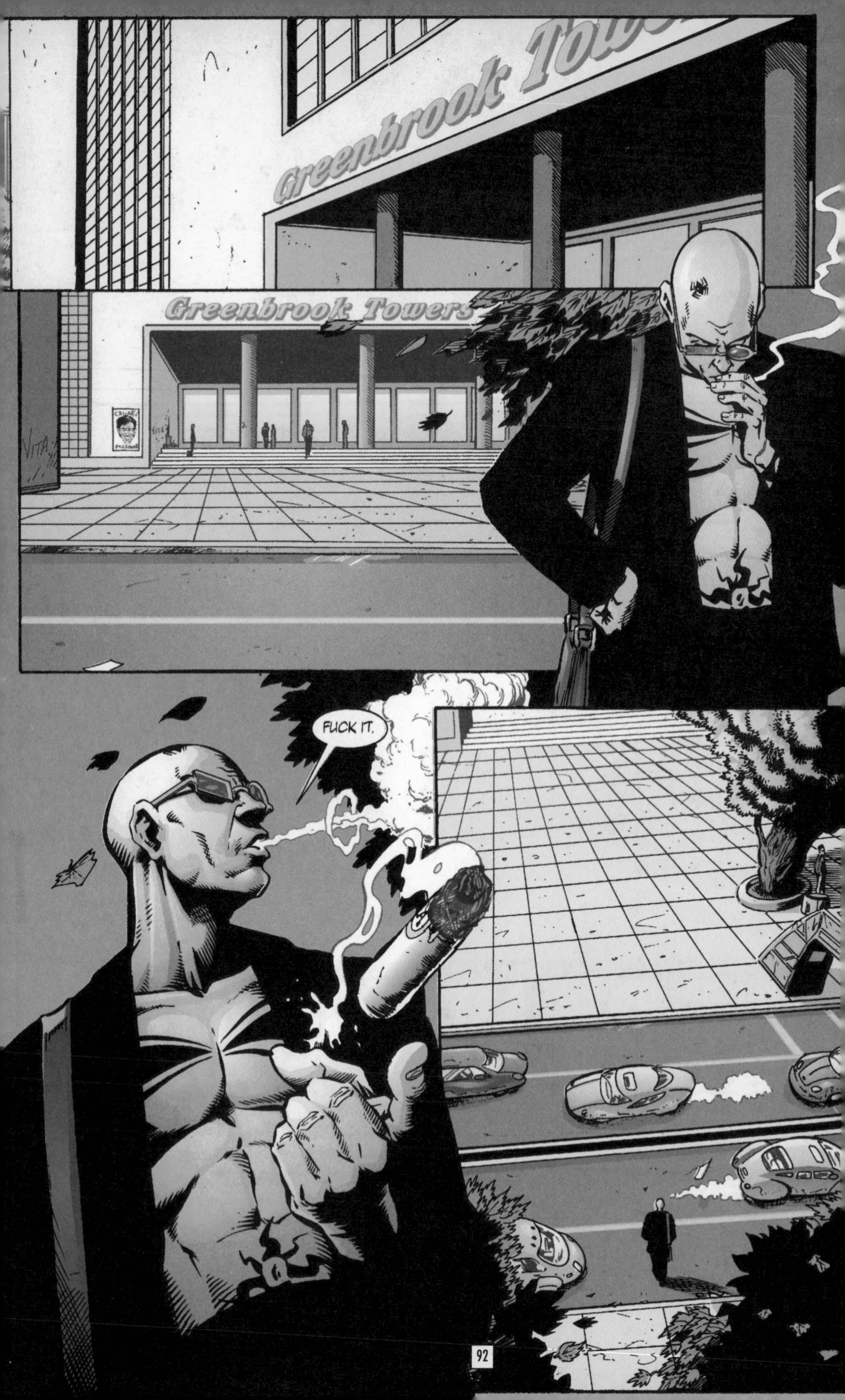
Greenbrook Towers
Greenbrook Towers
FUCK IT.

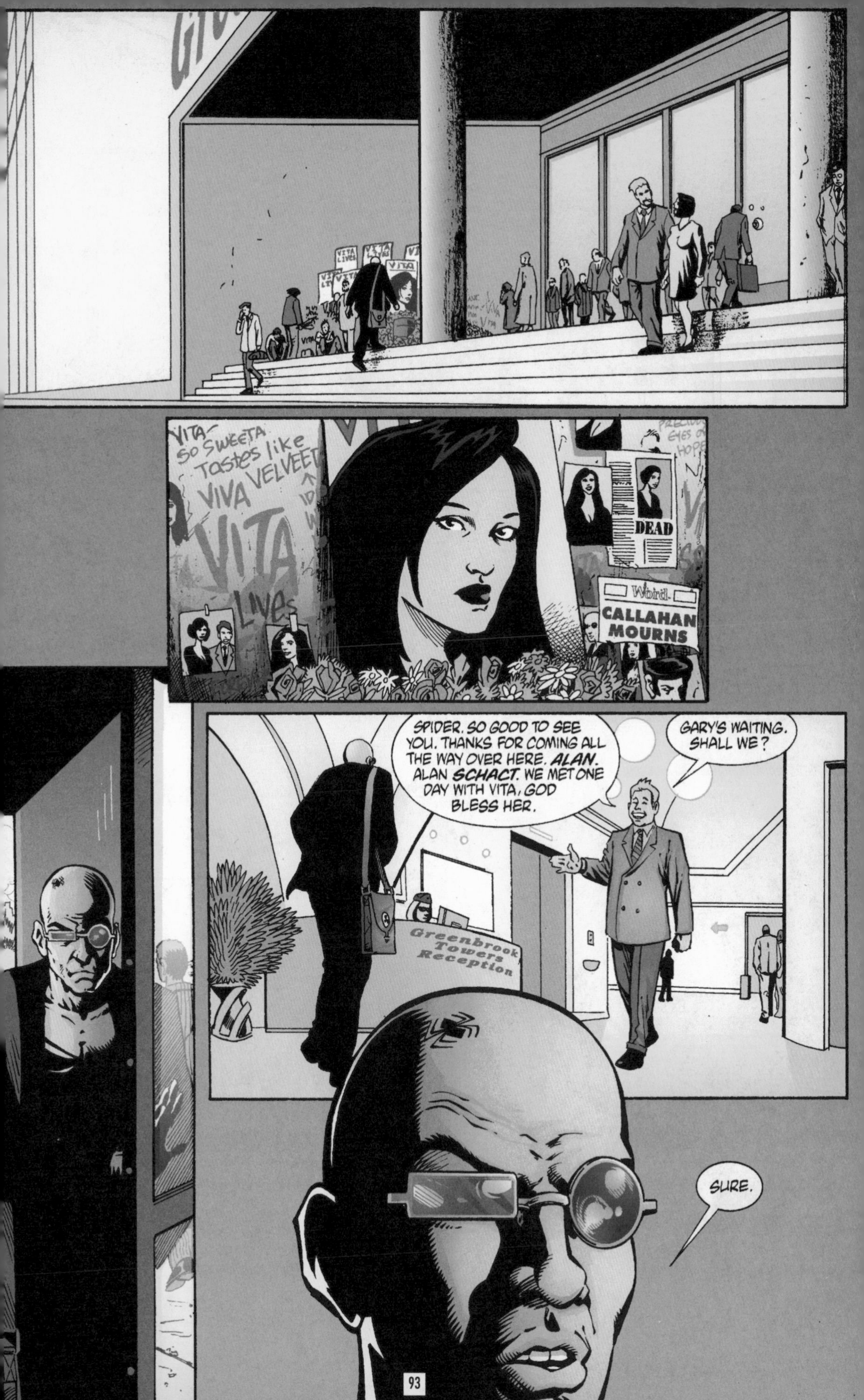
VITA LIVES
VITA
VITA-
So SWEETA
Tastes like
VIVA VELVEETA
VIVA
VITA
LIVES
PRECIOUS
EYES OF
HOPE
DEAD
Word
CALLAHAN
MOURNS
SPIDER. SO GOOD TO SEE YOU. THANKS FOR COMING ALL THE WAY OVER HERE. ALAN. ALAN SCHACT. WE MET ONE DAY WITH VITA, GOD BLESS HER.
GARY'S WAITING. SHALL WE?
Greenbrook Towers Reception
SURE.

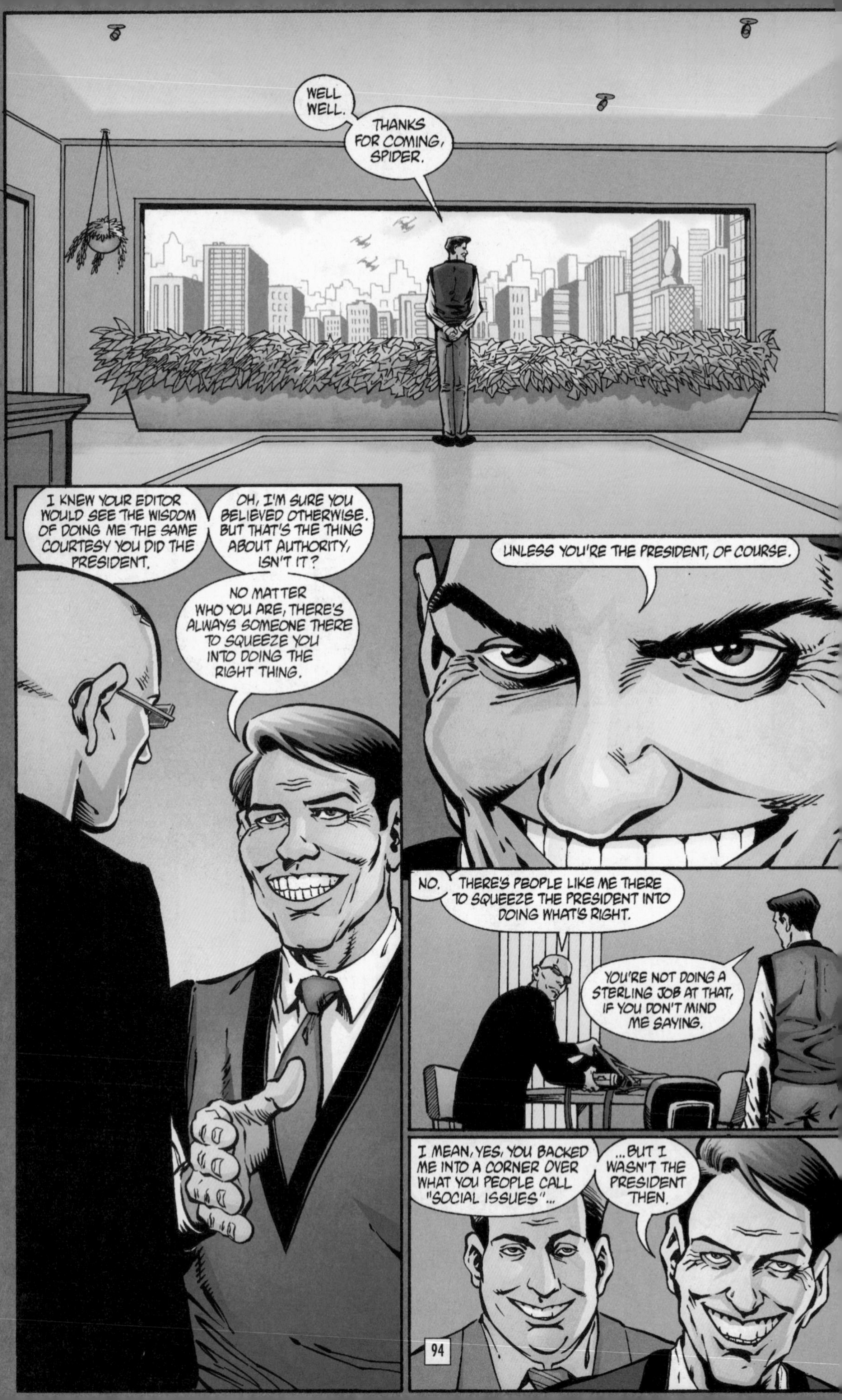
WELL WELL.
THANKS FOR COMING, SPIDER.
I KNEW YOUR EDITOR WOULD SEE THE WISDOM OF DOING ME THE SAME COURTESY YOU DID THE PRESIDENT.
OH, I'M SURE YOU BELIEVED OTHERWISE. BUT THAT'S THE THING ABOUT AUTHORITY, ISN'T IT?
NO MATTER WHO YOU ARE, THERE'S ALWAYS SOMEONE THERE TO SQUEEZE YOU INTO DOING THE RIGHT THING.
UNLESS YOU'RE THE PRESIDENT, OF COURSE.
NO.
THERE'S PEOPLE LIKE ME THERE TO SQUEEZE THE PRESIDENT INTO DOING WHAT'S RIGHT.
YOU'RE NOT DOING A STERLING JOB AT THAT, IF YOU DON'T MIND ME SAYING.
I MEAN, YES, YOU BACKED ME INTO A CORNER OVER WHAT YOU PEOPLE CALL "SOCIAL ISSUES"...
...BUT I WASN'T THE PRESIDENT THEN.

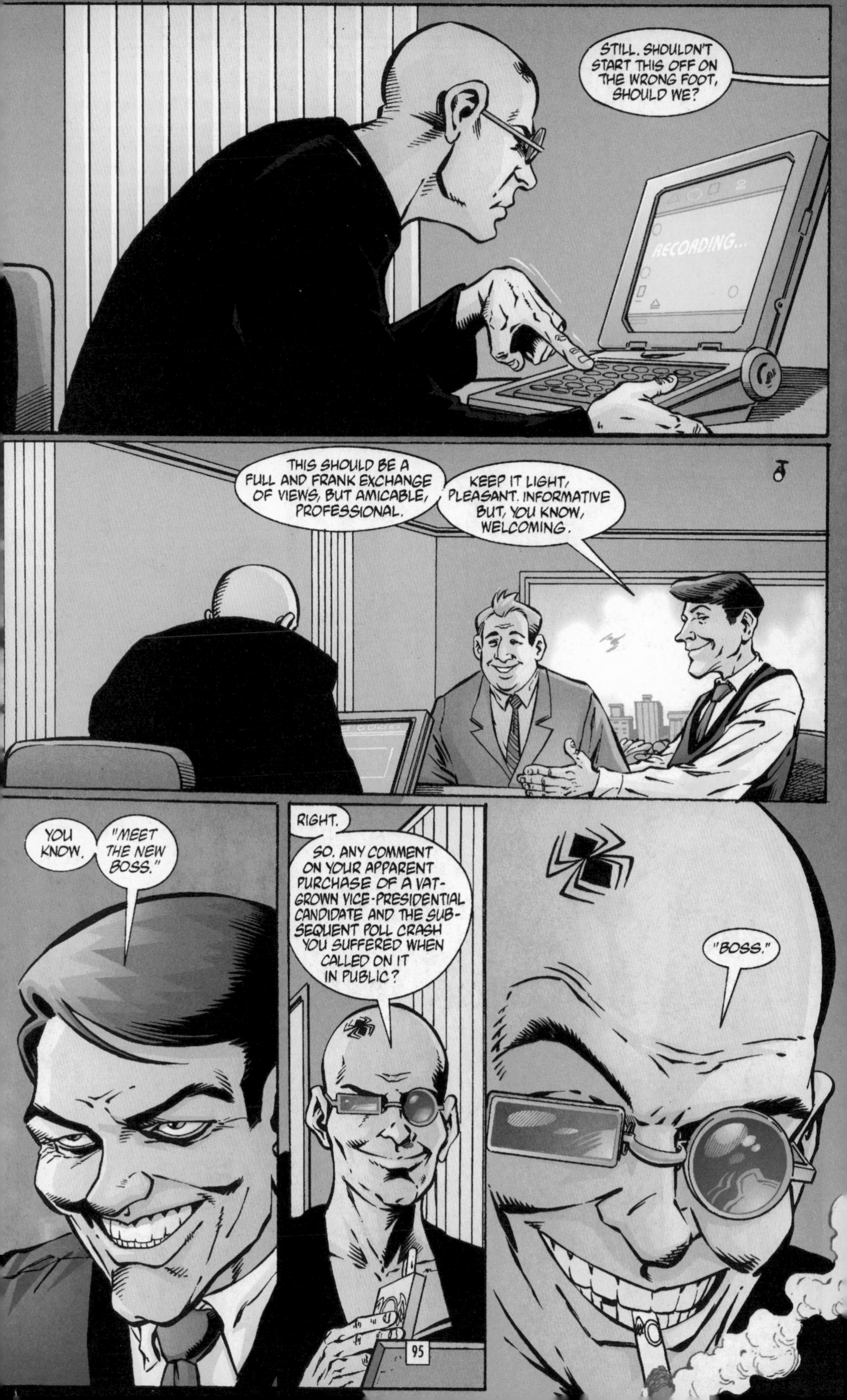
STILL. SHOULDN'T START THIS OFF ON THE WRONG FOOT, SHOULD WE?
RECORDING...
THIS SHOULD BE A FULL AND FRANK EXCHANGE OF VIEWS, BUT AMICABLE, PROFESSIONAL.
KEEP IT LIGHT, PLEASANT. INFORMATIVE BUT, YOU KNOW, WELCOMING.
YOU KNOW.
"MEET THE NEW BOSS."
RIGHT.
SO. ANY COMMENT ON YOUR APPARENT PURCHASE OF A VAT-GROWN VICE-PRESIDENTIAL CANDIDATE AND THE SUB-SEQUENT POLL CRASH YOU SUFFERED WHEN CALLED ON IT IN PUBLIC?
"BOSS."

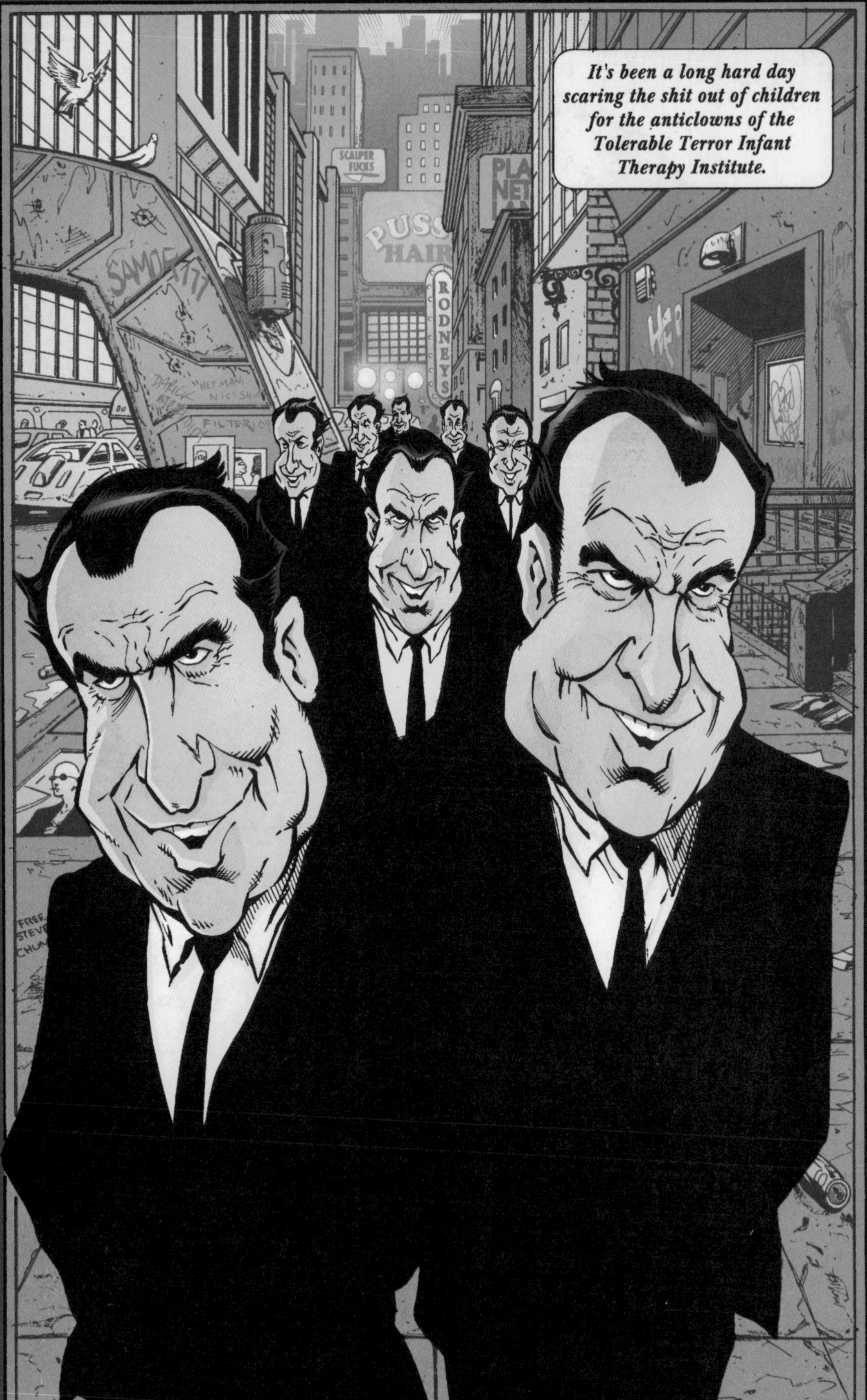
It's been a long hard day scaring the shit out of children for the anticlowns of the Tolerable Terror Infant Therapy Institute.
SCALPER FUCKS

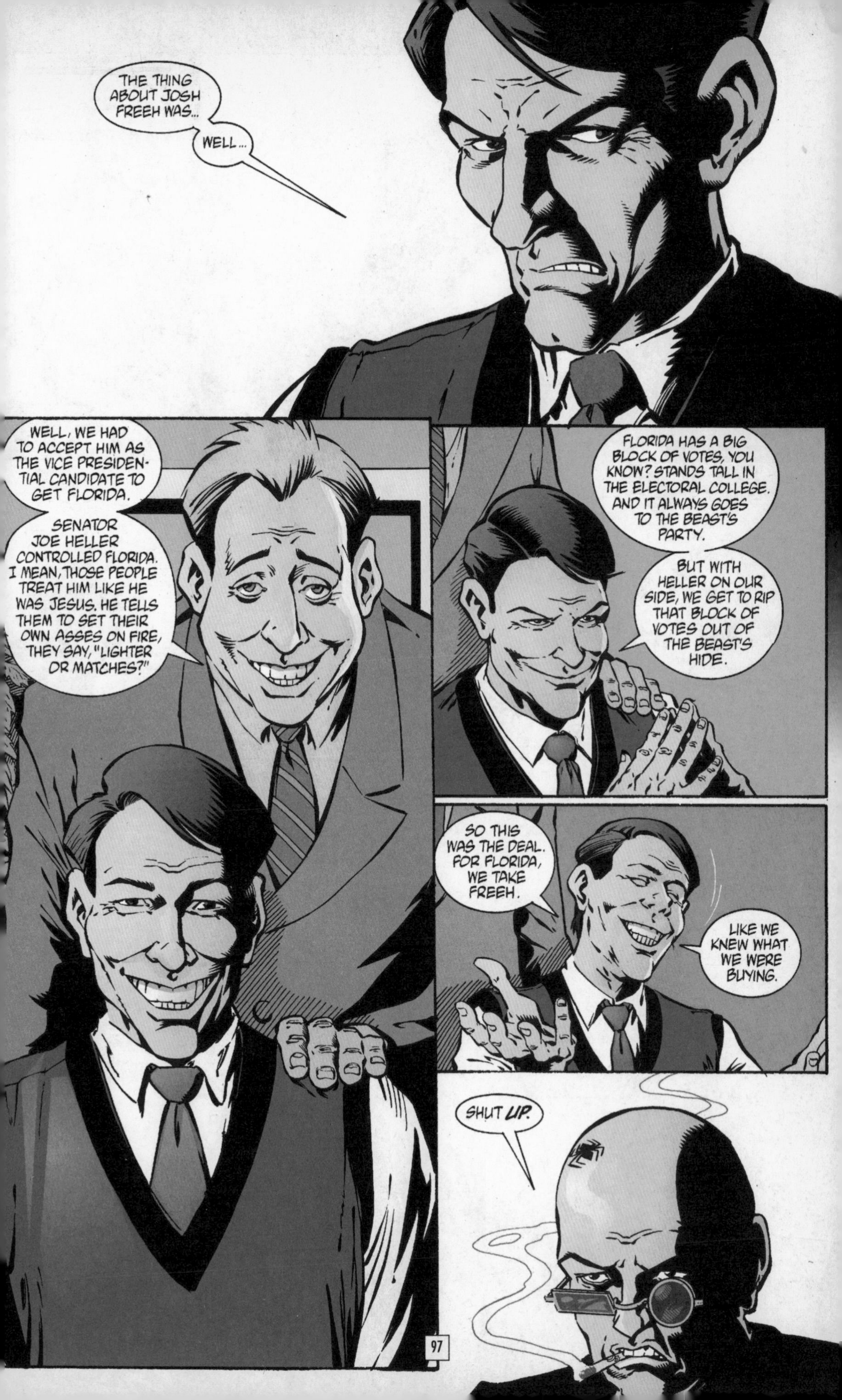
THE THING ABOUT JOSH FREEH WAS...
WELL...
WELL, WE HAD TO ACCEPT HIM AS THE VICE PRESIDENTIAL CANDIDATE TO GET FLORIDA.
SENATOR JOE HELLER CONTROLLED FLORIDA. I MEAN, THOSE PEOPLE TREAT HIM LIKE HE WAS JESUS. HE TELLS THEM TO SET THEIR OWN ASSES ON FIRE, THEY SAY, "LIGHTER OR MATCHES?"
FLORIDA HAS A BIG BLOCK OF VOTES, YOU KNOW? STANDS TALL IN THE ELECTORAL COLLEGE. AND IT ALWAYS GOES TO THE BEAST'S PARTY.
BUT WITH HELLER ON OUR SIDE, WE GET TO RIP THAT BLOCK OF VOTES OUT OF THE BEAST'S HIDE.
SO THIS WAS THE DEAL. FOR FLORIDA, WE TAKE FREEH.
LIKE WE KNEW WHAT WE WERE BUYING.
SHUT *UP*.

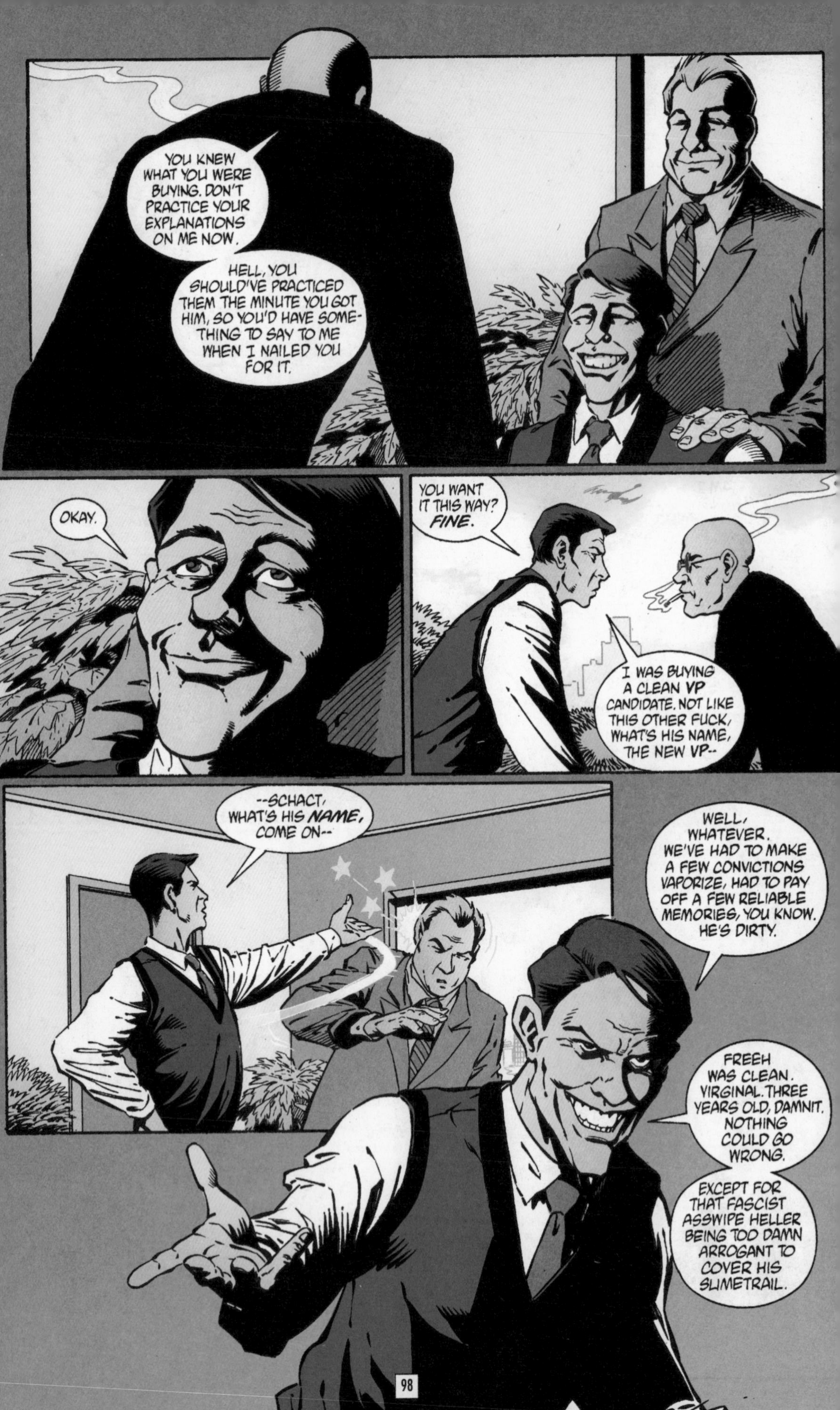
YOU KNEW WHAT YOU WERE BUYING. DON'T PRACTICE YOUR EXPLANATIONS ON ME NOW.
HELL, YOU SHOULD'VE PRACTICED THEM THE MINUTE YOU GOT HIM, SO YOU'D HAVE SOME-THING TO SAY TO ME WHEN I NAILED YOU FOR IT.
OKAY.
YOU WANT IT THIS WAY? FINE.
I WAS BUYING A CLEAN VP CANDIDATE. NOT LIKE THIS OTHER FUCK, WHAT'S HIS NAME, THE NEW VP--
--SCHACT, WHAT'S HIS NAME, COME ON--
WELL, WHATEVER. WE'VE HAD TO MAKE A FEW CONVICTIONS VAPORIZE, HAD TO PAY OFF A FEW RELIABLE MEMORIES, YOU KNOW. HE'S DIRTY.
FREEH WAS CLEAN. VIRGINAL. THREE YEARS OLD, DAMNIT. NOTHING COULD GO WRONG.
EXCEPT FOR THAT FASCIST ASSWIPE HELLER BEING TOO DAMN ARROGANT TO COVER HIS SLIMETRAIL.

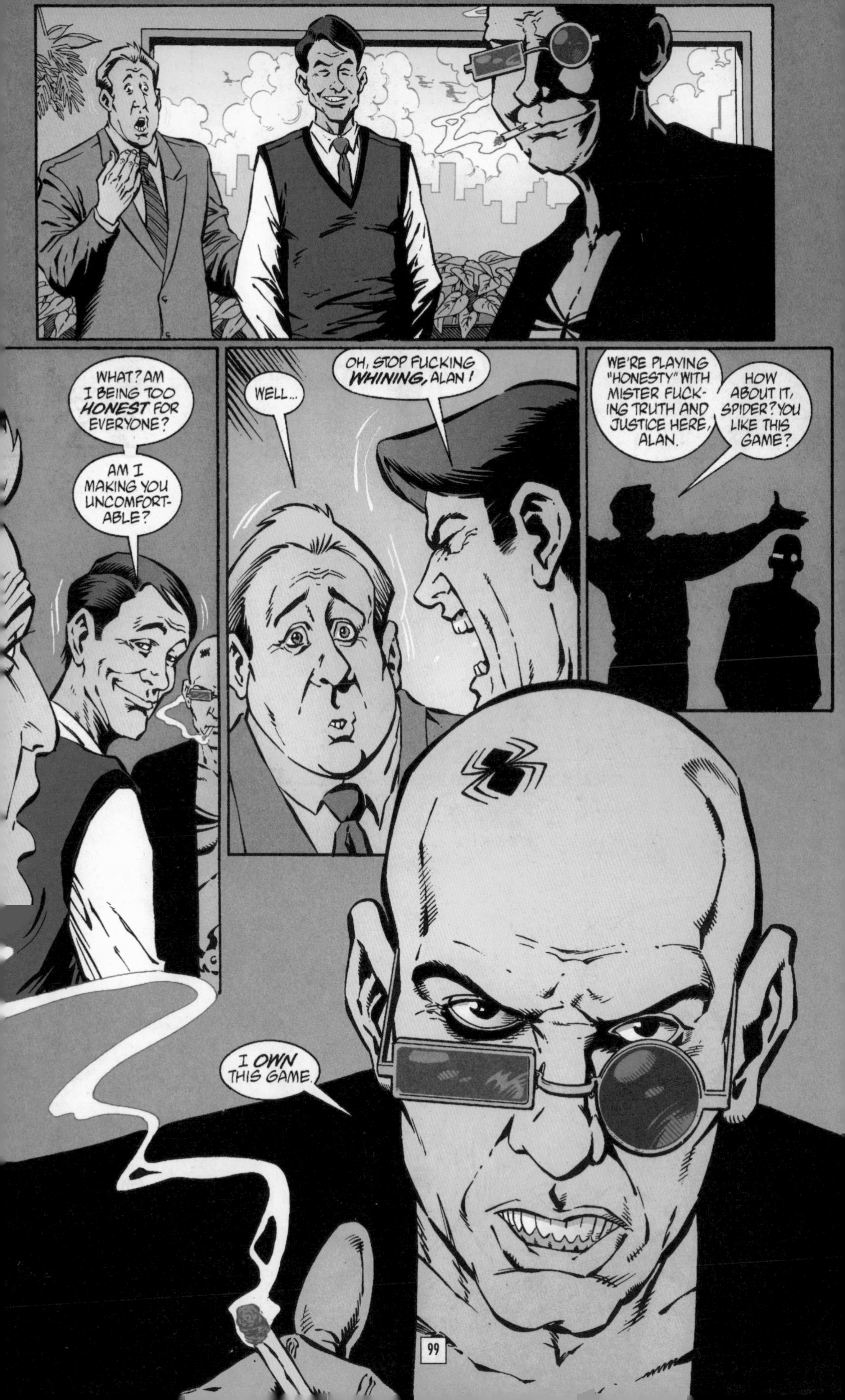
WHAT? AM I BEING TOO HONEST FOR EVERYONE?
AM I MAKING YOU UNCOMFORT-ABLE?
WELL...
OH, STOP FUCKING WHINING, ALAN!
WE'RE PLAYING "HONESTY" WITH MISTER FUCK-ING TRUTH AND JUSTICE HERE, ALAN.
HOW ABOUT IT, SPIDER? YOU LIKE THIS GAME?
I OWN THIS GAME.

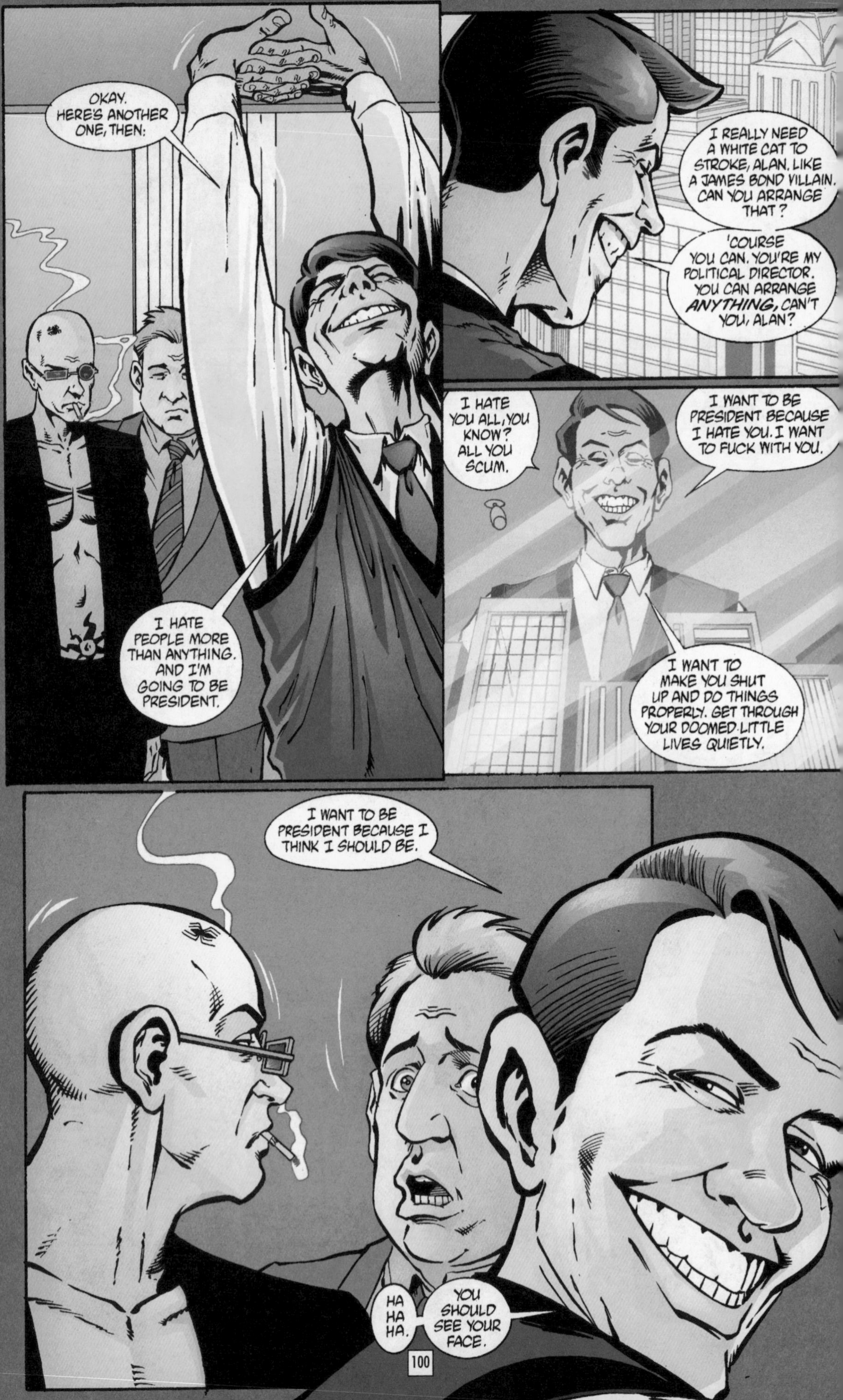
OKAY. HERE'S ANOTHER ONE, THEN:
I HATE PEOPLE MORE THAN ANYTHING. AND I'M GOING TO BE PRESIDENT.
I REALLY NEED A WHITE CAT TO STROKE, ALAN. LIKE A JAMES BOND VILLAIN. CAN YOU ARRANGE THAT?
'COURSE YOU CAN. YOU'RE MY POLITICAL DIRECTOR. YOU CAN ARRANGE ANYTHING, CAN'T YOU, ALAN?
I HATE YOU ALL, YOU KNOW? ALL YOU SCUM.
I WANT TO BE PRESIDENT BECAUSE I HATE YOU. I WANT TO FUCK WITH YOU.
I WANT TO MAKE YOU SHUT UP AND DO THINGS PROPERLY. GET THROUGH YOUR DOOMED LITTLE LIVES QUIETLY.
I WANT TO BE PRESIDENT BECAUSE I THINK I SHOULD BE.
HA HA HA.
YOU SHOULD SEE YOUR FACE.

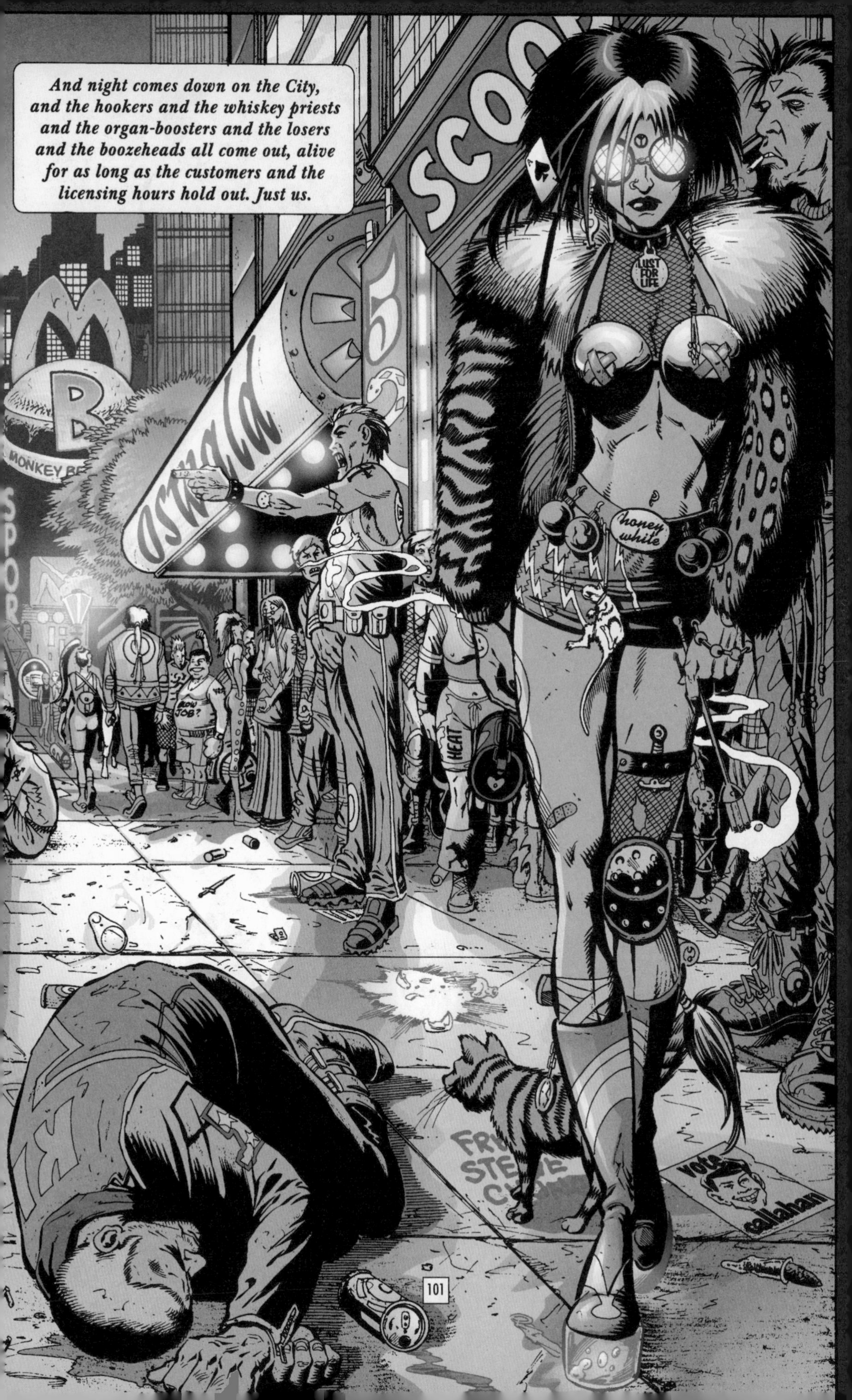
And night comes down on the City, and the hookers and the whiskey priests and the organ-boosters and the losers and the boozeheads all come out, alive for as long as the customers and the licensing hours hold out. Just us.
Oswald
LUST FOR LIFE
honey white
BLOW JOB?
HEAT
vote
callahan

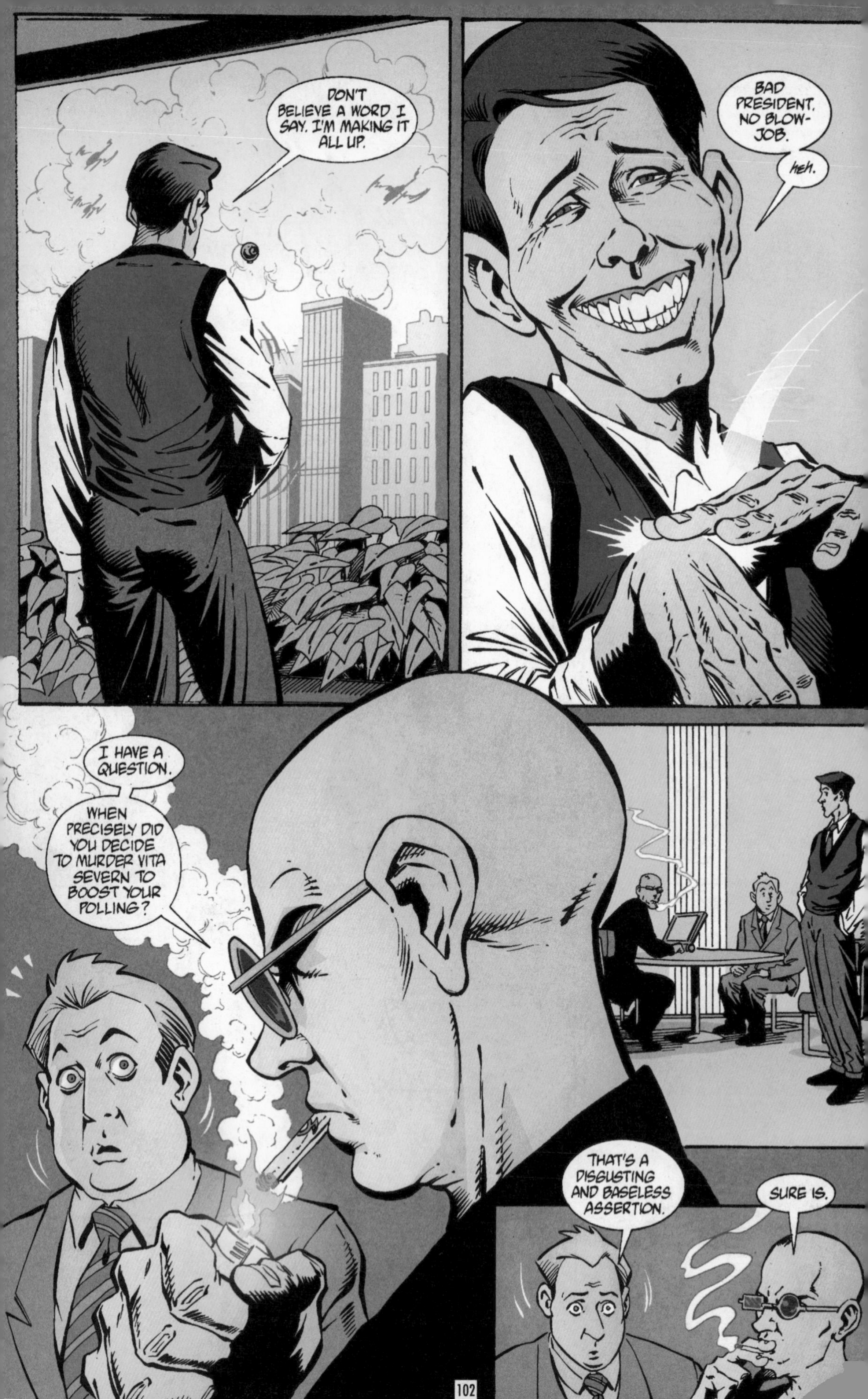
DON'T BELIEVE A WORD I SAY. I'M MAKING IT ALL UP.
BAD PRESIDENT. NO BLOW-JOB.
heh.
I HAVE A QUESTION.
WHEN PRECISELY DID YOU DECIDE TO MURDER VITA SEVERN TO BOOST YOUR POLLING?
THAT'S A DISGUSTING AND BASELESS ASSERTION.
SURE IS.

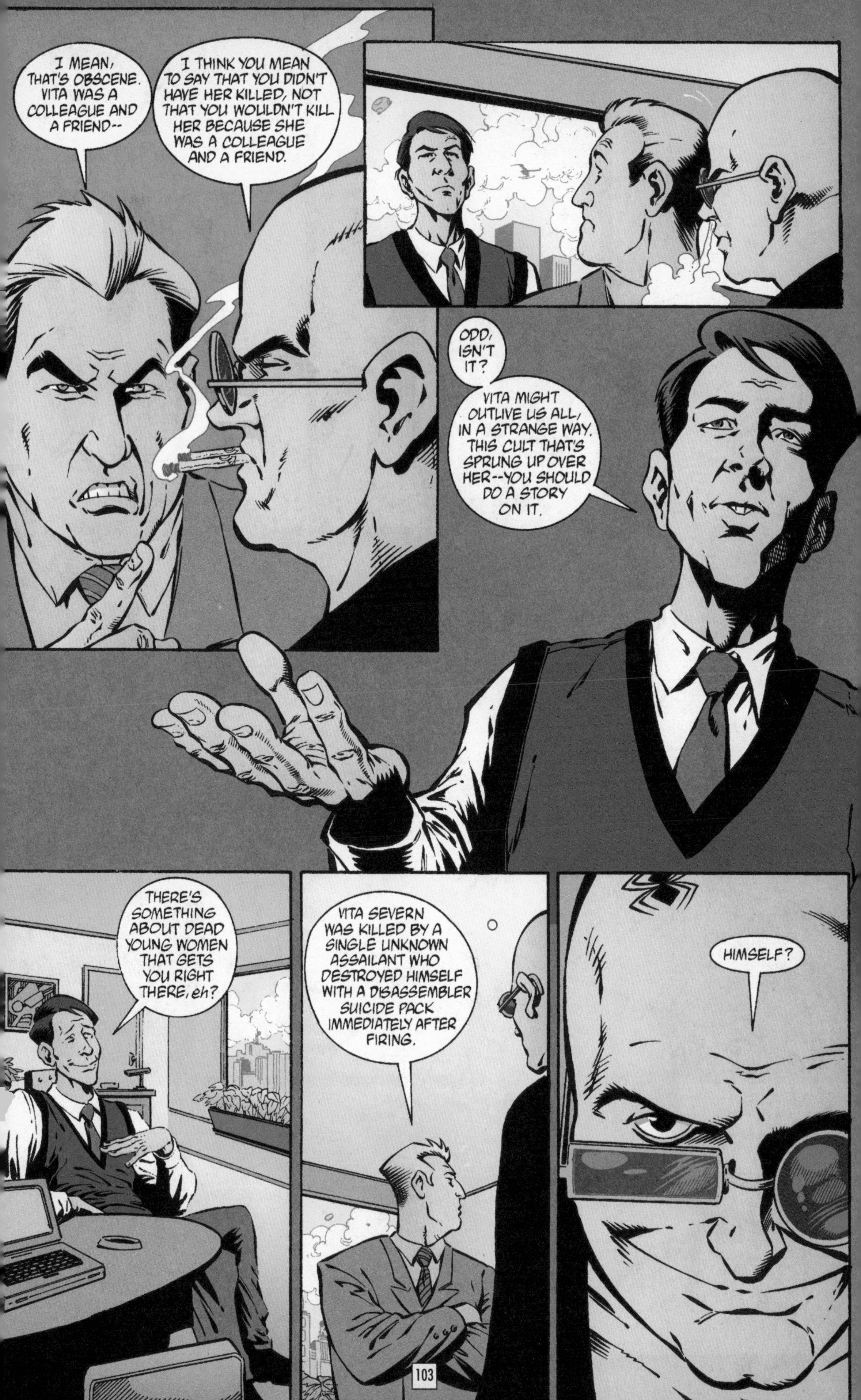
I MEAN, THAT'S OBSCENE. VITA WAS A COLLEAGUE AND A FRIEND--
I THINK YOU MEAN TO SAY THAT YOU DIDN'T HAVE HER KILLED, NOT THAT YOU WOULDN'T KILL HER BECAUSE SHE WAS A COLLEAGUE AND A FRIEND.
ODD, ISN'T IT?
VITA MIGHT OUTLIVE US ALL, IN A STRANGE WAY. THIS CULT THAT'S SPRUNG UP OVER HER--YOU SHOULD DO A STORY ON IT.
THERE'S SOMETHING ABOUT DEAD YOUNG WOMEN THAT GETS YOU RIGHT THERE, eh?
VITA SEVERN WAS KILLED BY A SINGLE UNKNOWN ASSAILANT WHO DESTROYED HIMSELF WITH A DISASSEMBLER SUICIDE PACK IMMEDIATELY AFTER FIRING.
HIMSELF?

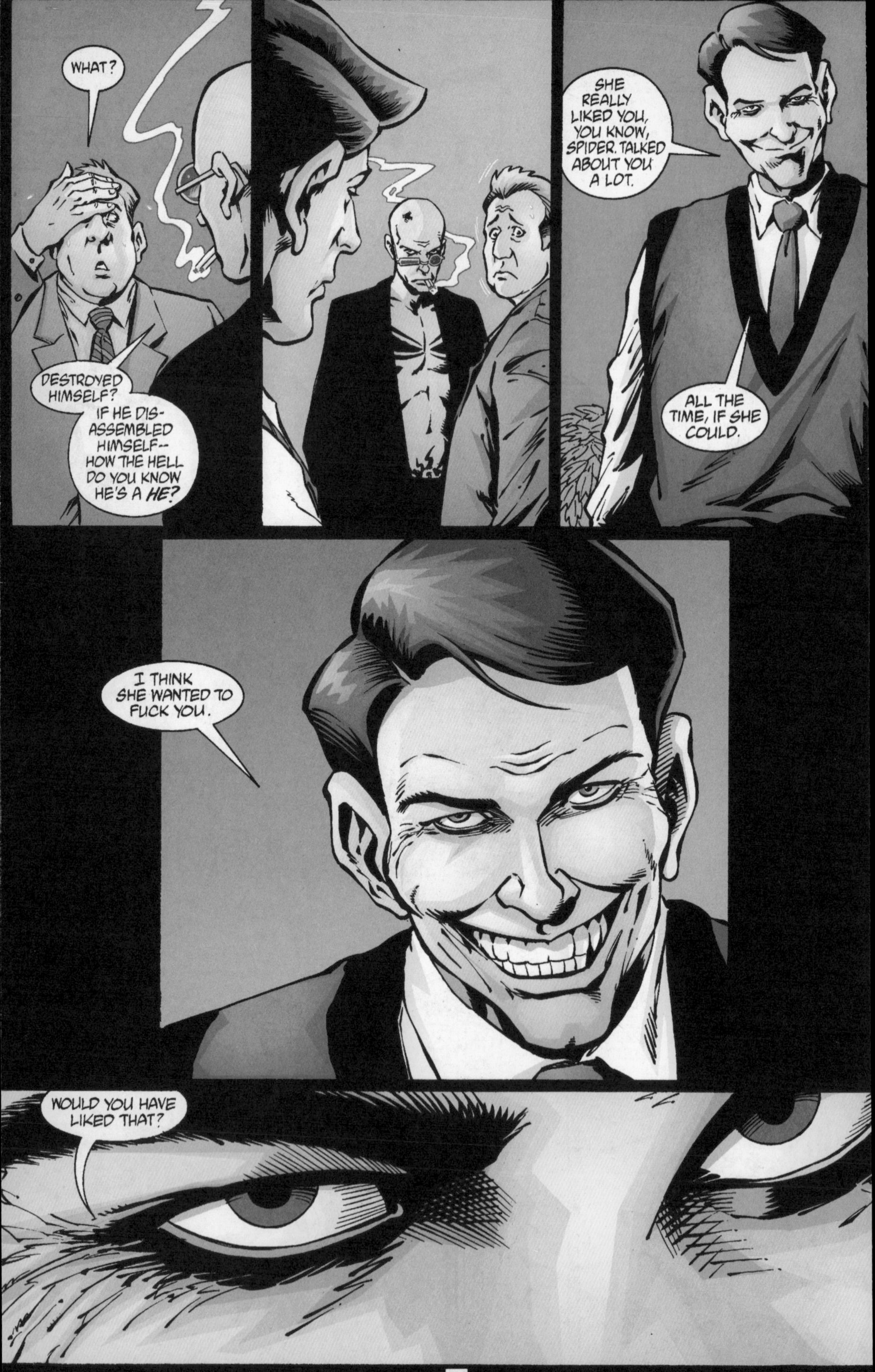
WHAT?
DESTROYED HIMSELF?
IF HE DIS-ASSEMBLED HIMSELF-- HOW THE HELL DO YOU KNOW HE'S A *HE?*
SHE REALLY LIKED YOU, YOU KNOW, SPIDER. TALKED ABOUT YOU A LOT.
ALL THE TIME, IF SHE COULD.
I THINK SHE WANTED TO FUCK YOU.
WOULD YOU HAVE LIKED THAT?

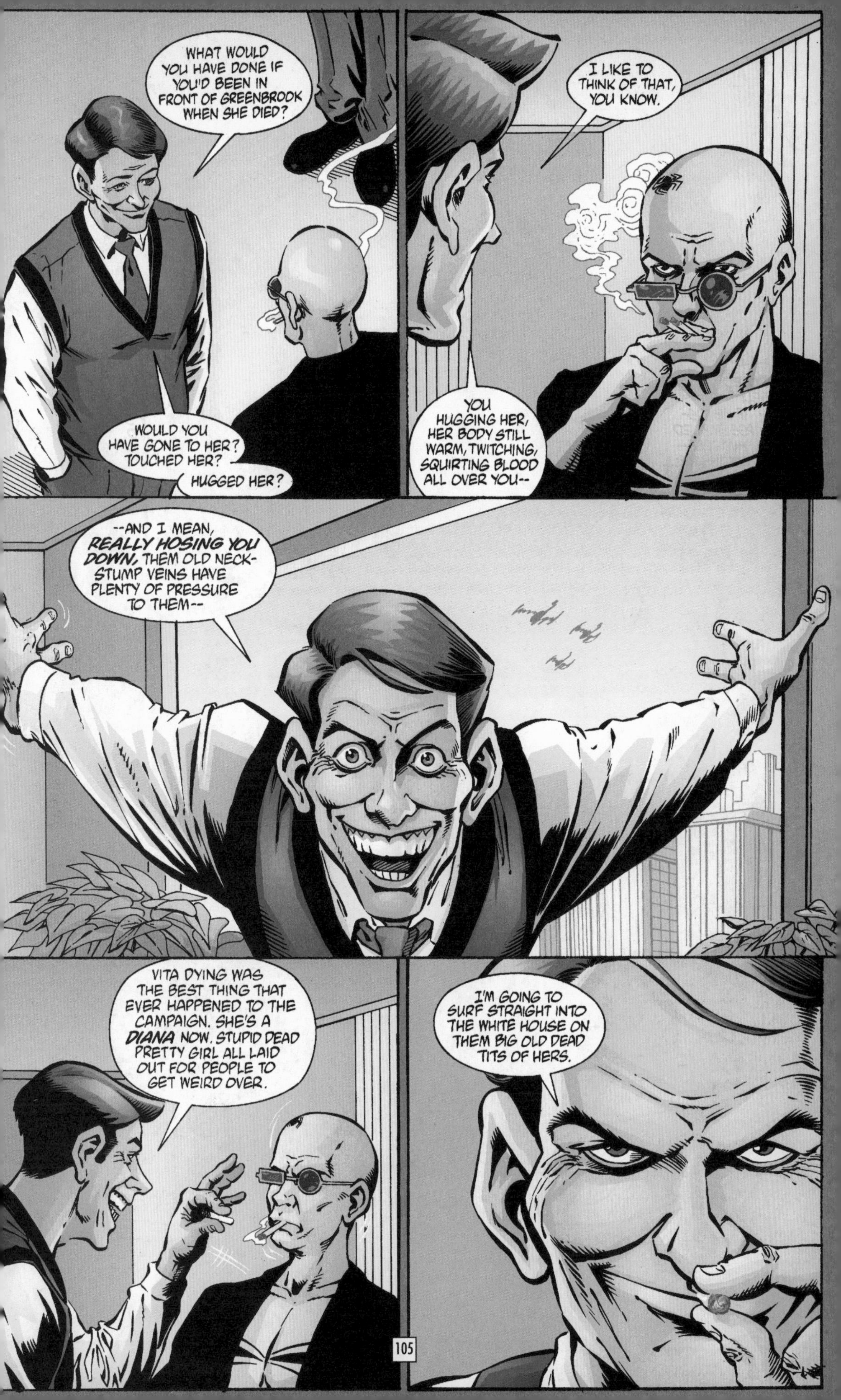

WHAT WOULD YOU HAVE DONE IF YOU'D BEEN IN FRONT OF GREENBROOK WHEN SHE DIED?
WOULD YOU HAVE GONE TO HER? TOUCHED HER?
HUGGED HER?
I LIKE TO THINK OF THAT, YOU KNOW.
YOU HUGGING HER, HER BODY STILL WARM, TWITCHING, SQUIRTING BLOOD ALL OVER YOU--
--AND I MEAN, REALLY HOSING YOU DOWN. THEM OLD NECK-STUMP VEINS HAVE PLENTY OF PRESSURE TO THEM--
VITA DYING WAS THE BEST THING THAT EVER HAPPENED TO THE CAMPAIGN. SHE'S A DIANA NOW. STUPID DEAD PRETTY GIRL ALL LAID OUT FOR PEOPLE TO GET WEIRD OVER.
I'M GOING TO SURF STRAIGHT INTO THE WHITE HOUSE ON THEM BIG OLD DEAD TITS OF HERS.

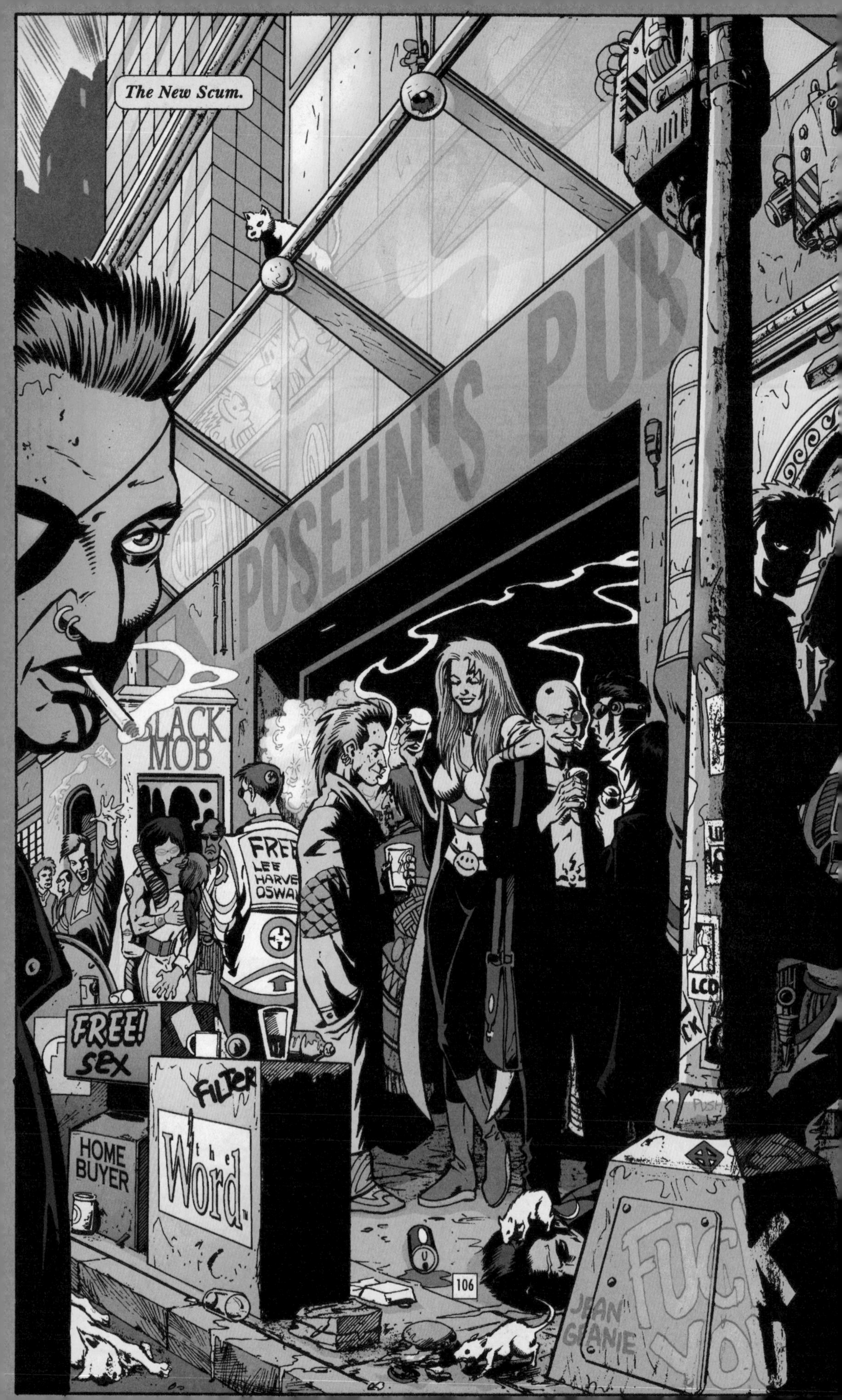
The New Scum.
POSEHN'S PUB
BLACK MOB
FREE LEE HARVE OSWA
FREE! sex
FILTER
the Word
HOME BUYER
LCD
JEAN GENIE

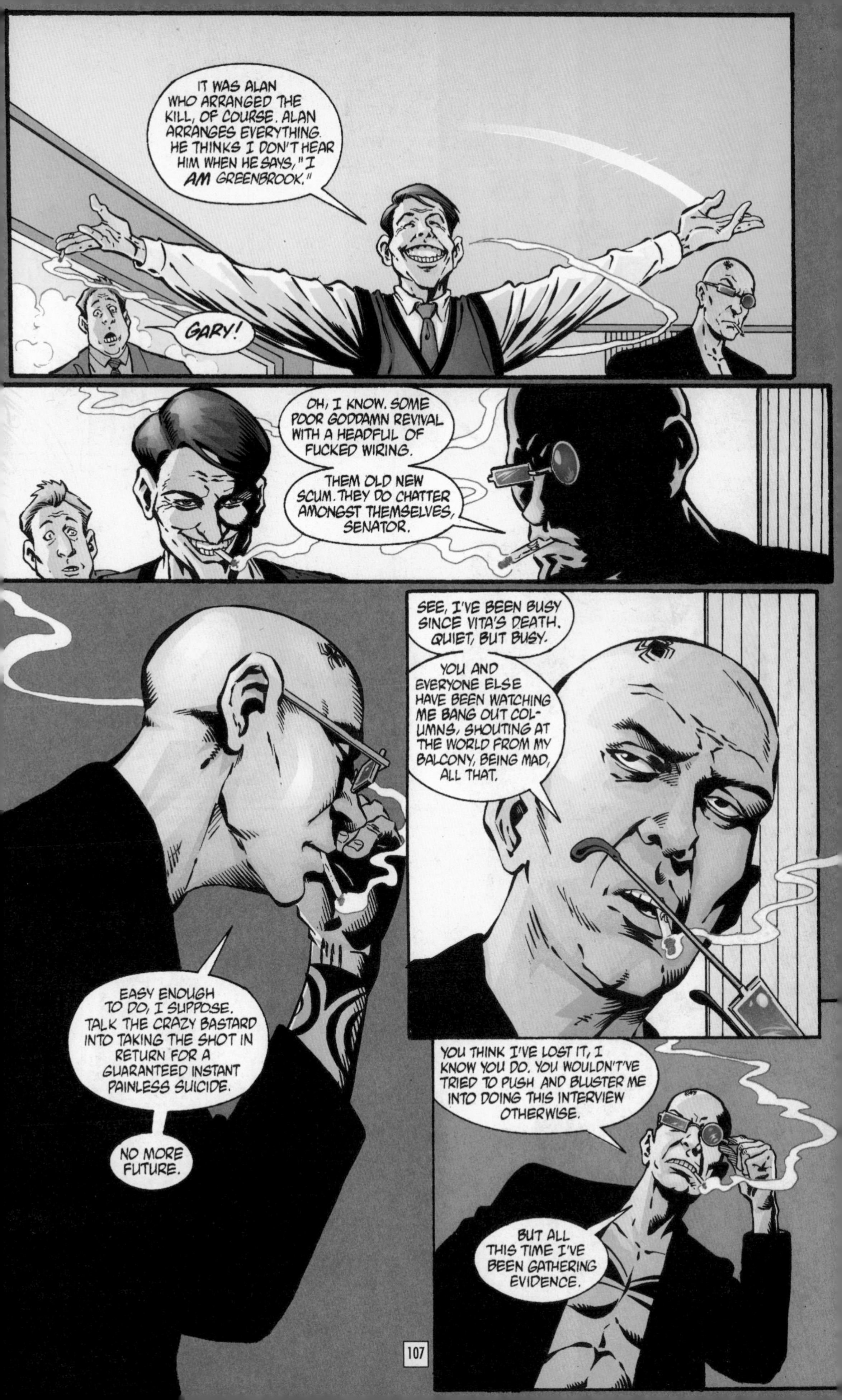
IT WAS ALAN WHO ARRANGED THE KILL, OF COURSE. ALAN ARRANGES EVERYTHING. HE THINKS I DON'T HEAR HIM WHEN HE SAYS, "I AM GREENBROOK."
GARY!
OH, I KNOW. SOME POOR GODDAMN REVIVAL WITH A HEADFUL OF FUCKED WIRING.
THEM OLD NEW SCUM. THEY DO CHATTER AMONGST THEMSELVES, SENATOR.
EASY ENOUGH TO DO, I SUPPOSE. TALK THE CRAZY BASTARD INTO TAKING THE SHOT IN RETURN FOR A GUARANTEED INSTANT PAINLESS SUICIDE.
NO MORE FUTURE.
SEE, I'VE BEEN BUSY SINCE VITA'S DEATH. QUIET, BUT BUSY.
YOU AND EVERYONE ELSE HAVE BEEN WATCHING ME BANG OUT COL-UMNS, SHOUTING AT THE WORLD FROM MY BALCONY, BEING MAD, ALL THAT.
YOU THINK I'VE LOST IT, I KNOW YOU DO. YOU WOULDN'T'VE TRIED TO PUSH AND BLUSTER ME INTO DOING THIS INTERVIEW OTHERWISE.
BUT ALL THIS TIME I'VE BEEN GATHERING EVIDENCE.

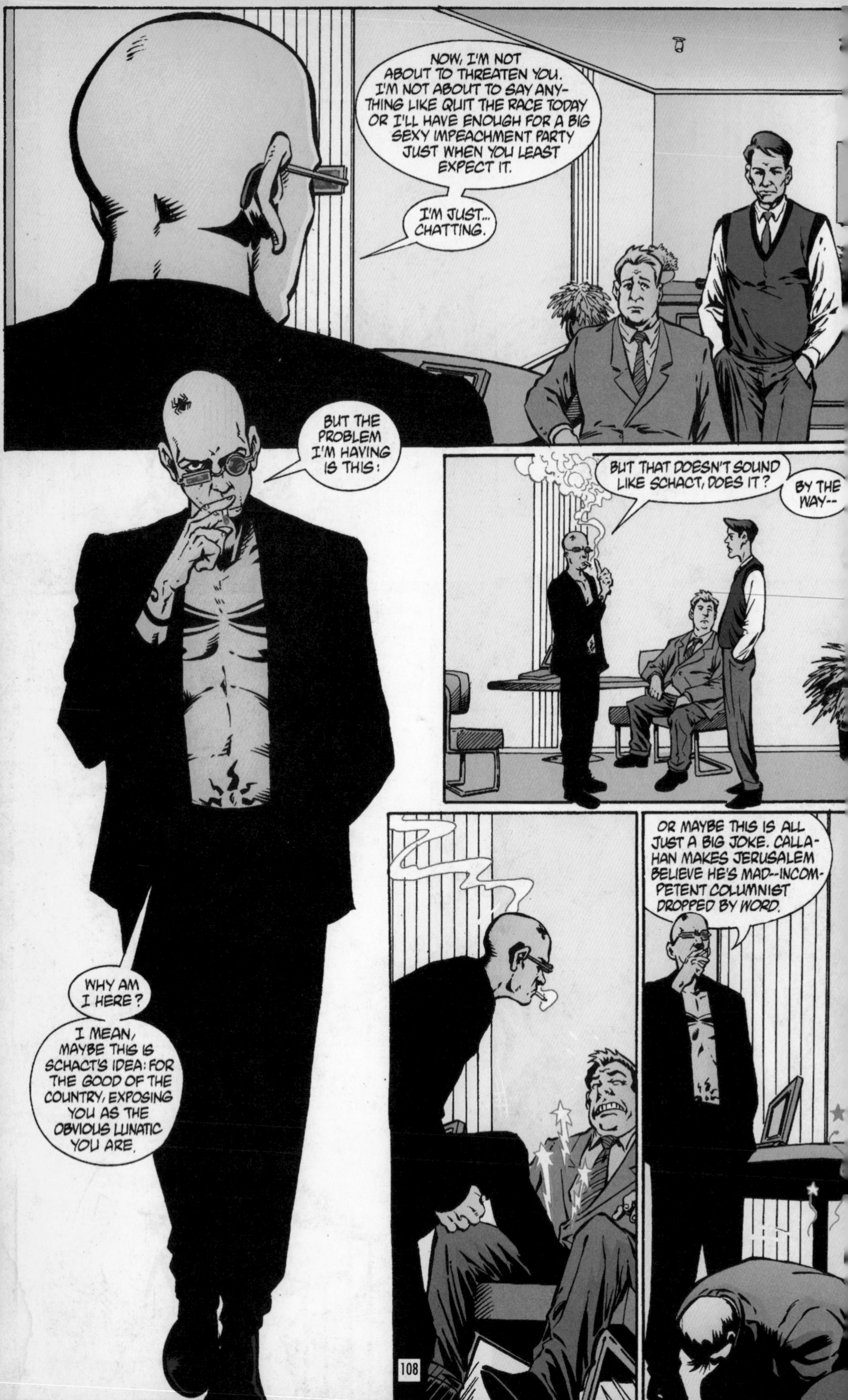
NOW, I'M NOT ABOUT TO THREATEN YOU. I'M NOT ABOUT TO SAY ANYTHING LIKE QUIT THE RACE TODAY OR I'LL HAVE ENOUGH FOR A BIG SEXY IMPEACHMENT PARTY JUST WHEN YOU LEAST EXPECT IT.
I'M JUST... CHATTING.
BUT THE PROBLEM I'M HAVING IS THIS:
WHY AM I HERE?
I MEAN, MAYBE THIS IS SCHACT'S IDEA: FOR THE GOOD OF THE COUNTRY, EXPOSING YOU AS THE OBVIOUS LUNATIC YOU ARE.
BUT THAT DOESN'T SOUND LIKE SCHACT, DOES IT?
BY THE WAY--
OR MAYBE THIS IS ALL JUST A BIG JOKE. CALLAHAN MAKES JERUSALEM BELIEVE HE'S MAD--INCOMPETENT COLUMNIST DROPPED BY WORD.

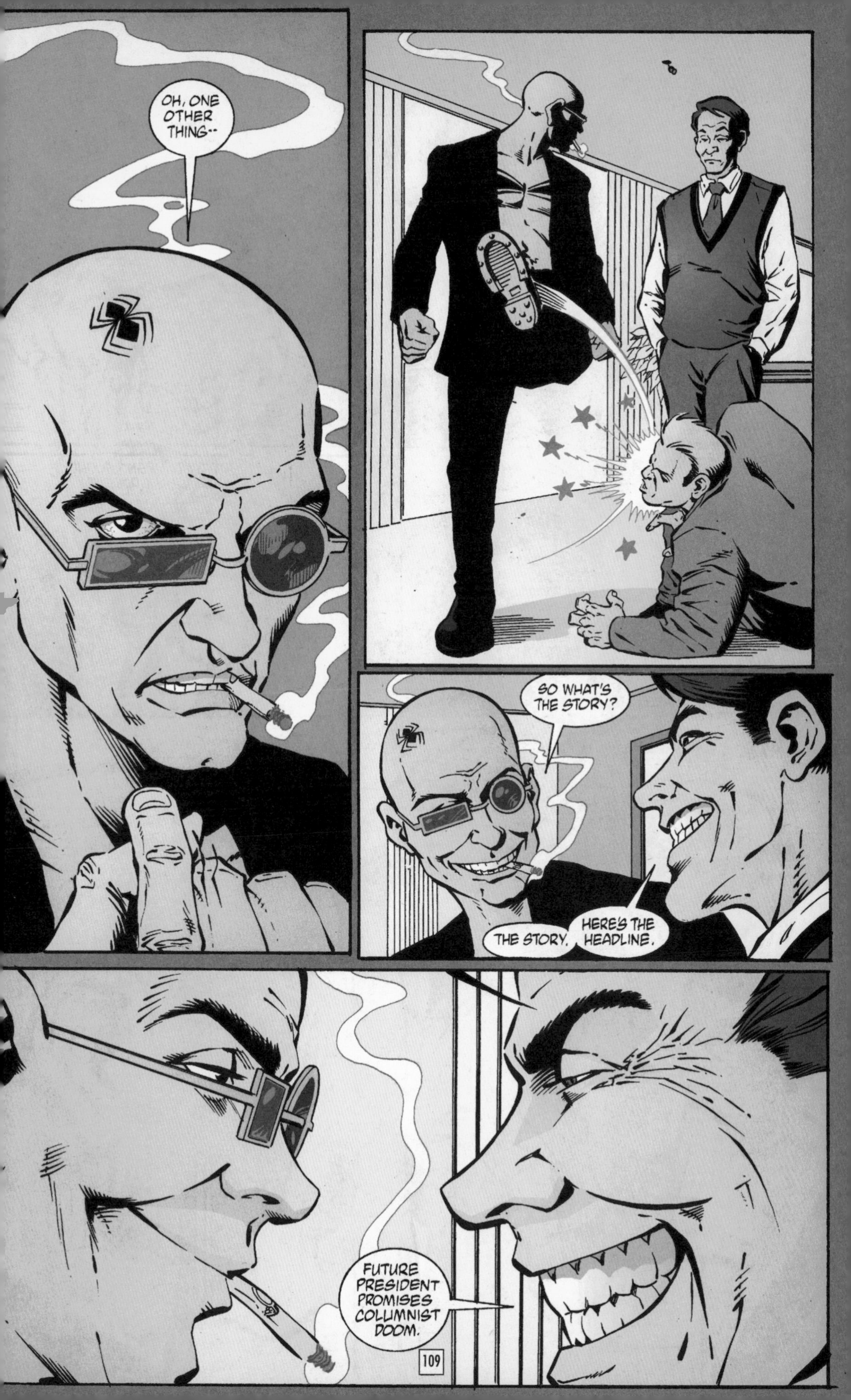
OH, ONE OTHER THING--
SO WHAT'S THE STORY?
THE STORY.
HERE'S THE HEADLINE.
FUTURE PRESIDENT PROMISES COLUMNIST DOOM.

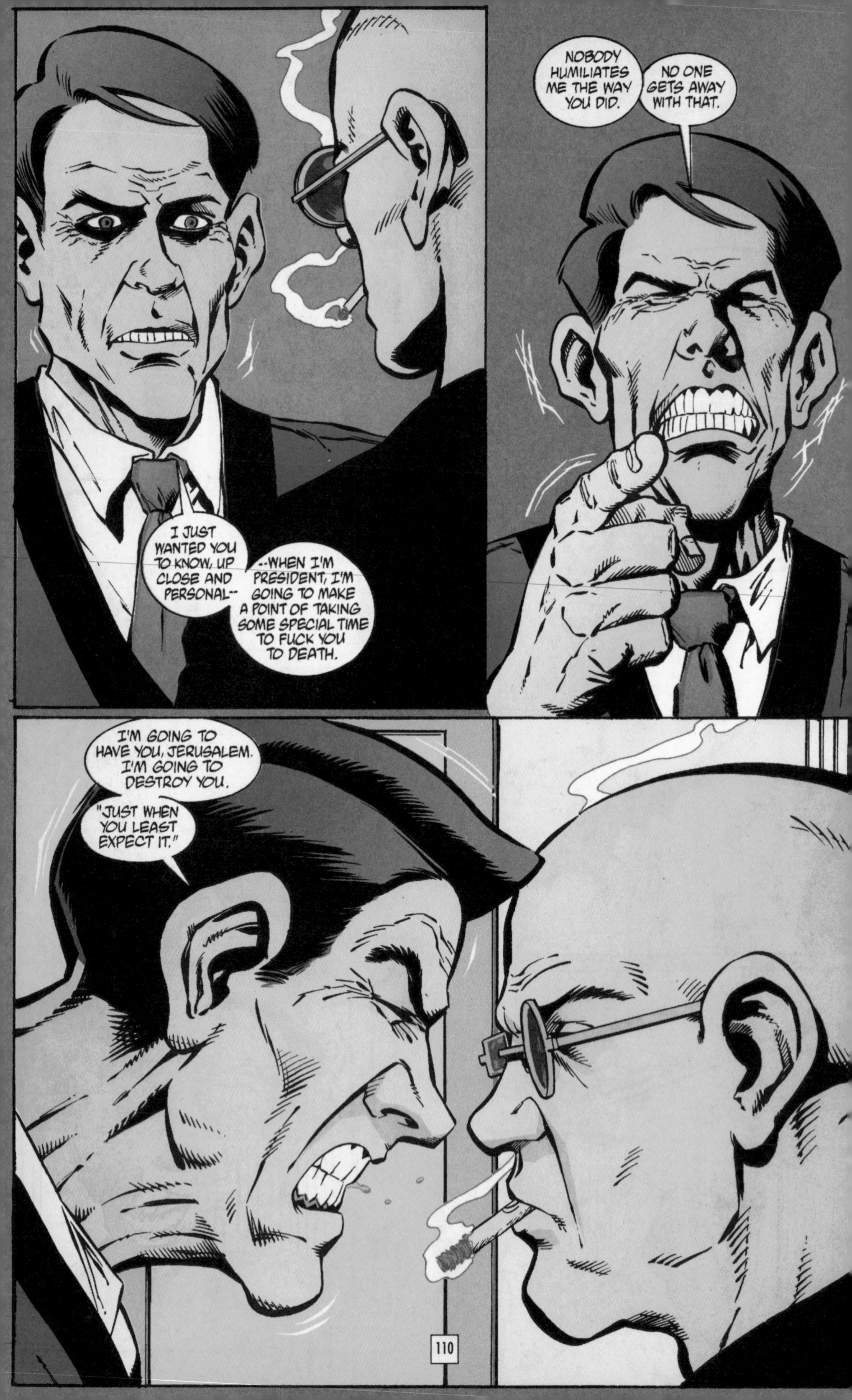
I JUST WANTED YOU TO KNOW, UP CLOSE AND PERSONAL--
--WHEN I'M PRESIDENT, I'M GOING TO MAKE A POINT OF TAKING SOME SPECIAL TIME TO FUCK YOU TO DEATH.
NOBODY HUMILIATES ME THE WAY YOU DID.
NO ONE GETS AWAY WITH THAT.
I'M GOING TO HAVE YOU, JERUSALEM. I'M GOING TO DESTROY YOU.
"JUST WHEN YOU LEAST EXPECT IT."

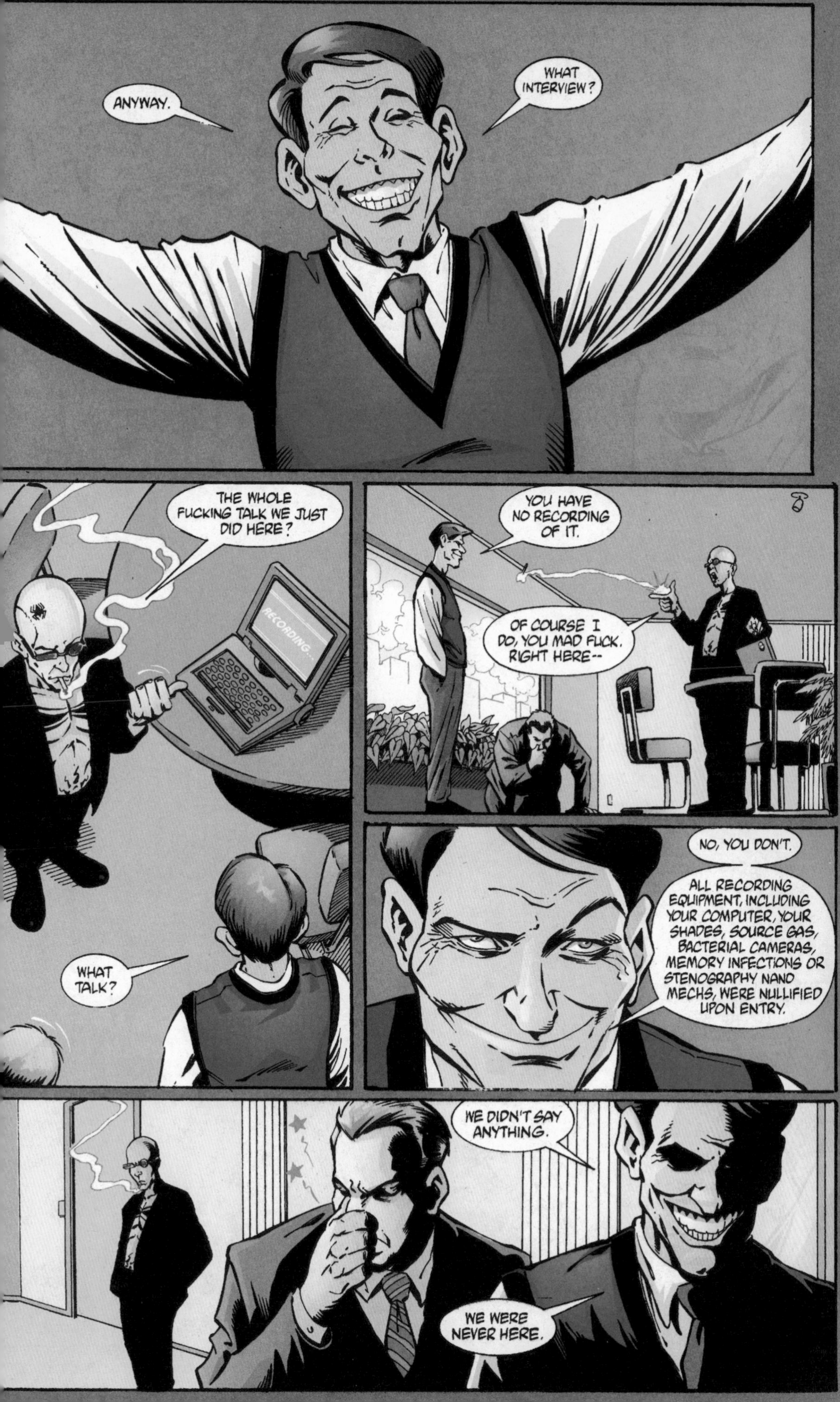
ANYWAY.
WHAT INTERVIEW?
THE WHOLE FUCKING TALK WE JUST DID HERE?
RECORDING...
YOU HAVE NO RECORDING OF IT.
OF COURSE I DO, YOU MAD FUCK. RIGHT HERE--
WHAT TALK?
NO, YOU DON'T.
ALL RECORDING EQUIPMENT, INCLUDING YOUR COMPUTER, YOUR SHADES, SOURCE GAS, BACTERIAL CAMERAS, MEMORY INFECTIONS OR STENOGRAPHY NANO MECHS, WERE NULLIFIED UPON ENTRY.
WE DIDN'T SAY ANYTHING.
WE WERE NEVER HERE.

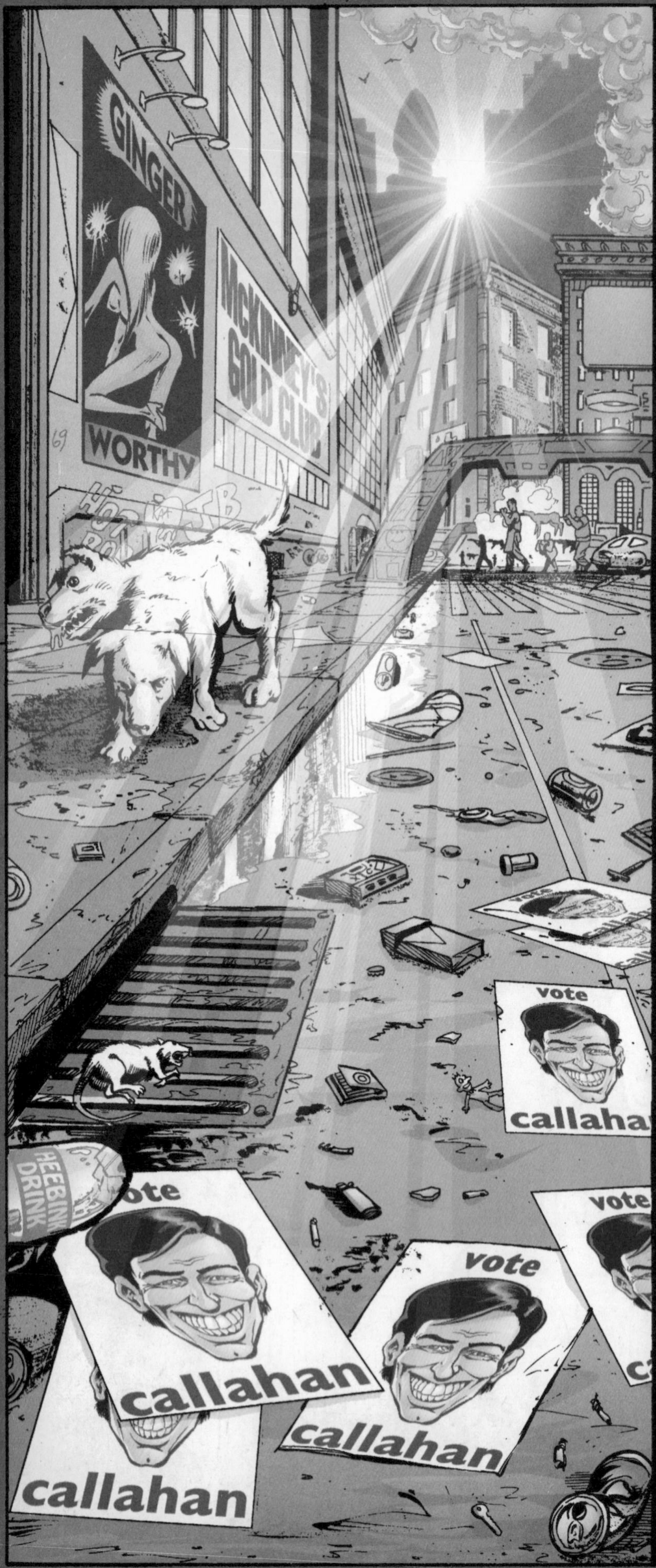
GINGER
WORTHY
McKINNEY'S GOLD CLUB
vote
callahan
HEEBINK DRINK
vote
callahan
vote
callahan
callahan

The Presidential Election is tomorrow.

Lots to do.

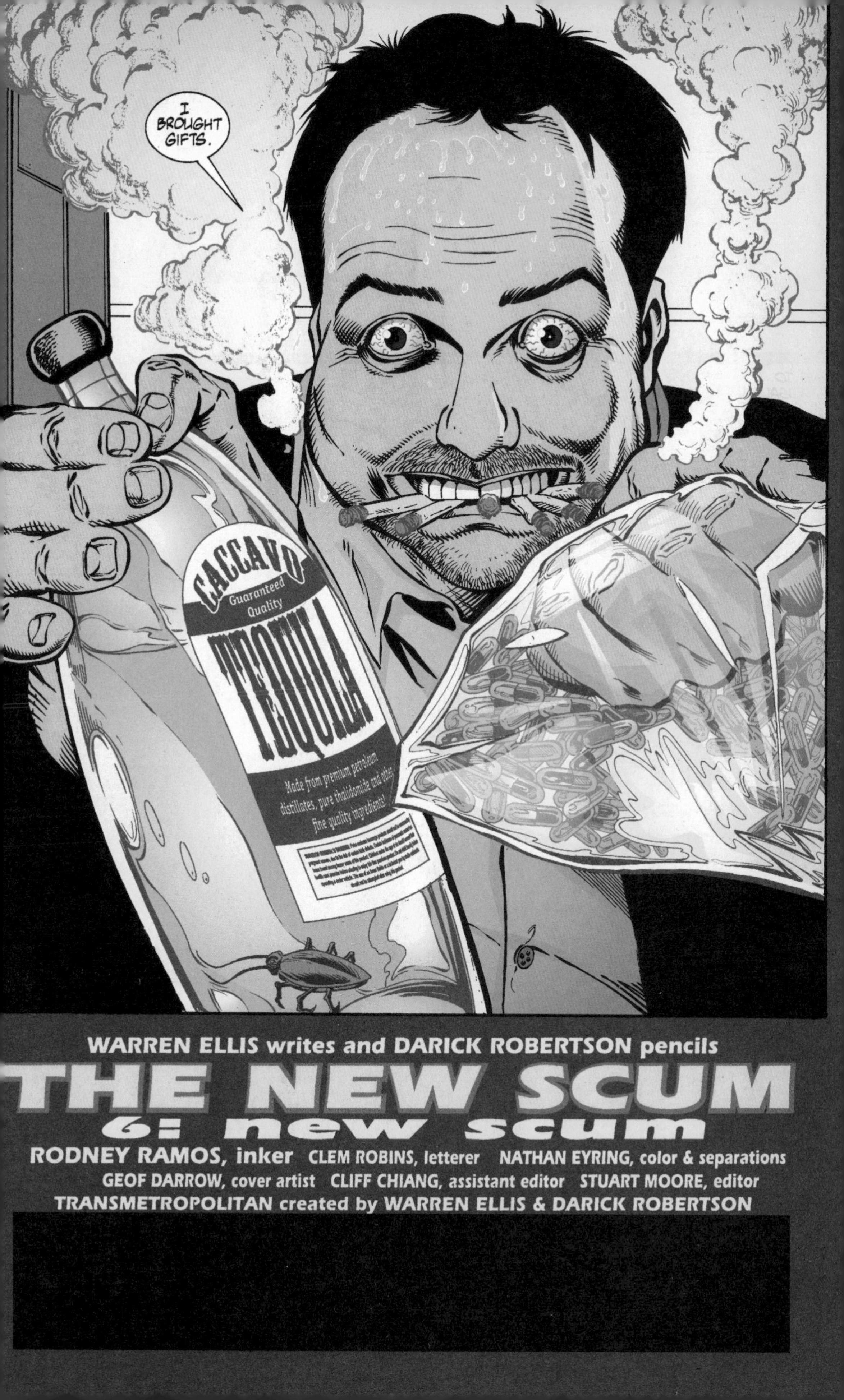
I BROUGHT GIFTS.
CACCAVO
Guaranteed Quality
TEQUILA
Made from premium petroleum distillates, pure thalidomide and other fine quality ingredients!

WARREN ELLIS writes and **DARICK ROBERTSON** pencils

THE NEW SCUM

6: new scum

RODNEY RAMOS, inker **CLEM ROBINS**, letterer **NATHAN EYRING**, color & separations
GEOF DARROW, cover artist **CLIFF CHIANG**, assistant editor **STUART MOORE**, editor
TRANSMETROPOLITAN created by **WARREN ELLIS & DARICK ROBERTSON**

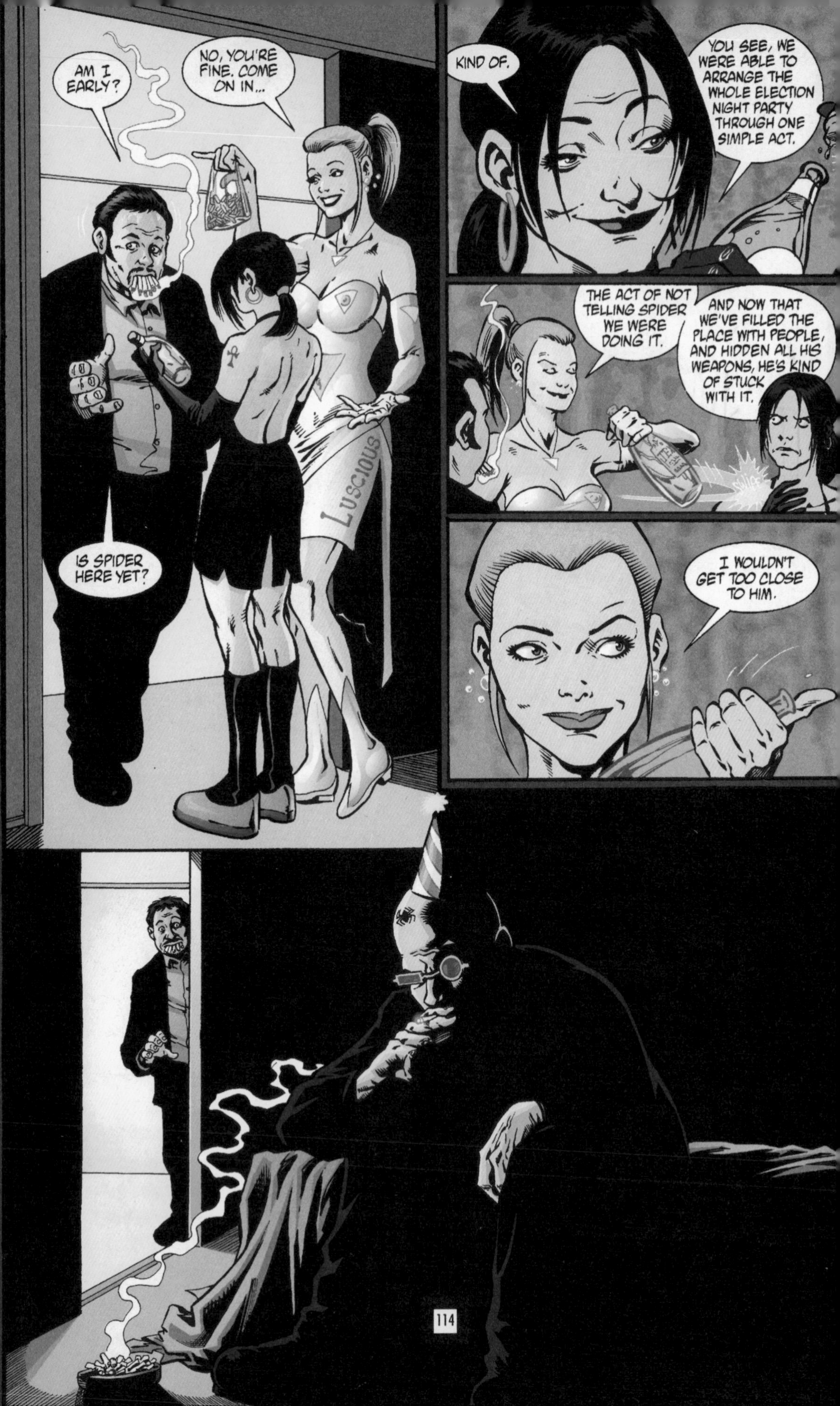

AM I EARLY?
NO, YOU'RE FINE. COME ON IN...
LUSCIOUS
IS SPIDER HERE YET?
KIND OF.
YOU SEE, WE WERE ABLE TO ARRANGE THE WHOLE ELECTION NIGHT PARTY THROUGH ONE SIMPLE ACT.
THE ACT OF NOT TELLING SPIDER WE WERE DOING IT.
AND NOW THAT WE'VE FILLED THE PLACE WITH PEOPLE, AND HIDDEN ALL HIS WEAPONS, HE'S KIND OF STUCK WITH IT.
I WOULDN'T GET TOO CLOSE TO HIM.

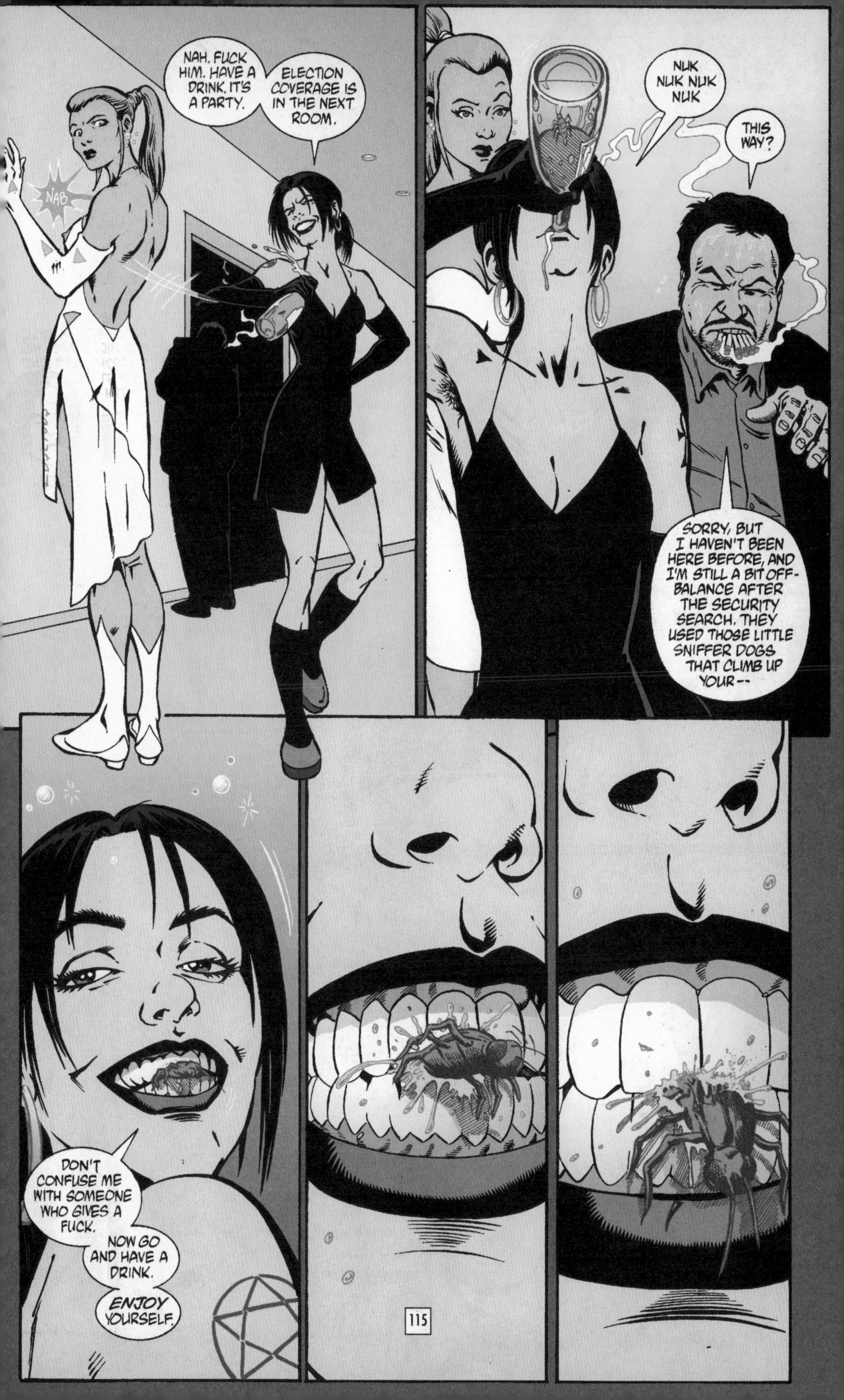

NAB
NAH. FUCK HIM. HAVE A DRINK. IT'S A PARTY.
ELECTION COVERAGE IS IN THE NEXT ROOM.
NUK NUK NUK NUK
THIS WAY?
SORRY, BUT I HAVEN'T BEEN HERE BEFORE, AND I'M STILL A BIT OFF-BALANCE AFTER THE SECURITY SEARCH. THEY USED THOSE LITTLE SNIFFER DOGS THAT CLIMB UP YOUR--
DON'T CONFUSE ME WITH SOMEONE WHO GIVES A FUCK.
NOW GO AND HAVE A DRINK.
ENJOY YOURSELF.

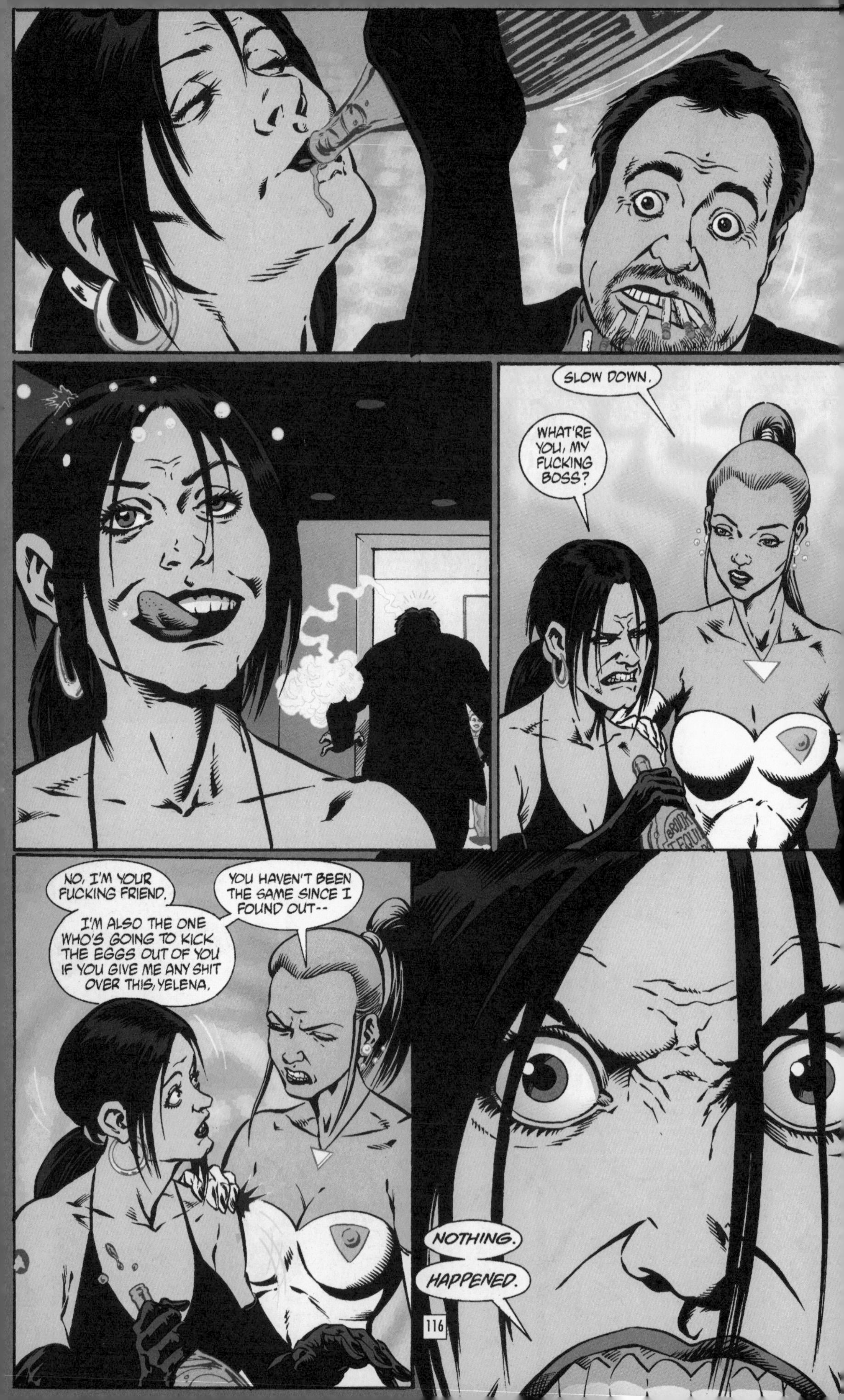
SLOW DOWN.
WHAT'RE YOU, MY FUCKING BOSS?
NO, I'M YOUR FUCKING FRIEND.
I'M ALSO THE ONE WHO'S GOING TO KICK THE EGGS OUT OF YOU IF YOU GIVE ME ANY SHIT OVER THIS, YELENA.
YOU HAVEN'T BEEN THE SAME SINCE I FOUND OUT--
NOTHING.
HAPPENED.

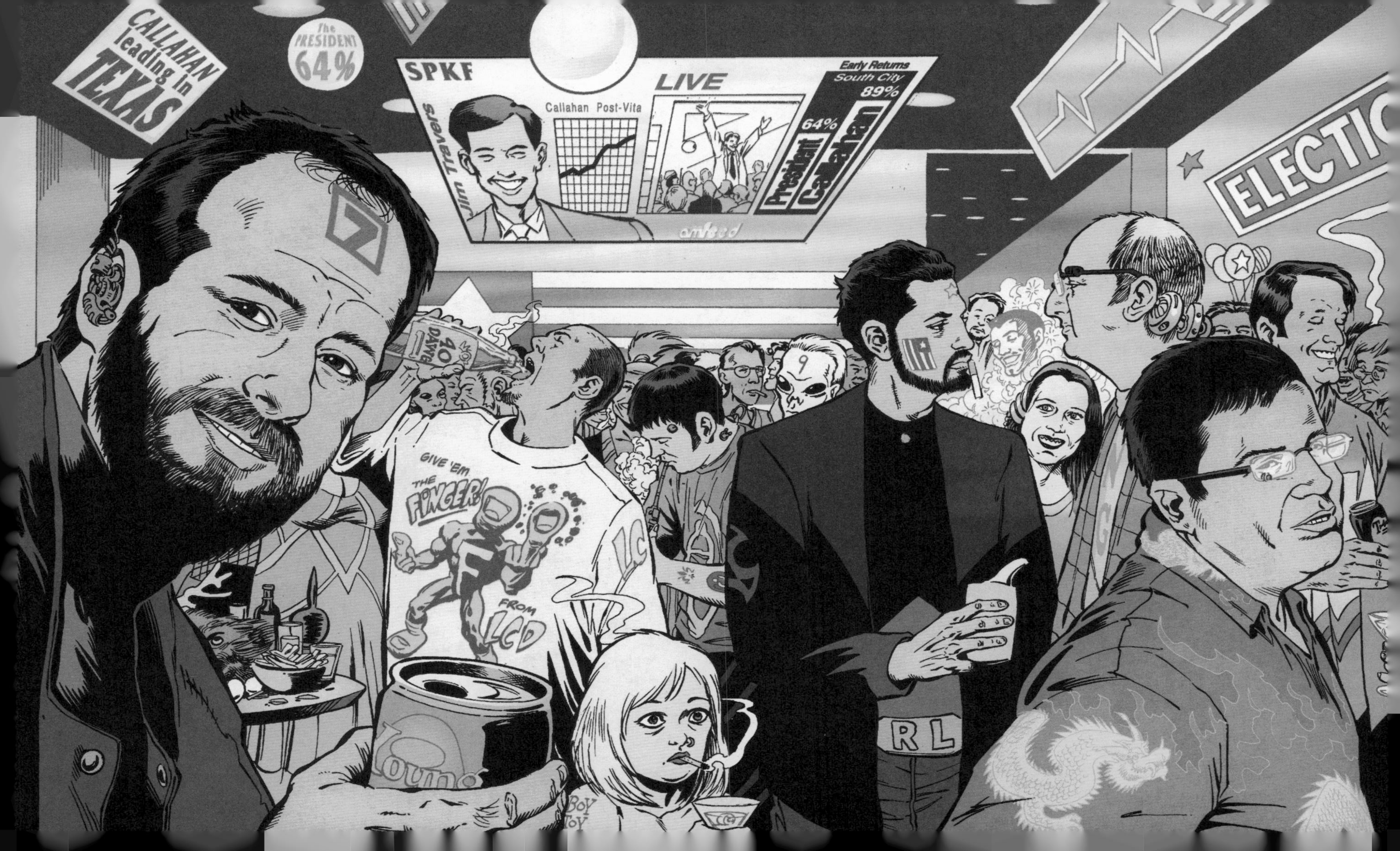

CALLAHAN leading in TEXAS
The PRESIDENT 64%
SPKF
Jim Travers
Callahan Post-Vita
LIVE
Early Returns
South City
89%
President Callahan
64%
ELECTIO
40 DAWG
GIVE 'EM THE FINGER!
FROM LCD
LC
RL
BOY TOY

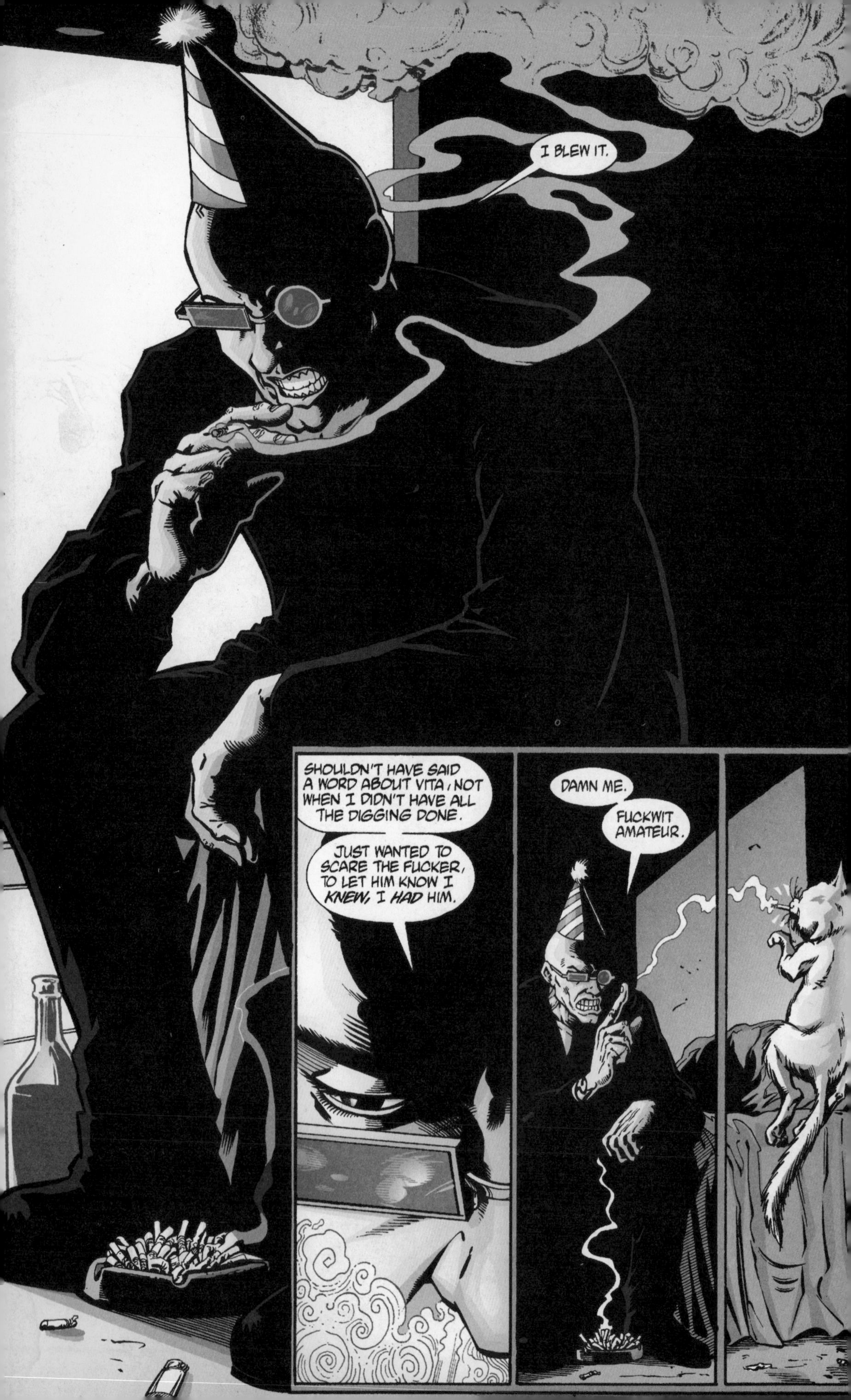
I BLEW IT.
SHOULDN'T HAVE SAID A WORD ABOUT VITA, NOT WHEN I DIDN'T HAVE ALL THE DIGGING DONE.
JUST WANTED TO SCARE THE FUCKER, TO LET HIM KNOW I KNEW, I HAD HIM.
DAMN ME.
FUCKWIT AMATEUR.

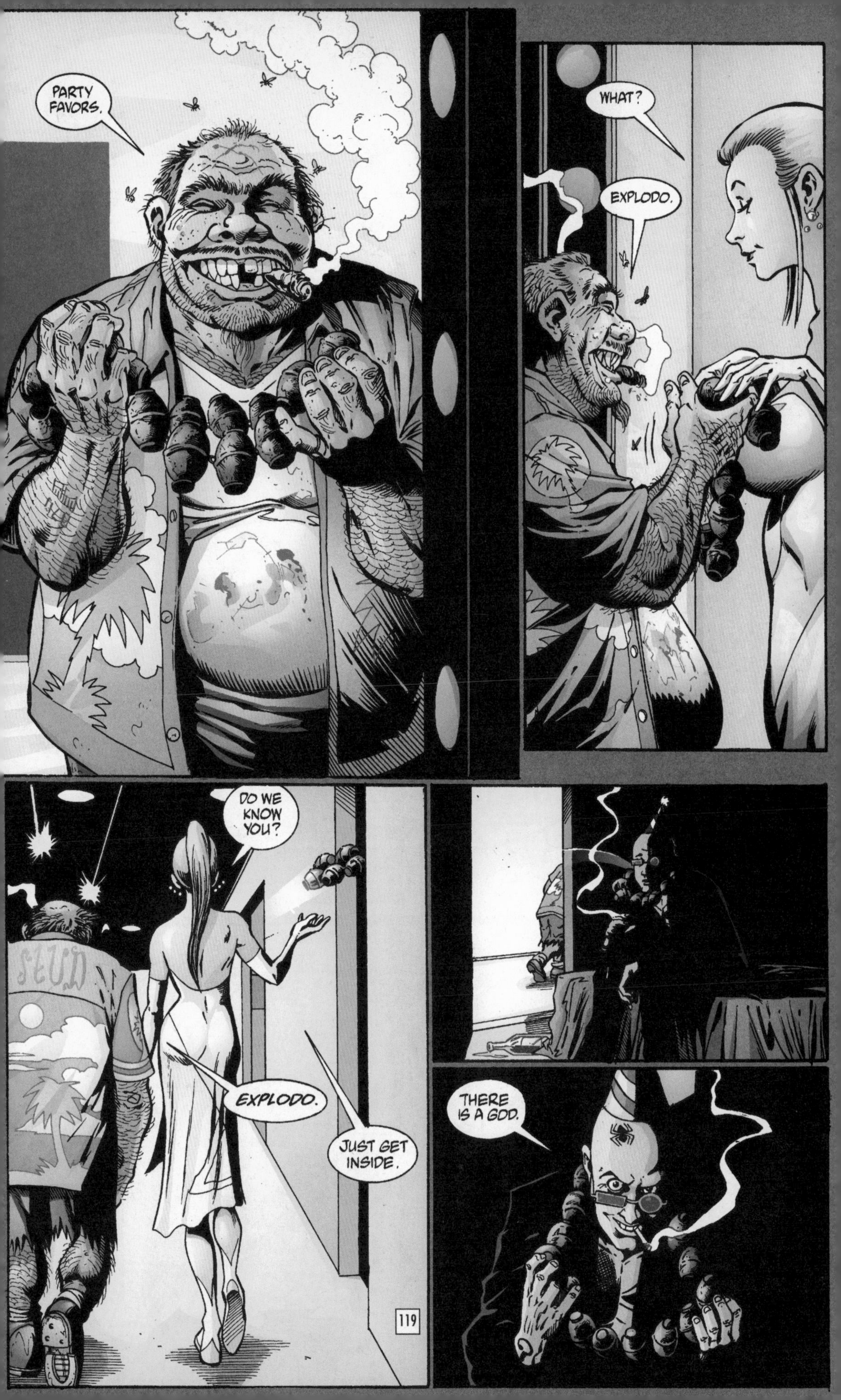
PARTY FAVORS.
WHAT?
EXPLODO.
DO WE KNOW YOU?
EXPLODO.
JUST GET INSIDE.
THERE IS A GOD.
STUD

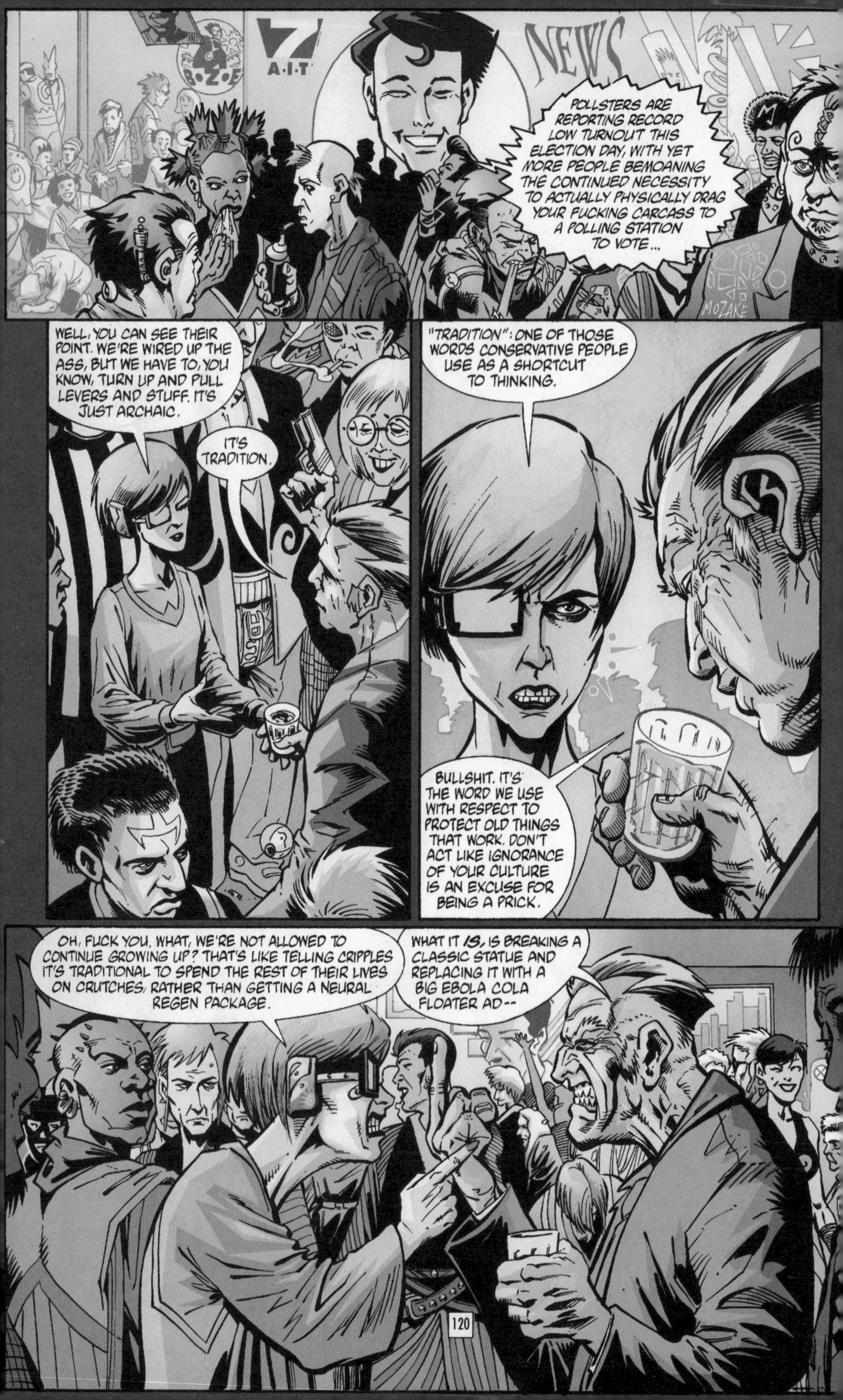
A·I·T
B·O·Z·E
NEWS
POLLSTERS ARE REPORTING RECORD LOW TURNOUT THIS ELECTION DAY, WITH YET MORE PEOPLE BEMOANING THE CONTINUED NECESSITY TO ACTUALLY PHYSICALLY DRAG YOUR FUCKING CARCASS TO A POLLING STATION TO VOTE...
MOZAKE
WELL, YOU CAN SEE THEIR POINT. WE'RE WIRED UP THE ASS, BUT WE HAVE TO, YOU KNOW, TURN UP AND PULL LEVERS AND STUFF. IT'S JUST ARCHAIC.
IT'S TRADITION.
"TRADITION": ONE OF THOSE WORDS CONSERVATIVE PEOPLE USE AS A SHORTCUT TO THINKING.
BULLSHIT. IT'S THE WORD WE USE WITH RESPECT TO PROTECT OLD THINGS THAT WORK. DON'T ACT LIKE IGNORANCE OF YOUR CULTURE IS AN EXCUSE FOR BEING A PRICK.
OH, FUCK YOU. WHAT, WE'RE NOT ALLOWED TO CONTINUE GROWING UP? THAT'S LIKE TELLING CRIPPLES IT'S TRADITIONAL TO SPEND THE REST OF THEIR LIVES ON CRUTCHES, RATHER THAN GETTING A NEURAL REGEN PACKAGE.
WHAT IT *IS*, IS BREAKING A CLASSIC STATUE AND REPLACING IT WITH A BIG EBOLA COLA FLOATER AD--

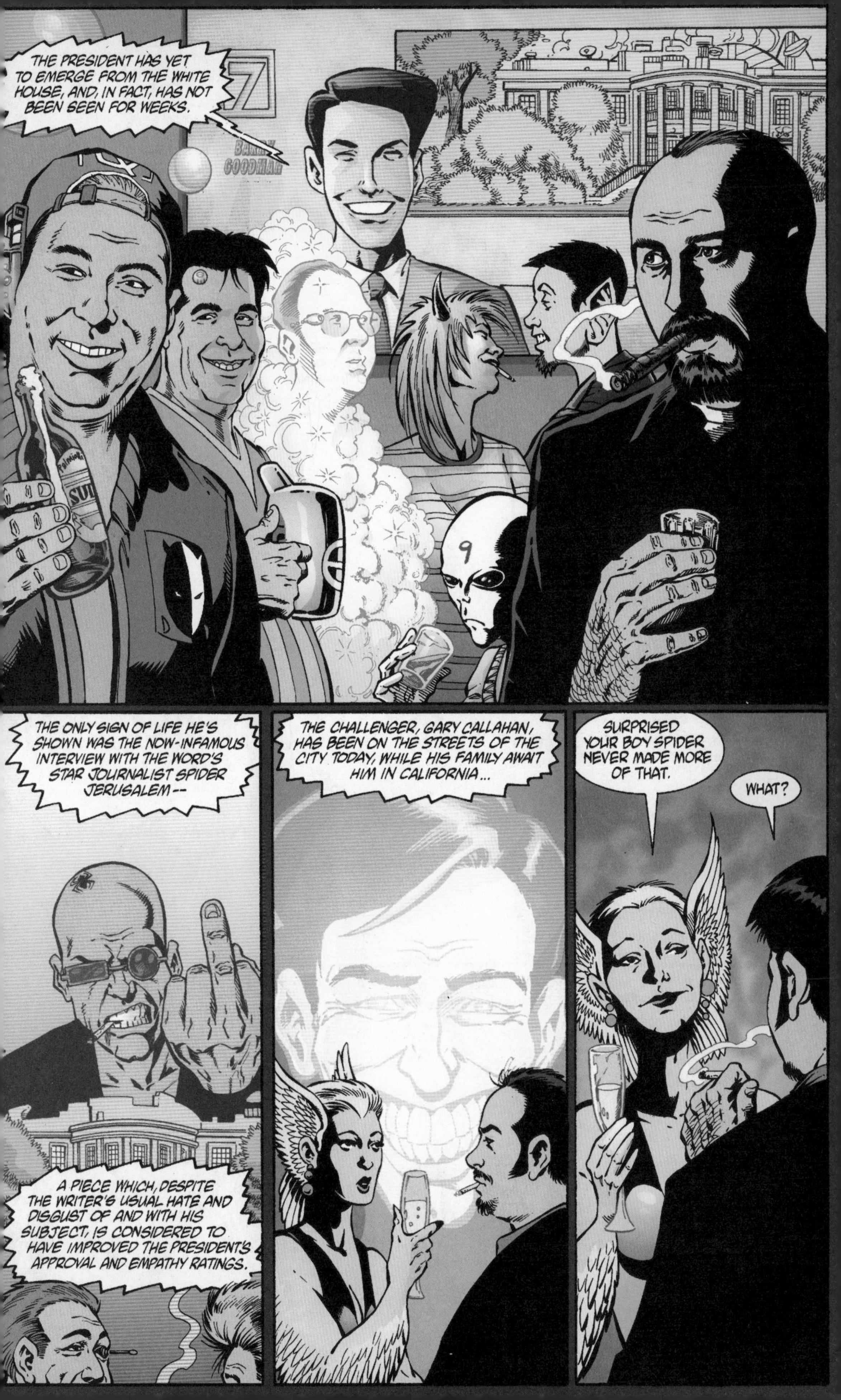
THE PRESIDENT HAS YET TO EMERGE FROM THE WHITE HOUSE, AND, IN FACT, HAS NOT BEEN SEEN FOR WEEKS.
7
GOODMAN
THE ONLY SIGN OF LIFE HE'S SHOWN WAS THE NOW-INFAMOUS INTERVIEW WITH THE WORD'S STAR JOURNALIST SPIDER JERUSALEM--
A PIECE WHICH, DESPITE THE WRITER'S USUAL HATE AND DISGUST OF AND WITH HIS SUBJECT, IS CONSIDERED TO HAVE IMPROVED THE PRESIDENT'S APPROVAL AND EMPATHY RATINGS.
THE CHALLENGER, GARY CALLAHAN, HAS BEEN ON THE STREETS OF THE CITY TODAY, WHILE HIS FAMILY AWAIT HIM IN CALIFORNIA...
SURPRISED YOUR BOY SPIDER NEVER MADE MORE OF THAT.
WHAT?

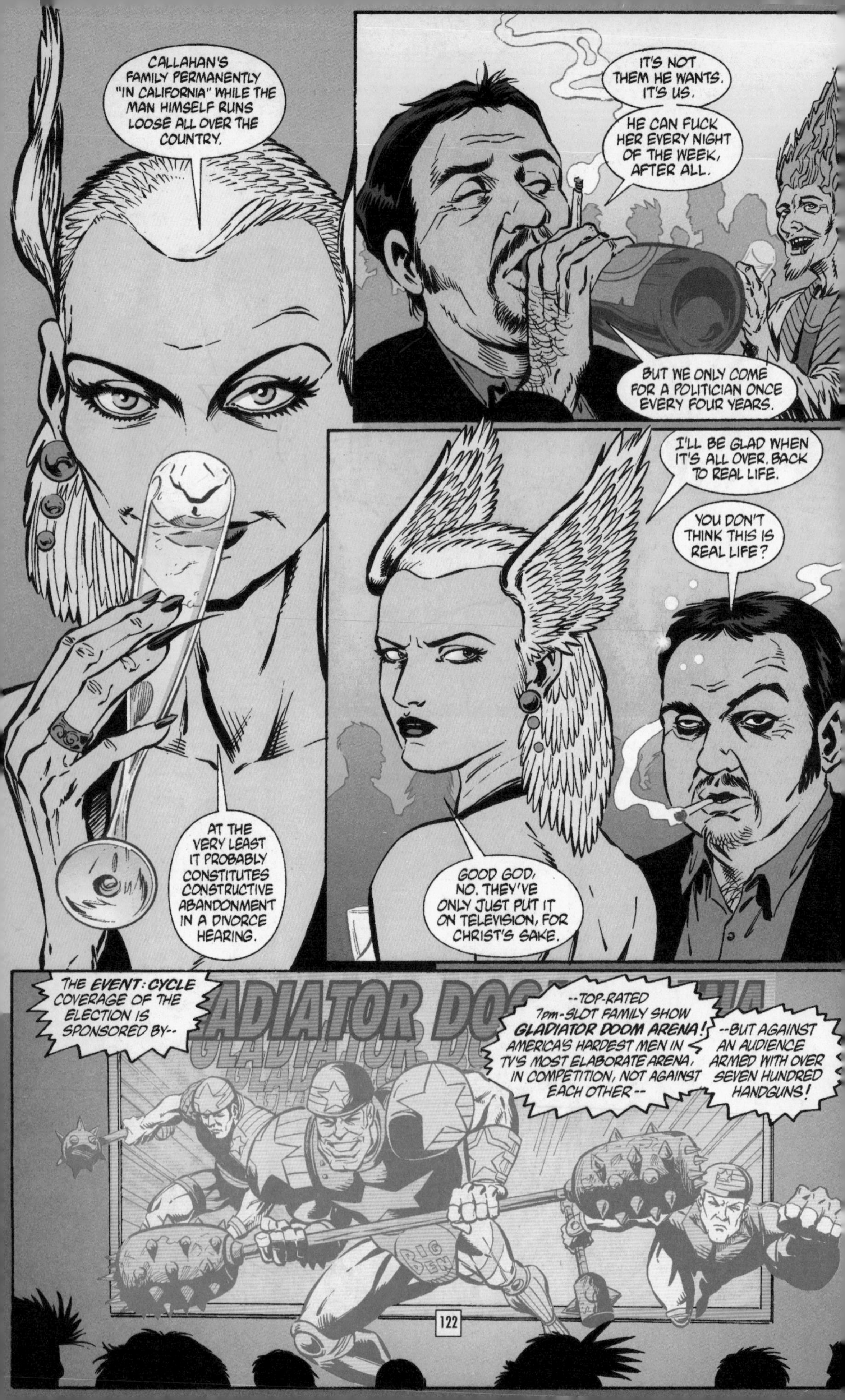
CALLAHAN'S FAMILY PERMANENTLY "IN CALIFORNIA" WHILE THE MAN HIMSELF RUNS LOOSE ALL OVER THE COUNTRY.
AT THE VERY LEAST IT PROBABLY CONSTITUTES CONSTRUCTIVE ABANDONMENT IN A DIVORCE HEARING.
IT'S NOT THEM HE WANTS. IT'S US.
HE CAN FUCK HER EVERY NIGHT OF THE WEEK, AFTER ALL.
BUT WE ONLY COME FOR A POLITICIAN ONCE EVERY FOUR YEARS.
I'LL BE GLAD WHEN IT'S ALL OVER. BACK TO REAL LIFE.
YOU DON'T THINK THIS IS REAL LIFE?
GOOD GOD, NO. THEY'VE ONLY JUST PUT IT ON TELEVISION, FOR CHRIST'S SAKE.
THE EVENT: CYCLE COVERAGE OF THE ELECTION IS SPONSORED BY--
--TOP-RATED 7pm-SLOT FAMILY SHOW GLADIATOR DOOM ARENA! AMERICA'S HARDEST MEN IN TV'S MOST ELABORATE ARENA, IN COMPETITION, NOT AGAINST EACH OTHER--
--BUT AGAINST AN AUDIENCE ARMED WITH OVER SEVEN HUNDRED HANDGUNS!
BIG BEN

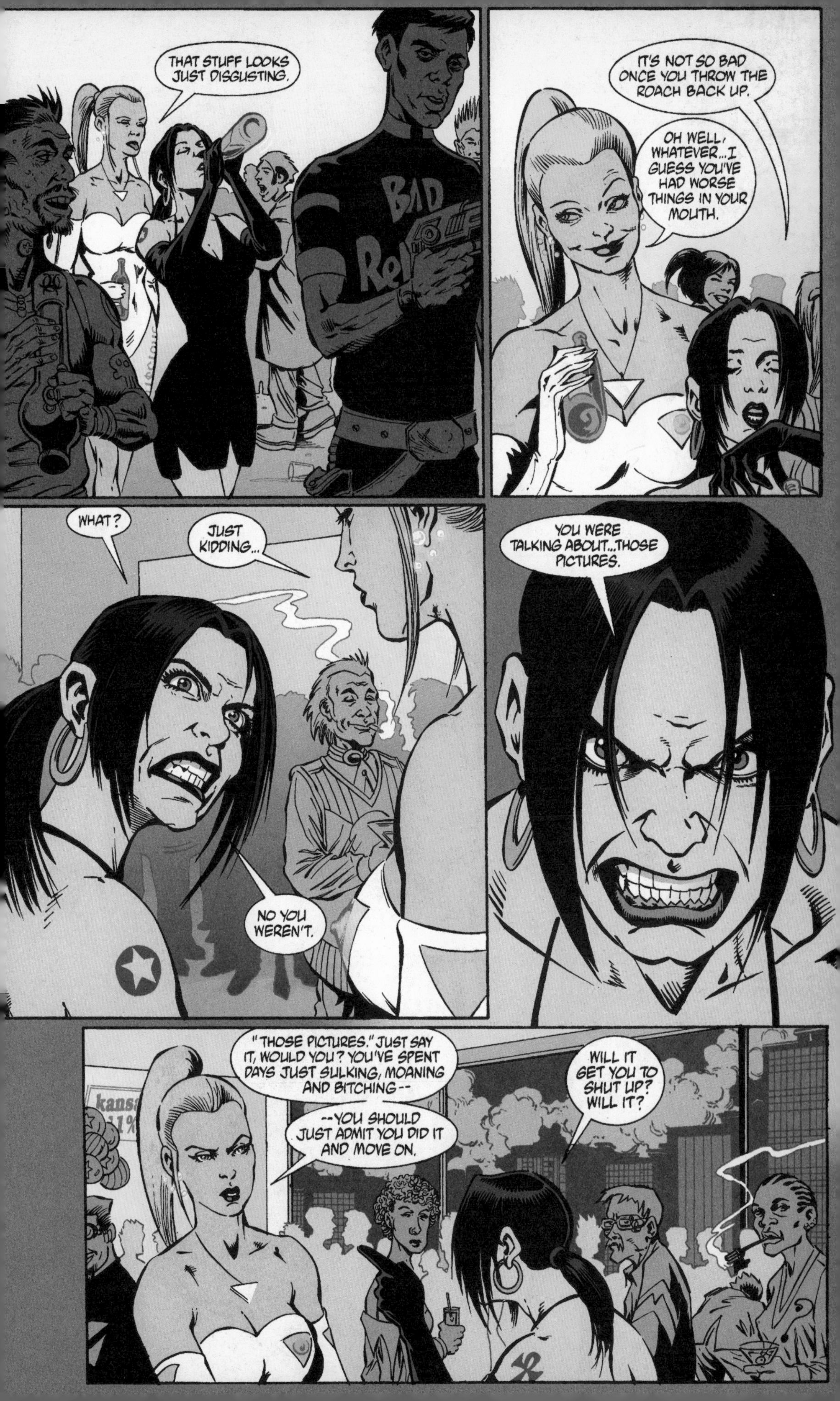

THAT STUFF LOOKS JUST DISGUSTING.
BAD Rel
IT'S NOT SO BAD ONCE YOU THROW THE ROACH BACK UP.
OH WELL, WHATEVER...I GUESS YOU'VE HAD WORSE THINGS IN YOUR MOUTH.
WHAT?
JUST KIDDING...
NO YOU WEREN'T.
YOU WERE TALKING ABOUT...THOSE PICTURES.
"THOSE PICTURES." JUST SAY IT, WOULD YOU? YOU'VE SPENT DAYS JUST SULKING, MOANING AND BITCHING--
--YOU SHOULD JUST ADMIT YOU DID IT AND MOVE ON.
WILL IT GET YOU TO SHUT UP? WILL IT?

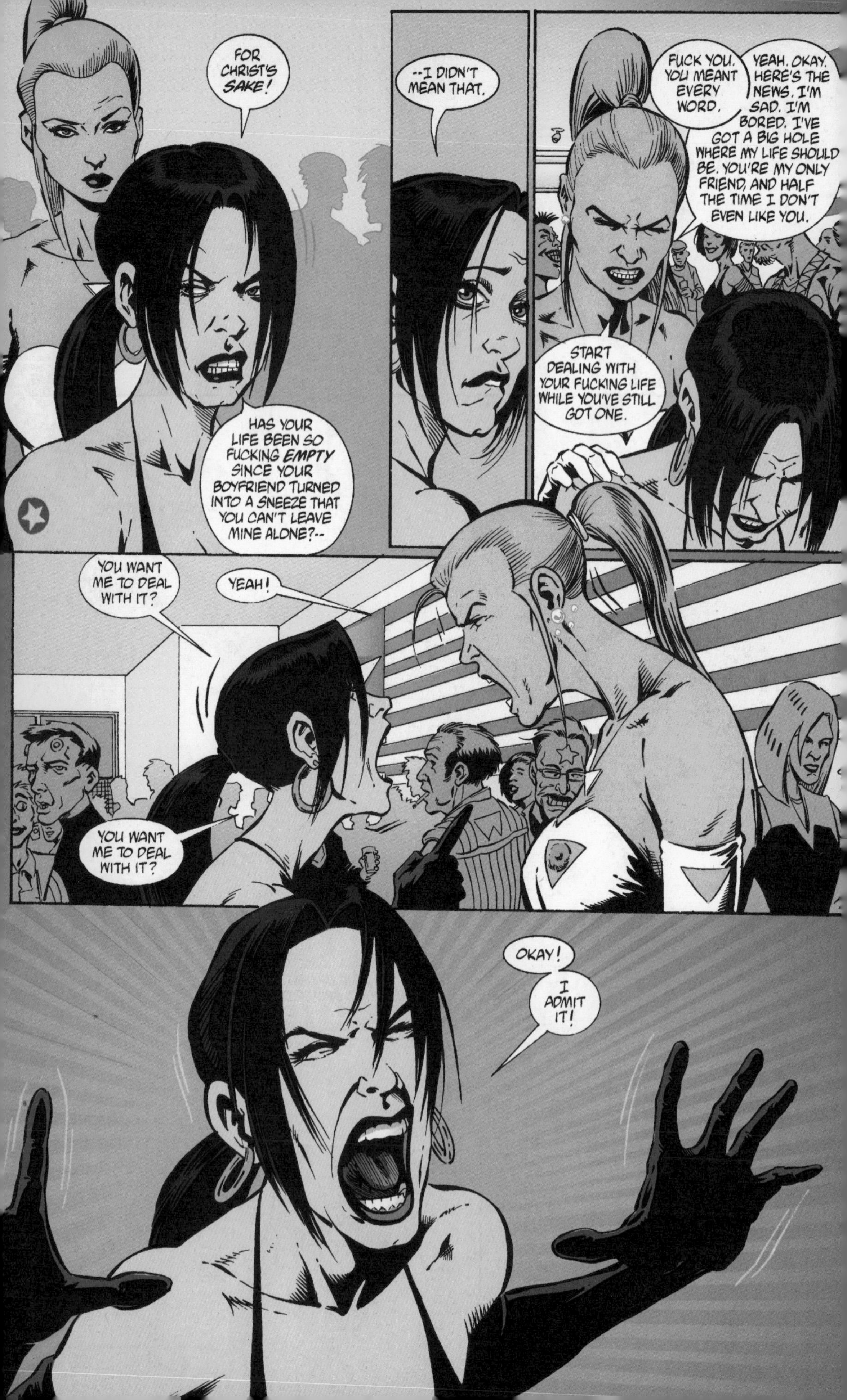
FOR CHRIST'S SAKE!
HAS YOUR LIFE BEEN SO FUCKING EMPTY SINCE YOUR BOYFRIEND TURNED INTO A SNEEZE THAT YOU CAN'T LEAVE MINE ALONE?--
--I DIDN'T MEAN THAT.
FUCK YOU. YOU MEANT EVERY WORD.
YEAH. OKAY. HERE'S THE NEWS. I'M SAD. I'M BORED. I'VE GOT A BIG HOLE WHERE MY LIFE SHOULD BE. YOU'RE MY ONLY FRIEND, AND HALF THE TIME I DON'T EVEN LIKE YOU.
START DEALING WITH YOUR FUCKING LIFE WHILE YOU'VE STILL GOT ONE.
YOU WANT ME TO DEAL WITH IT?
YEAH!
YOU WANT ME TO DEAL WITH IT?
OKAY!
I ADMIT IT!

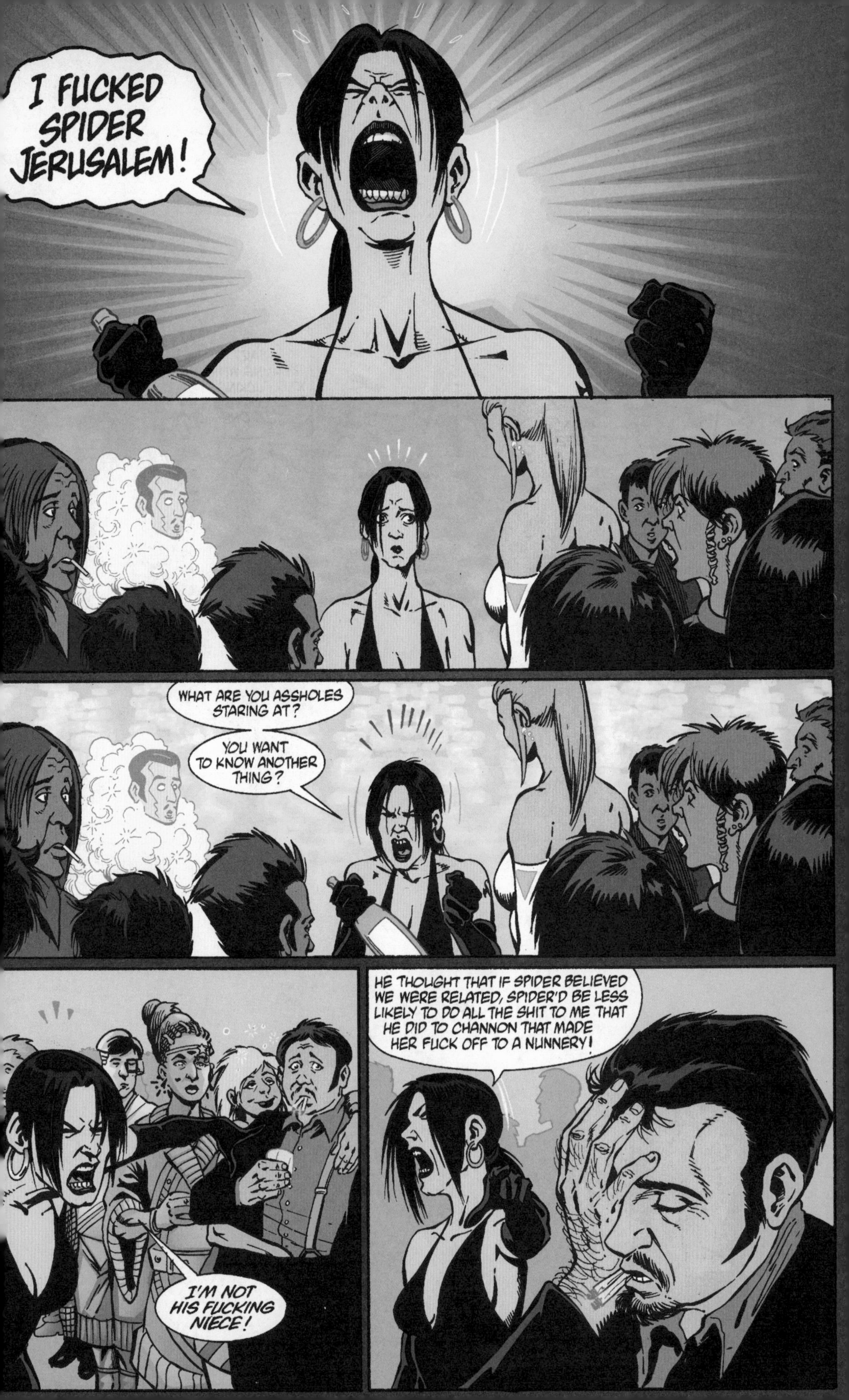
I FUCKED SPIDER JERUSALEM!
WHAT ARE YOU ASSHOLES STARING AT?
YOU WANT TO KNOW ANOTHER THING?
I'M NOT HIS FUCKING NIECE!
HE THOUGHT THAT IF SPIDER BELIEVED WE WERE RELATED, SPIDER'D BE LESS LIKELY TO DO ALL THE SHIT TO ME THAT HE DID TO CHANNON THAT MADE HER FUCK OFF TO A NUNNERY!

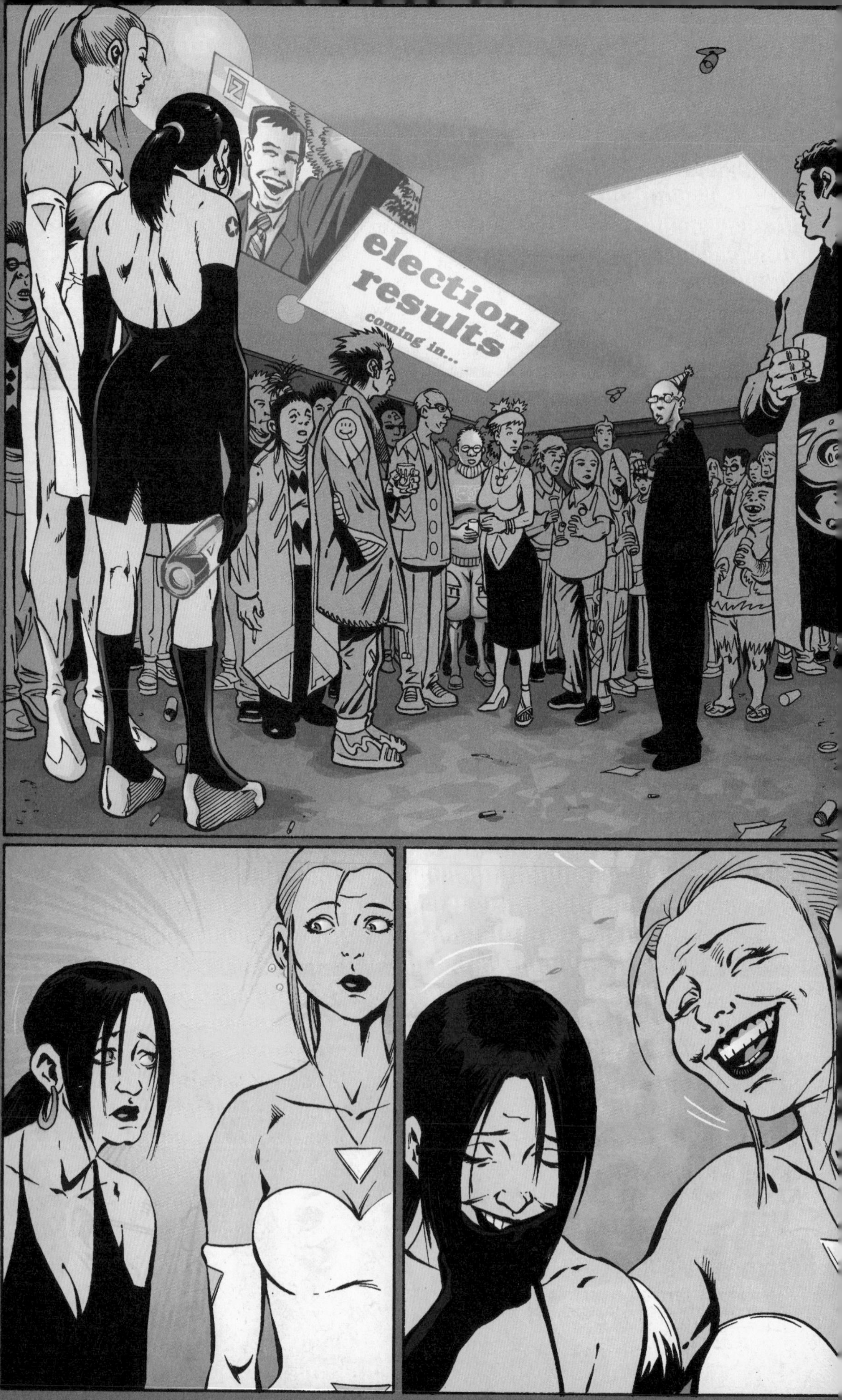
election results
coming in...

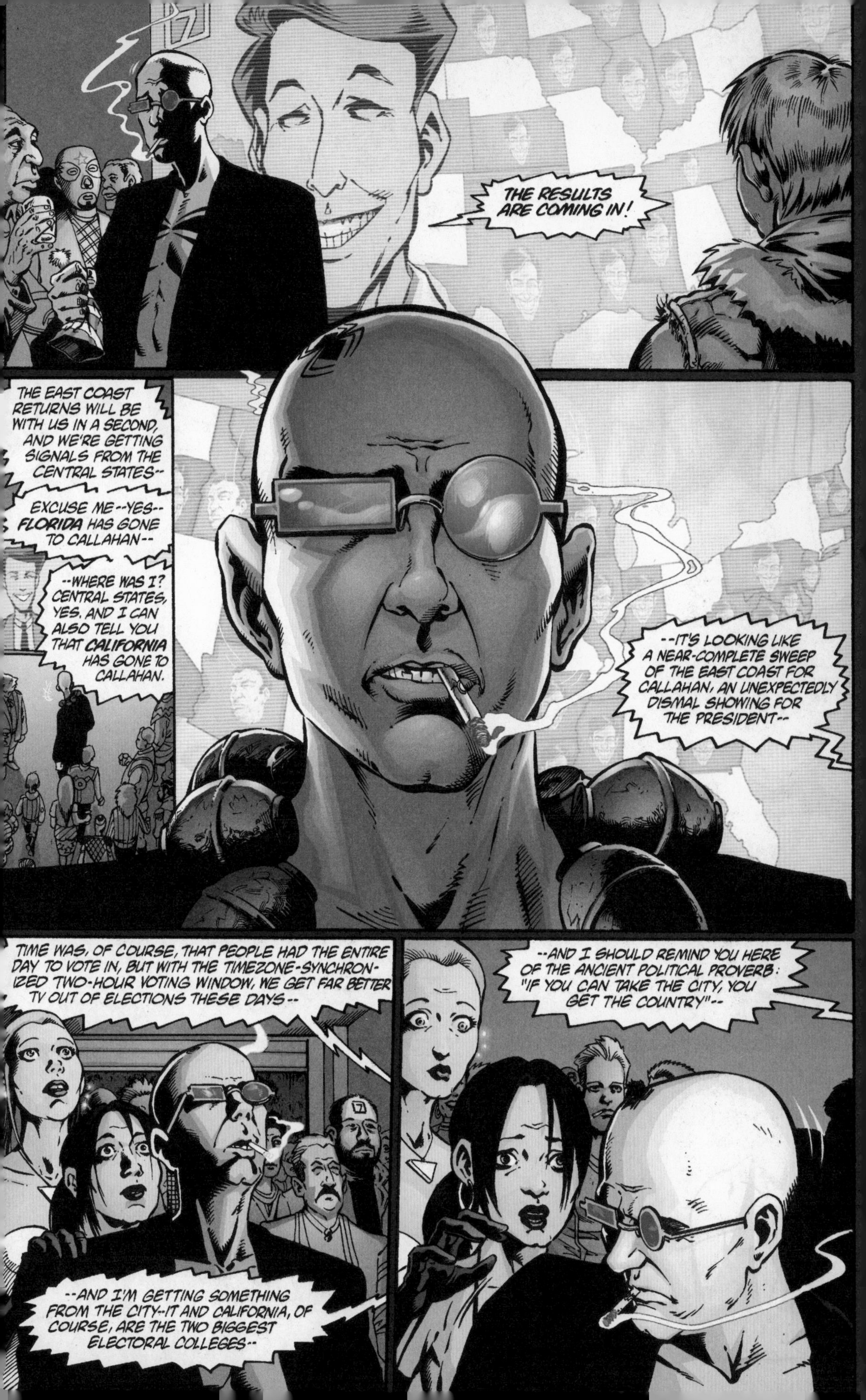
THE RESULTS ARE COMING IN!
THE EAST COAST RETURNS WILL BE WITH US IN A SECOND, AND WE'RE GETTING SIGNALS FROM THE CENTRAL STATES--
EXCUSE ME--YES-- FLORIDA HAS GONE TO CALLAHAN--
--WHERE WAS I? CENTRAL STATES, YES. AND I CAN ALSO TELL YOU THAT CALIFORNIA HAS GONE TO CALLAHAN.
--IT'S LOOKING LIKE A NEAR-COMPLETE SWEEP OF THE EAST COAST FOR CALLAHAN, AN UNEXPECTEDLY DISMAL SHOWING FOR THE PRESIDENT--
TIME WAS, OF COURSE, THAT PEOPLE HAD THE ENTIRE DAY TO VOTE IN, BUT WITH THE TIMEZONE-SYNCHRONIZED TWO-HOUR VOTING WINDOW, WE GET FAR BETTER TV OUT OF ELECTIONS THESE DAYS--
--AND I'M GETTING SOMETHING FROM THE CITY--IT AND CALIFORNIA, OF COURSE, ARE THE TWO BIGGEST ELECTORAL COLLEGES--
--AND I SHOULD REMIND YOU HERE OF THE ANCIENT POLITICAL PROVERB: "IF YOU CAN TAKE THE CITY, YOU GET THE COUNTRY"--

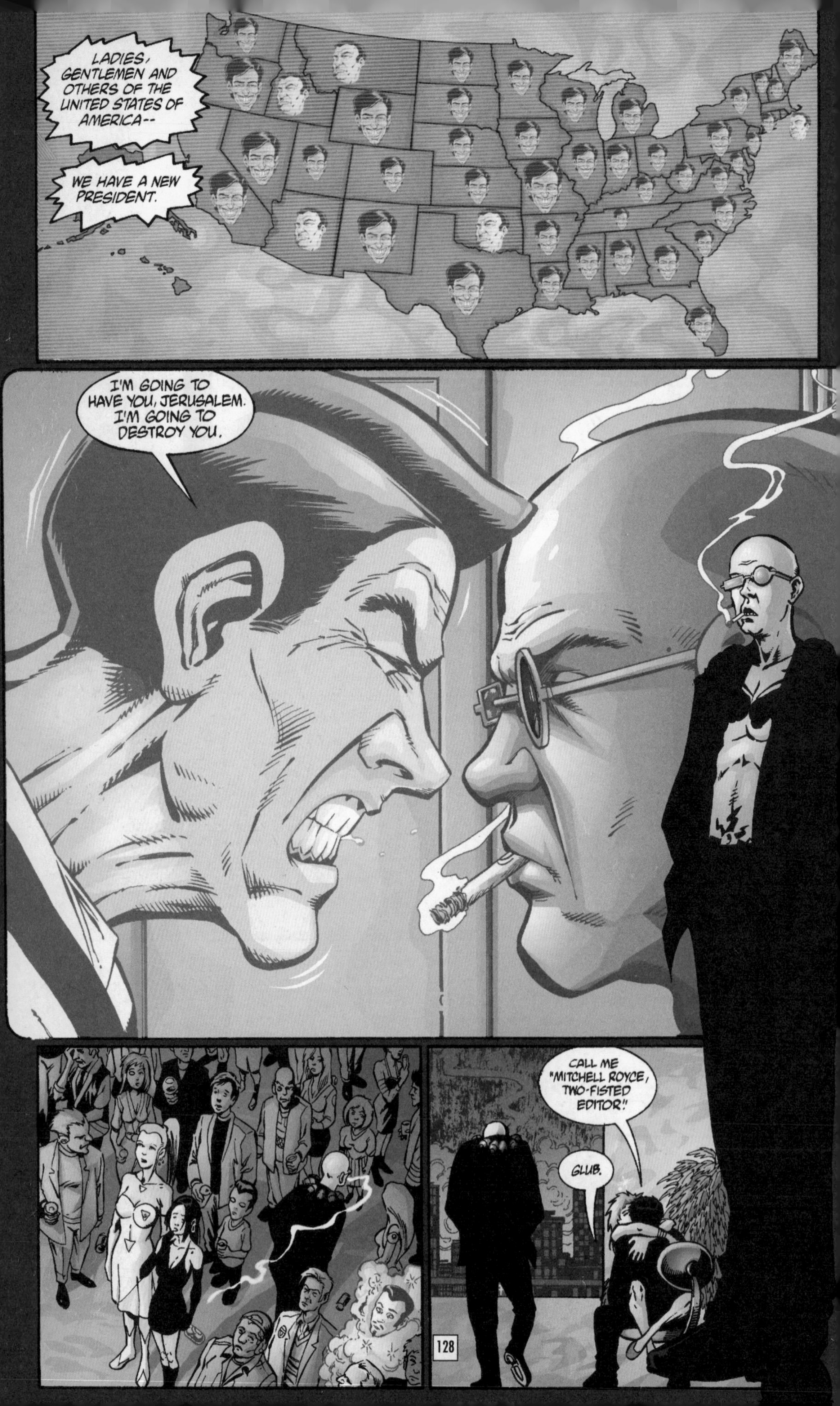
LADIES, GENTLEMEN AND OTHERS OF THE UNITED STATES OF AMERICA--
WE HAVE A NEW PRESIDENT.
I'M GOING TO HAVE YOU, JERUSALEM. I'M GOING TO DESTROY YOU.
CALL ME "MITCHELL ROYCE, TWO-FISTED EDITOR."
GLUB.

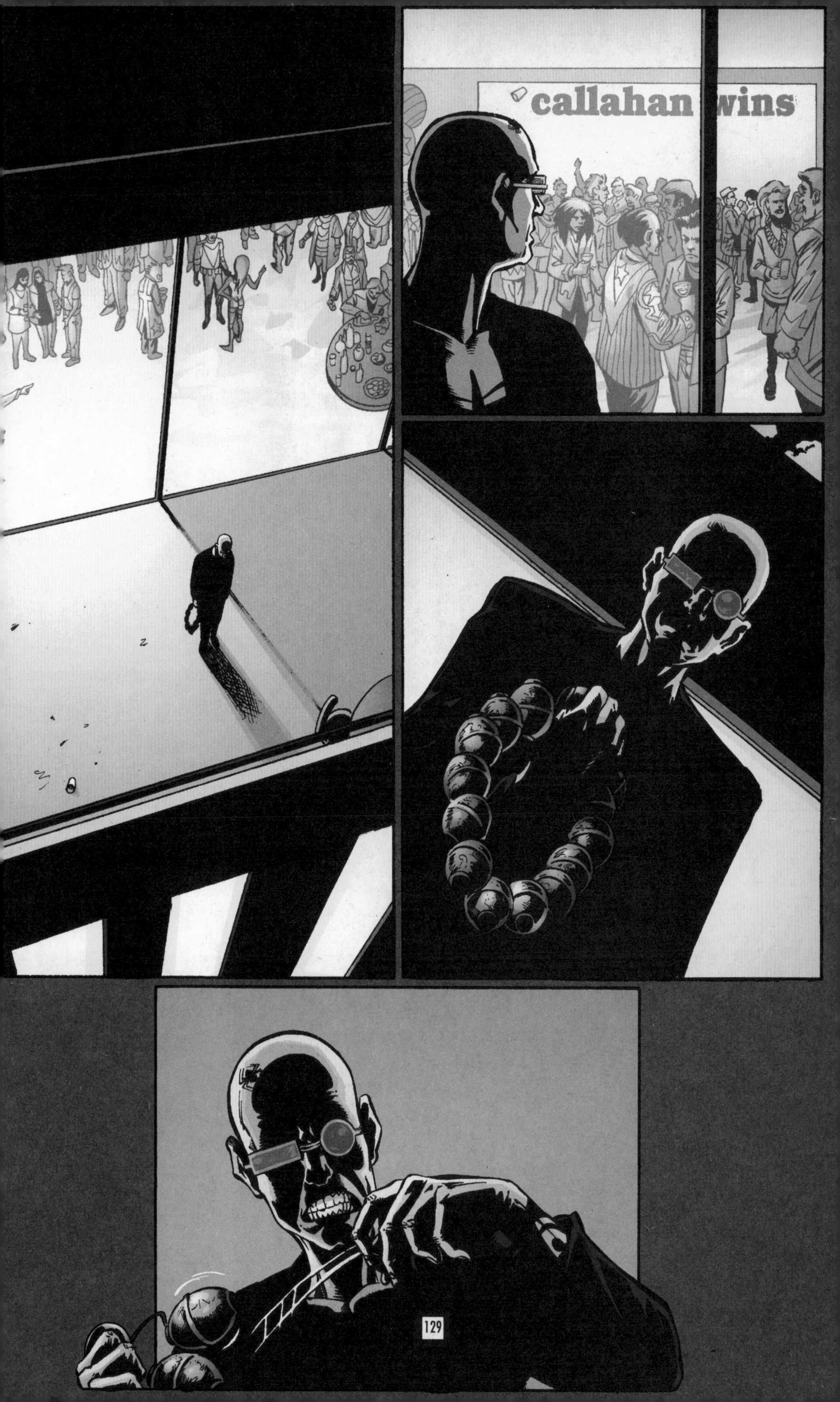
callahan wins

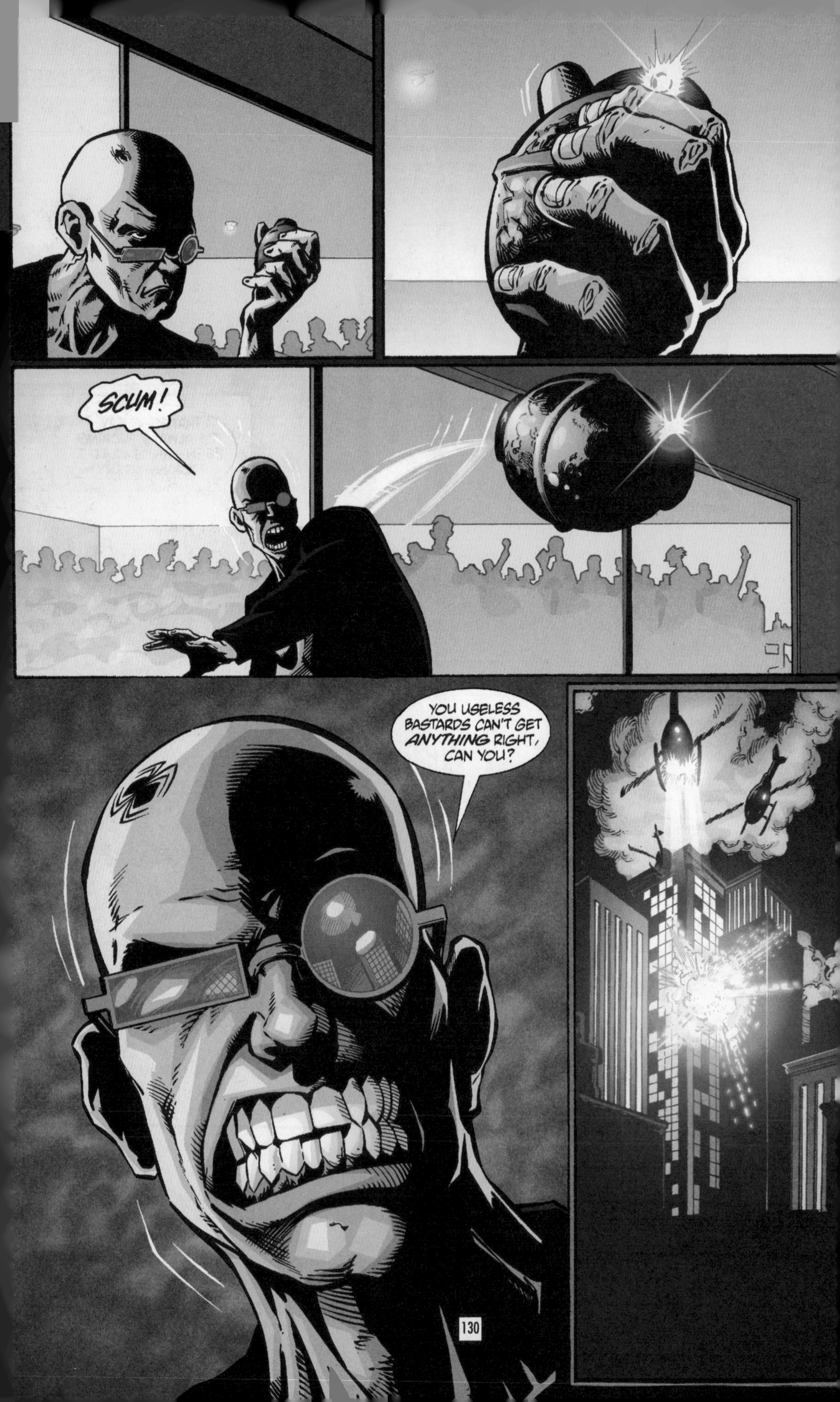

SCUM!
YOU USELESS BASTARDS CAN'T GET ANYTHING RIGHT, CAN YOU?

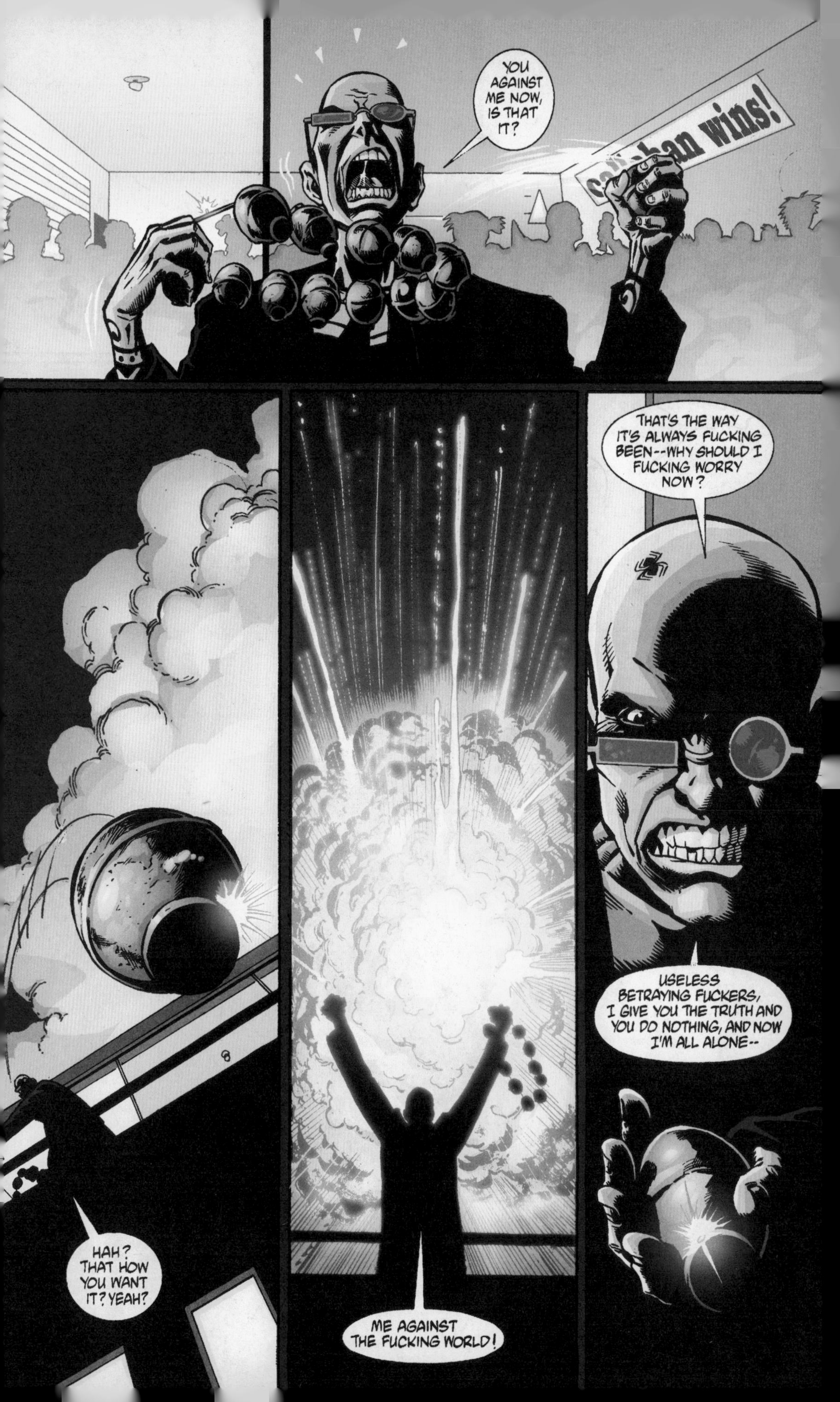
YOU AGAINST ME NOW, IS THAT IT?
THAT'S THE WAY IT'S ALWAYS FUCKING BEEN--WHY SHOULD I FUCKING WORRY NOW?
USELESS BETRAYING FUCKERS, I GIVE YOU THE TRUTH AND YOU DO NOTHING, AND NOW I'M ALL ALONE--
HAH? THAT HOW YOU WANT IT? YEAH?
ME AGAINST THE FUCKING WORLD!

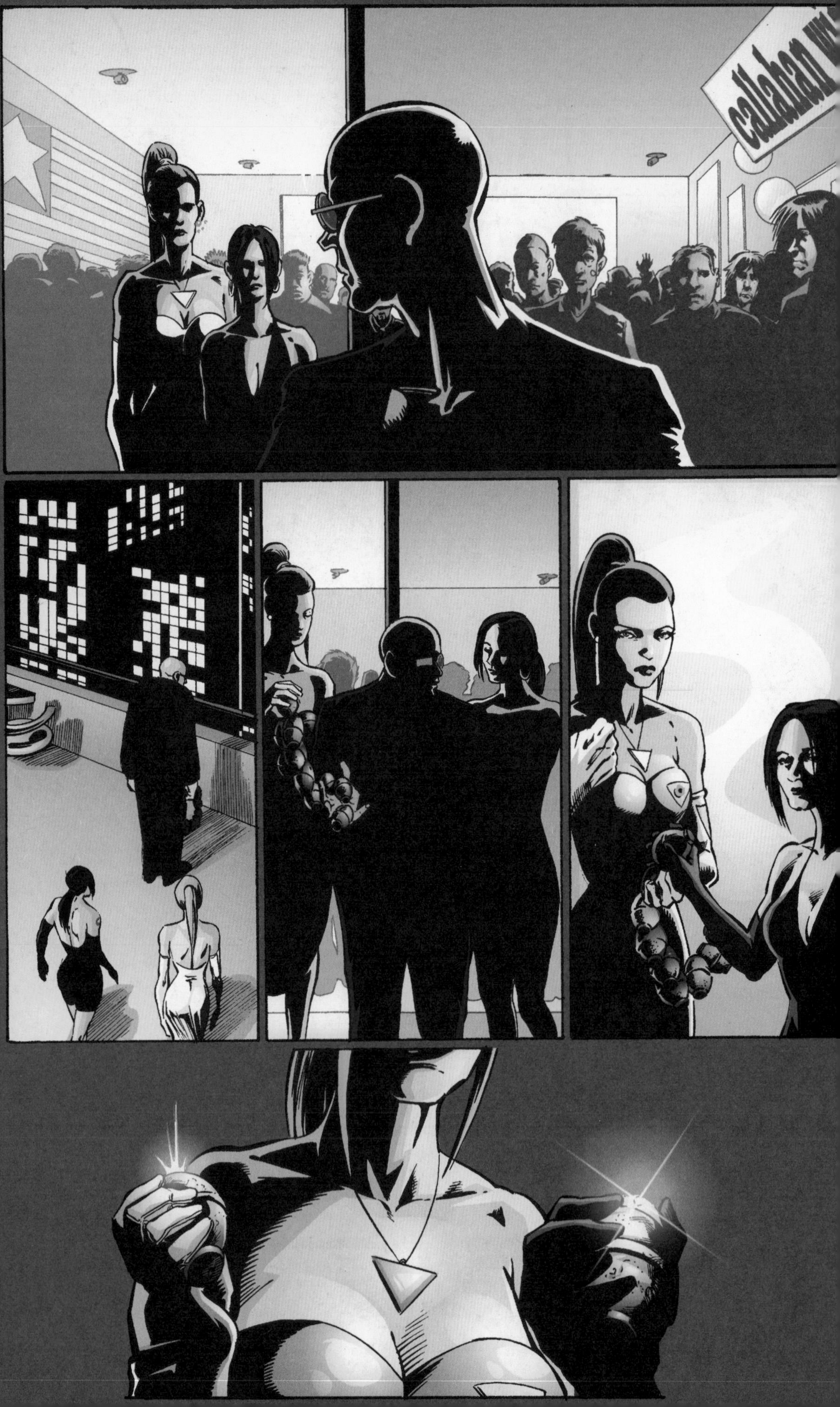

callahan w

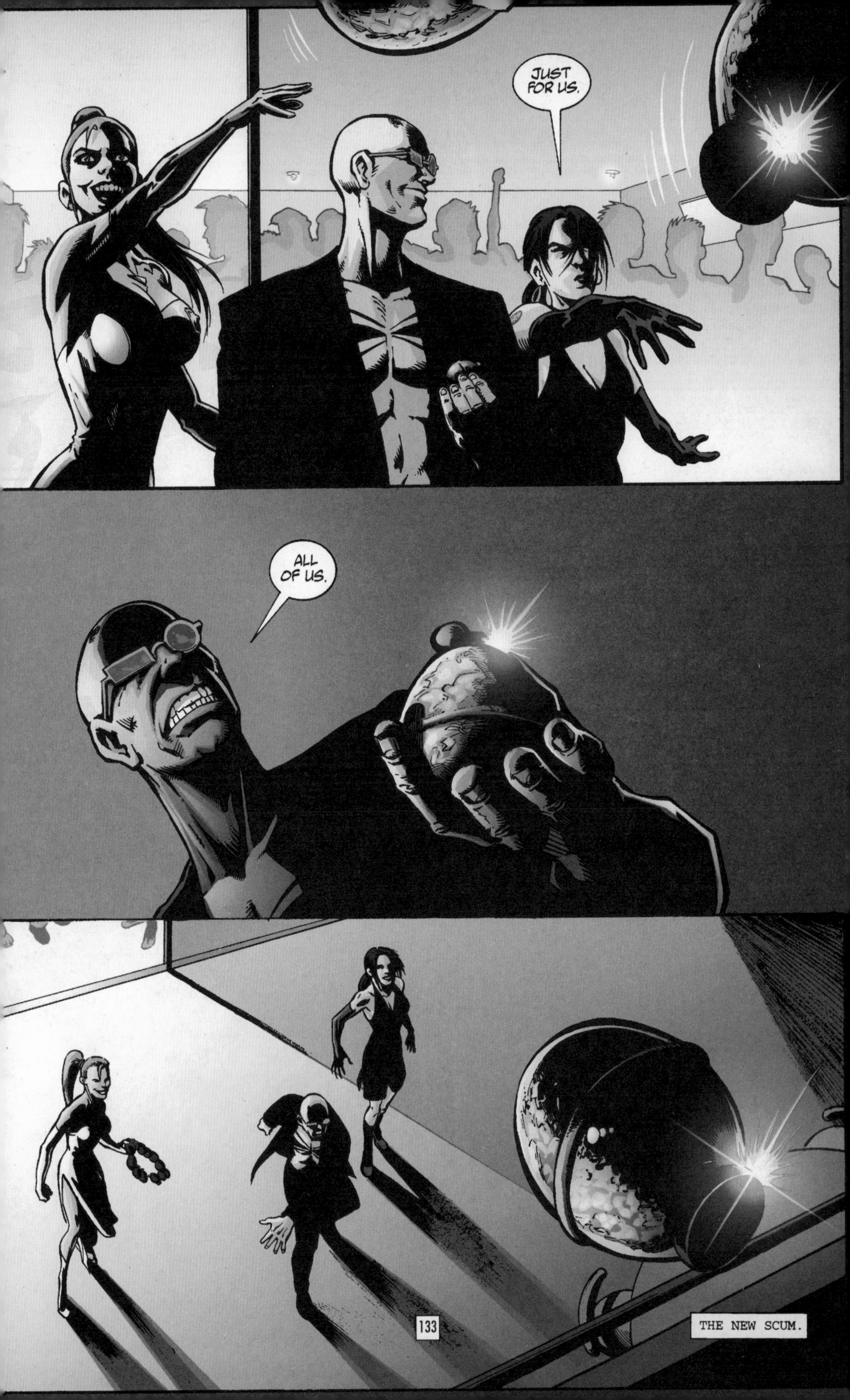
JUST FOR US.
ALL OF US.
THE NEW SCUM.

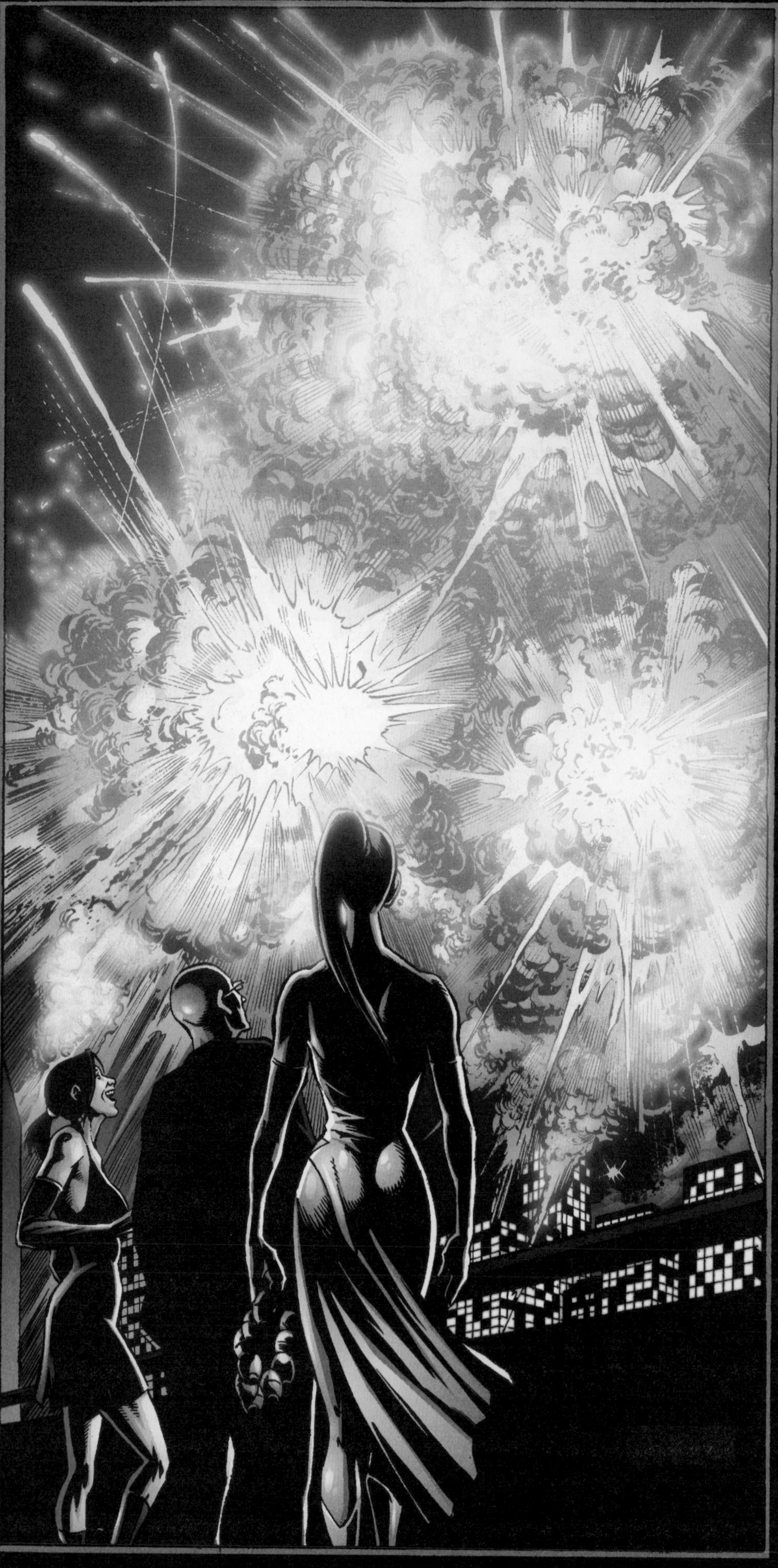

NEXT WINTERS

A TRANSMETROPOLITAN STORY

WRITTEN BY WARREN ELLIS AND
PENCILLED BY DARICK ROBERTSON INKED BY KEITH AIKEN
COLORED BY NATHAN EYRING SEPARATED BY JAMISON
LETTERED BY CLEM ROBINS EDITED BY SHELLY ROEBERG & CLIFF CHIANG
TRANSMETROPOLITAN CREATED BY WARREN ELLIS & DARICK ROBERTSON

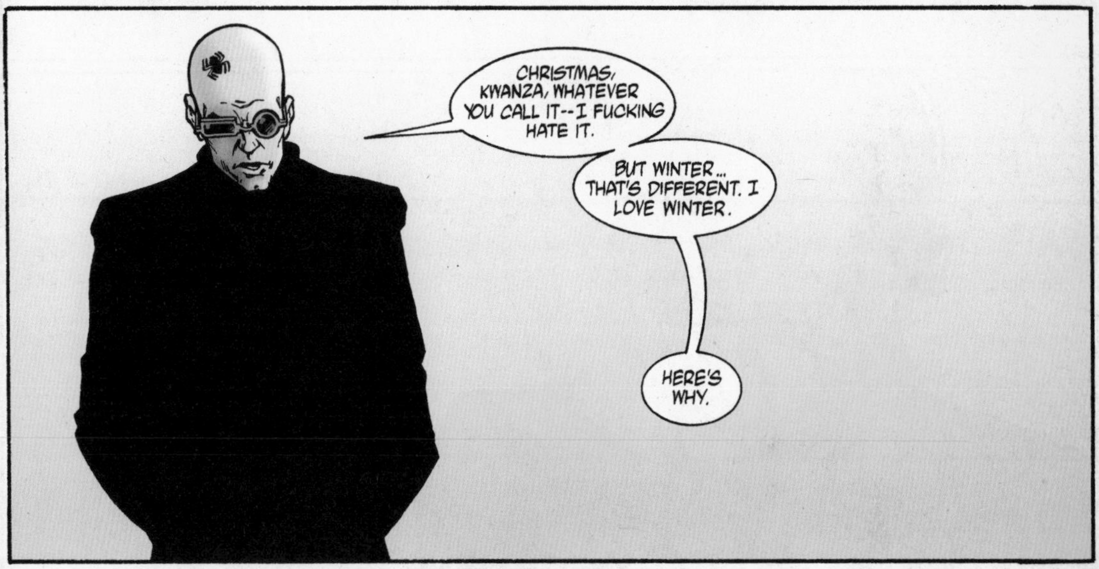

CHRISTMAS, KWANZA, WHATEVER YOU CALL IT--I FUCKING HATE IT.
BUT WINTER... THAT'S DIFFERENT. I LOVE WINTER.
HERE'S WHY.

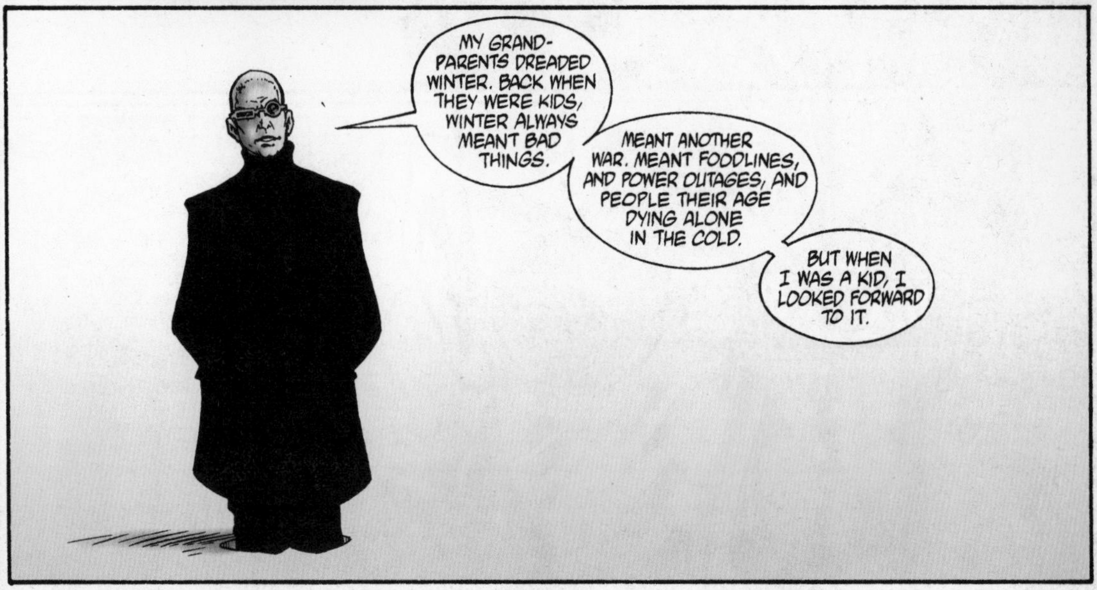

MY GRAND-PARENTS DREADED WINTER. BACK WHEN THEY WERE KIDS, WINTER ALWAYS MEANT BAD THINGS.
MEANT ANOTHER WAR. MEANT FOODLINES, AND POWER OUTAGES, AND PEOPLE THEIR AGE DYING ALONE IN THE COLD.
BUT WHEN I WAS A KID, I LOOKED FORWARD TO IT.

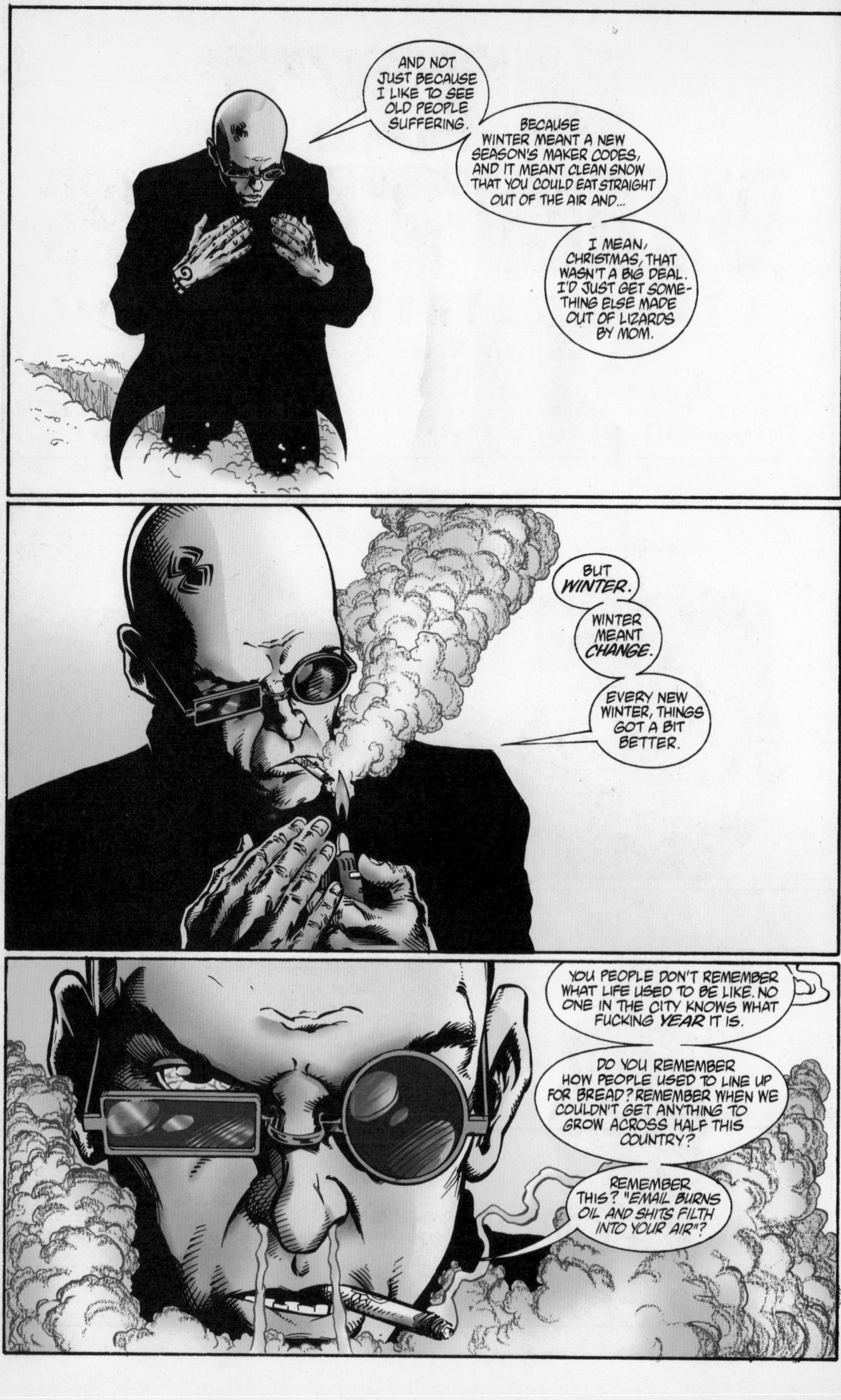
AND NOT JUST BECAUSE I LIKE TO SEE OLD PEOPLE SUFFERING.
BECAUSE WINTER MEANT A NEW SEASON'S MAKER CODES, AND IT MEANT CLEAN SNOW THAT YOU COULD EAT STRAIGHT OUT OF THE AIR AND...
I MEAN, CHRISTMAS, THAT WASN'T A BIG DEAL. I'D JUST GET SOME-THING ELSE MADE OUT OF LIZARDS BY MOM.
BUT WINTER.
WINTER MEANT CHANGE.
EVERY NEW WINTER, THINGS GOT A BIT BETTER.
YOU PEOPLE DON'T REMEMBER WHAT LIFE USED TO BE LIKE. NO ONE IN THE CITY KNOWS WHAT FUCKING YEAR IT IS.
DO YOU REMEMBER HOW PEOPLE USED TO LINE UP FOR BREAD? REMEMBER WHEN WE COULDN'T GET ANYTHING TO GROW ACROSS HALF THIS COUNTRY?
REMEMBER THIS? "EMAIL BURNS OIL AND SHITS FILTH INTO YOUR AIR"?

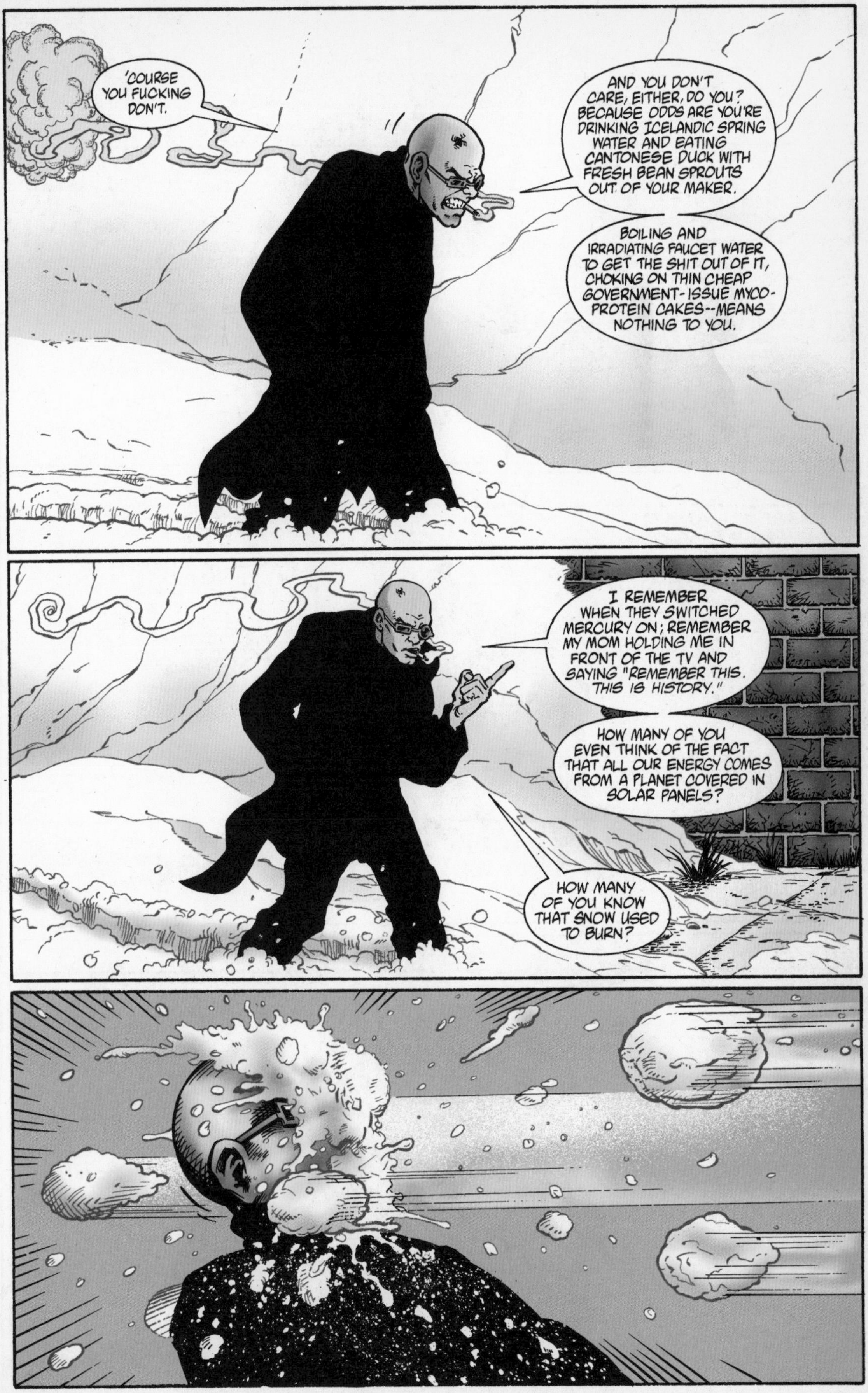
'COURSE YOU FUCKING DON'T.
AND YOU DON'T CARE, EITHER, DO YOU? BECAUSE ODDS ARE YOU'RE DRINKING ICELANDIC SPRING WATER AND EATING CANTONESE DUCK WITH FRESH BEAN SPROUTS OUT OF YOUR MAKER.
BOILING AND IRRADIATING FAUCET WATER TO GET THE SHIT OUT OF IT, CHOKING ON THIN CHEAP GOVERNMENT-ISSUE MYCO-PROTEIN CAKES--MEANS NOTHING TO YOU.
I REMEMBER WHEN THEY SWITCHED MERCURY ON; REMEMBER MY MOM HOLDING ME IN FRONT OF THE TV AND SAYING "REMEMBER THIS. THIS IS HISTORY."
HOW MANY OF YOU EVEN THINK OF THE FACT THAT ALL OUR ENERGY COMES FROM A PLANET COVERED IN SOLAR PANELS?
HOW MANY OF YOU KNOW THAT SNOW USED TO BURN?

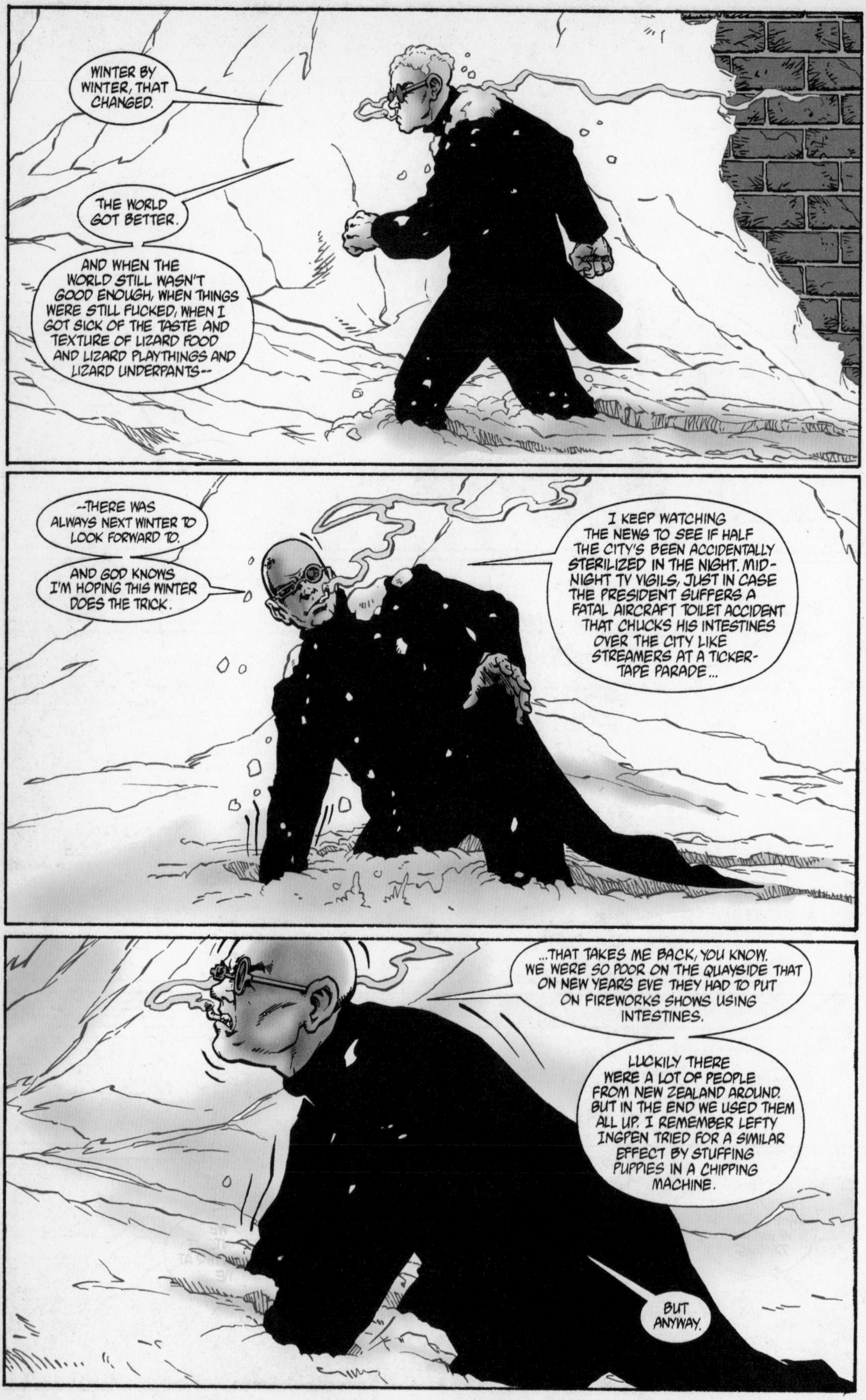
WINTER BY WINTER, THAT CHANGED.
THE WORLD GOT BETTER.
AND WHEN THE WORLD STILL WASN'T GOOD ENOUGH, WHEN THINGS WERE STILL FUCKED, WHEN I GOT SICK OF THE TASTE AND TEXTURE OF LIZARD FOOD AND LIZARD PLAYTHINGS AND LIZARD UNDERPANTS--
--THERE WAS ALWAYS NEXT WINTER TO LOOK FORWARD TO.
AND GOD KNOWS I'M HOPING THIS WINTER DOES THE TRICK.
I KEEP WATCHING THE NEWS TO SEE IF HALF THE CITY'S BEEN ACCIDENTALLY STERILIZED IN THE NIGHT. MID-NIGHT TV VIGILS, JUST IN CASE THE PRESIDENT SUFFERS A FATAL AIRCRAFT TOILET ACCIDENT THAT CHUCKS HIS INTESTINES OVER THE CITY LIKE STREAMERS AT A TICKER-TAPE PARADE...
...THAT TAKES ME BACK, YOU KNOW. WE WERE SO POOR ON THE QUAYSIDE THAT ON NEW YEAR'S EVE THEY HAD TO PUT ON FIREWORKS SHOWS USING INTESTINES.
LUCKILY THERE WERE A LOT OF PEOPLE FROM NEW ZEALAND AROUND. BUT IN THE END WE USED THEM ALL UP. I REMEMBER LEFTY INGPEN TRIED FOR A SIMILAR EFFECT BY STUFFING PUPPIES IN A CHIPPING MACHINE.
BUT ANYWAY.

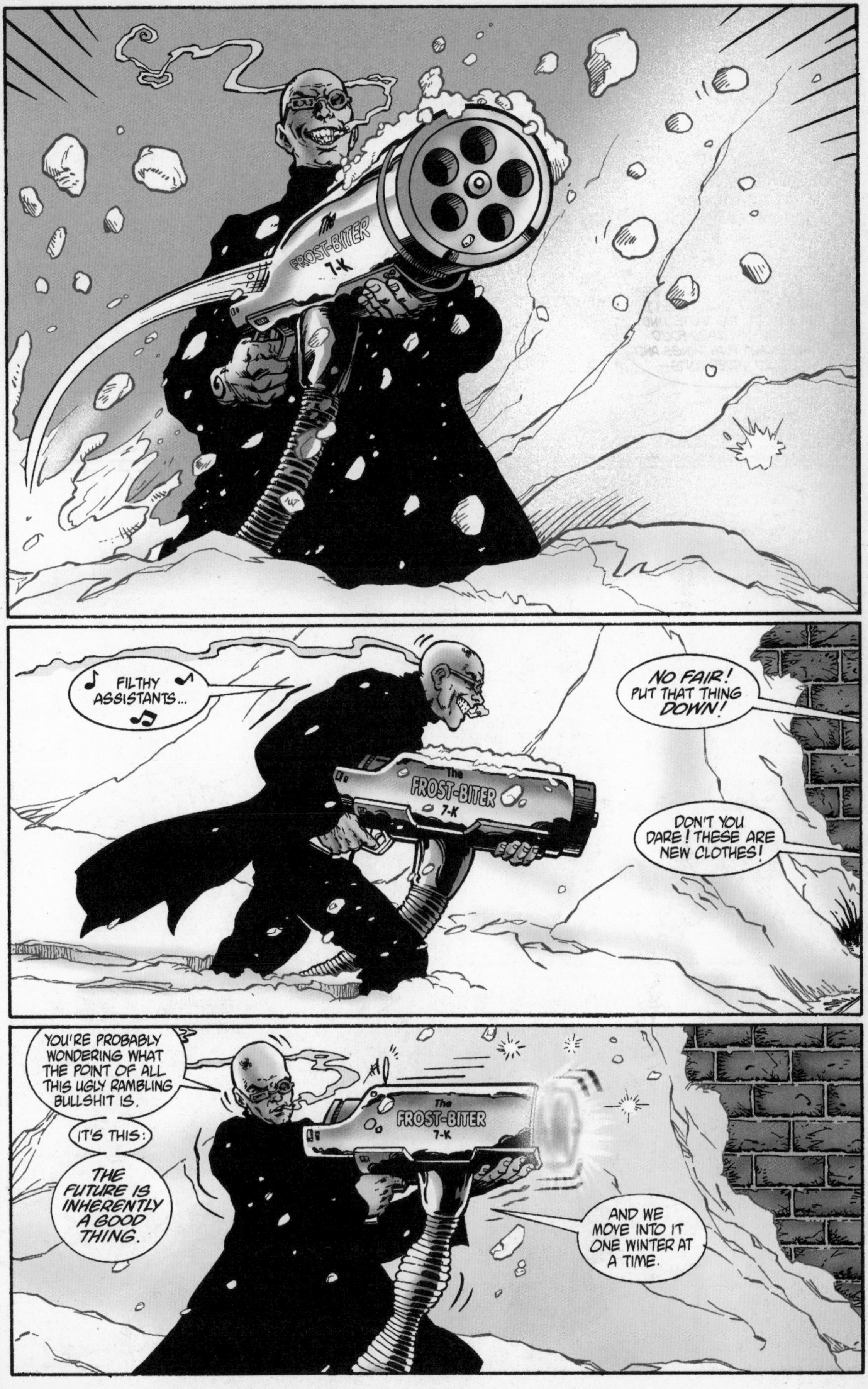
The FROST-BITER 7-K
FILTHY ASSISTANTS...
NO FAIR! PUT THAT THING DOWN!
The FROST-BITER 7-K
DON'T YOU DARE! THESE ARE NEW CLOTHES!
YOU'RE PROBABLY WONDERING WHAT THE POINT OF ALL THIS UGLY RAMBLING BULLSHIT IS.
IT'S THIS:
THE FUTURE IS INHERENTLY A GOOD THING.
The FROST-BITER 7-K
AND WE MOVE INTO IT ONE WINTER AT A TIME.

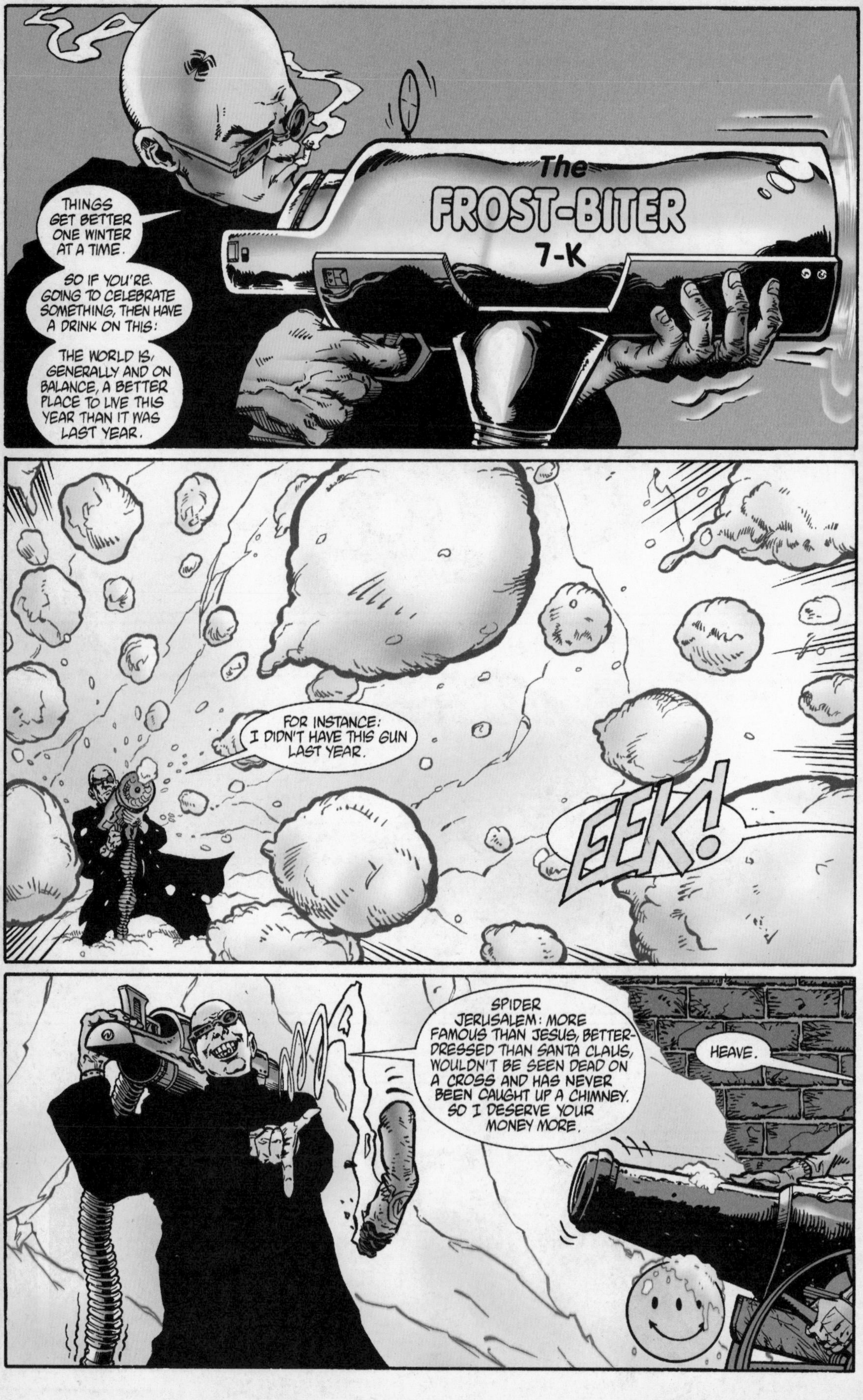
The
FROST-BITER
7-K
THINGS GET BETTER ONE WINTER AT A TIME.
SO IF YOU'RE GOING TO CELEBRATE SOMETHING, THEN HAVE A DRINK ON THIS:
THE WORLD IS, GENERALLY AND ON BALANCE, A BETTER PLACE TO LIVE THIS YEAR THAN IT WAS LAST YEAR.
FOR INSTANCE: I DIDN'T HAVE THIS GUN LAST YEAR.
EEK!
SPIDER JERUSALEM: MORE FAMOUS THAN JESUS, BETTER-DRESSED THAN SANTA CLAUS, WOULDN'T BE SEEN DEAD ON A CROSS AND HAS NEVER BEEN CAUGHT UP A CHIMNEY. SO I DESERVE YOUR MONEY MORE.
HEAVE.

COVER GALLERY

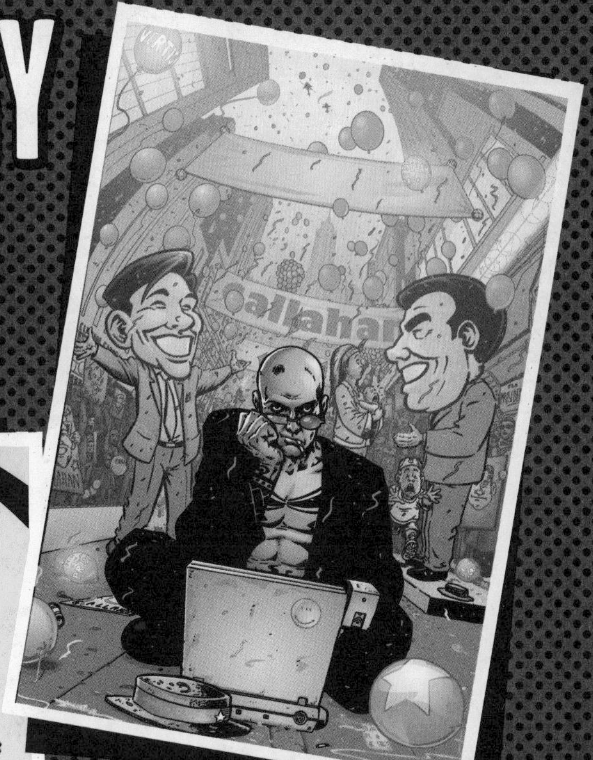

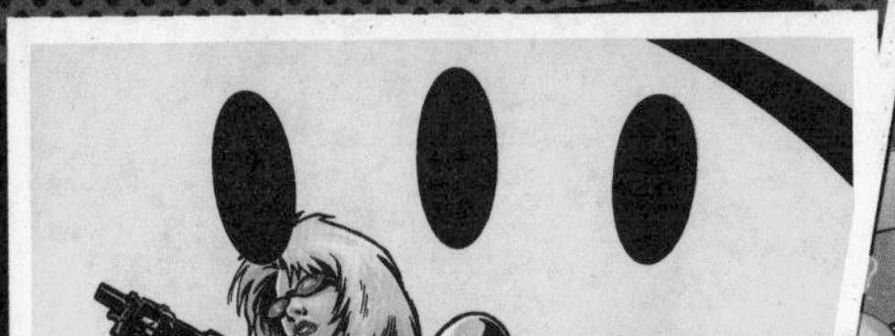

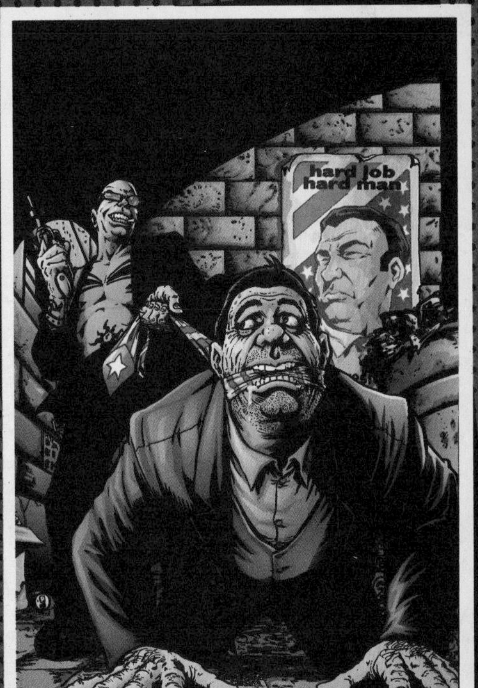
hard job
hard man

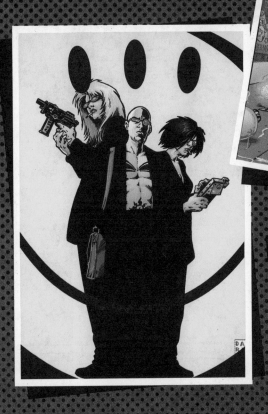

THE TRANSMETROPOLITAN LIBRARY

BY WARREN ELLIS, DARICK ROBERTSON, RODNEY RAMOS AND VARIOUS

An exuberant trip into a frenetic future, where outlaw journalist Spider Jerusalem battles hypocrisy, corruption, and sobriety.

Volume One:
BACK ON THE STREET

Volume Two:
LUST FOR LIFE

Volume Three:
YEAR OF THE BASTARD

Volume Four:
THE NEW SCUM

Volume Five:
LONELY CITY

Volume Six:
GOUGE AWAY

Volume Seven:
SPIDER'S THRASH

Volume Eight:
DIRGE

Volume Nine:
THE CURE

Volume Ten:
ONE MORE TIME

Volume Zero:
TALES OF HUMAN WASTE

ALSO FROM WRITER WARREN ELLIS

HELLBLAZER: HAUNTED
with John Higgins

HELLBLAZER: SETTING SUN
with Tim Bradstreet, Javier Pulido, Marcelo Frusin and various

ORBITER
with Colleen Doran

GLOBAL FREQUENCY: PLANET ABLAZE
with various

RELOAD/MEK
with various

RED/TOKYO STORM WARNING
with various

THE AUTHORITY: RELENTLESS
with Bryan Hitch and Paul Neary

THE AUTHORITY: UNDER NEW MANAGEMENT
with Mark Millar and various

PLANETARY: ALL OVER THE WORLD
with John Cassaday

PLANETARY: THE FOURTH MAN
with John Cassaday

PLANETARY: CROSSING WORLDS
with John Cassaday, Phil Jimenez and Jerry Ordway

STORMWATCH: FORCE OF NATURE
with Tom Raney and Randy Elliott

STORMWATCH: LIGHTNING STRIKES
with Tom Raney, Randy Elliott and Jim Lee

STORMWATCH: CHANGE OR DIE
with Tom Raney and Oscar Jimenez

STORMWATCH: A FINER WORLD
with Bryan Hitch and Paul Neary

STORMWATCH: FINAL ORBIT
with various

Look for these other VERTIGO books:

All Vertigo titles are Suggested for Mature Readers

100 BULLETS
Brian Azzarello/Eduardo Risso
With one special briefcase, Agent Graves gives you the chance to kill without retribution. But what is the real price for this chance —— and who is setting it?

Vol 1: FIRST SHOT, LAST CALL
Vol 2: SPLIT SECOND CHANCE
Vol 3: HANG UP ON THE HANG LOW
Vol 4: A FOREGONE TOMORROW
Vol 5: THE COUNTERFIFTH DETECTIVE
Vol 6: SIX FEET UNDER THE GUN
Vol 7: SAMURAI

AMERICAN CENTURY
Howard Chaykin/David Tischman/
Marc Laming/John Stokes
The 1950s were no picnic, but for a sharp operator like Harry Kraft opportunity still knocked all over the world — and usually brought trouble right through the door with it.

Vol 1: SCARS & STRIPES
Vol 2: HOLLYWOOD BABYLON

ANIMAL MAN
Grant Morrison/Chas Truog/
Doug Hazlewood/various
A minor super-hero's consciousness is raised higher and higher until he becomes aware of his own fictitious nature in this revolutionary and existential series.

Vol 1: ANIMAL MAN
Vol 2: ORIGIN OF THE SPECIES
Vol 3: DEUS EX MACHINA

DEATH: THE HIGH COST OF LIVING
Neil Gaiman/Chris Bachalo/
Mark Buckingham
One day every century, Death assumes mortal form to learn more about the lives she must take.

DEATH: THE TIME OF YOUR LIFE
Neil Gaiman/Chris Bachalo/
Mark Buckingham/Mark Pennington
A young lesbian mother strikes a deal with Death for the life of her son in a story about fame, relationships, and rock and roll.

DOOM PATROL
Grant Morrison/Richard Case/
John Nyberg/Doug Braithwaite/
various

The World's Strangest Heroes are reimagined even stranger and more otherworldly in this groundbreaking series exploring the mysteries of identity and madness.

Vol 1: CRAWLING FROM THE
WRECKAGE
Vol 2: THE PAINTING THAT ATE PARIS

FABLES
Bill Willingham/Lan Medina/
Mark Buckingham/Steve Leialoha
The immortal characters of popular fairy tales have been driven from their homelands, and now live hidden among us, trying to cope with life in 21st-century Manhattan.

Vol 1: LEGENDS IN EXILE
Vol 2: ANIMAL FARM
Vol 3: STORYBOOK LOVE
Vol 4: MARCH OF THE WOODEN
SOLDIERS

HELLBLAZER
Jamie Delano/Garth Ennis/Warren Ellis/
Steve Dillon/John Higgins/various
Where horror, dark magic, and bad luck meet, John Constantine is never far away.

ORIGINAL SINS
DANGEROUS HABITS
FEAR AND LOATHING
TAINTED LOVE
DAMNATION'S FLAME
RAKE AT THE GATES OF HELL
SON OF MAN
HARD TIMES
GOOD INTENTIONS
FREEZES OVER
HIGHWATER
RARE CUTS
ALL HIS ENGINES

THE INVISIBLES
Grant Morrison/various
The saga of a terrifying conspiracy and the resistance movement combating it —— a secret underground of ultra-cool guerrilla cells trained in ontological and physical anarchy.

Vol 1: SAY YOU WANT A REVOLUTION
Vol 2: APOCALIPSTICK
Vol 3: ENTROPY IN THE U.K.

Vol 4: BLOODY HELL IN AMERICA
Vol 5: COUNTING TO NONE
Vol 6: KISSING MR. QUIMPER
Vol 7: THE INVISIBLE KINGDOM

LUCIFER
Mike Carey/Peter Gross/
Scott Hampton/Chris Weston/
Dean Ormston/various
Walking out of Hell (and out of the pages of THE SANDMAN), an ambitious Lucifer Morningstar creates a new cosmos modeled after his own image.

Vol 1: DEVIL IN THE GATEWAY
Vol 2: CHILDREN AND MONSTERS
Vol 3: A DALLIANCE WITH THE DAMNED
Vol 4: THE DIVINE COMEDY
Vol 5: INFERNO
Vol 6: MANSIONS OF THE SILENCE
Vol 7: EXODUS

PREACHER
Garth Ennis/Steve Dillon/various
A modern American epic of life, death, God, love, and redemption —— filled with sex, booze, and blood.

Vol 1: GONE TO TEXAS
Vol 2: UNTIL THE END OF THE WORLD
Vol 3: PROUD AMERICANS
Vol 4: ANCIENT HISTORY
Vol 5: DIXIE FRIED
Vol 6: WAR IN THE SUN
Vol 7: SALVATION
Vol 8: ALL HELL'S A-COMING
Vol 9: ALAMO

THE SANDMAN
Neil Gaiman/various
One of the most acclaimed and celebrated comics titles ever published.

Vol 1: PRELUDES & NOCTURNES
Vol 2: THE DOLL'S HOUSE
Vol 3: DREAM COUNTRY
Vol 4: SEASON OF MISTS
Vol 5: A GAME OF YOU
Vol 6: FABLES & REFLECTIONS
Vol 7: BRIEF LIVES
Vol 8: WORLDS' END

Vol 9: THE KINDLY ONES
Vol 10: THE WAKE
Vol 11: ENDLESS NIGHTS

THE SANDMAN: THE DREAM HUNTERS
Neil Gaiman/Yoshitaka Amano
Set in Japan and told in illustrated prose, this adult fairy tale featuring the Lord of Dreams is beautifully painted by legendary artist Yoshitaka Amano.

**THE SANDMAN: DUST COVERS —
THE COLLECTED SANDMAN COVERS
1989-1997**
Dave McKean/Neil Gaiman
A complete portfolio of Dave McKean's celebrated SANDMAN cover art, together with commentary by McKean and Gaiman.

SWAMP THING: DARK GENESIS
Len Wein/Berni Wrightson
A gothic nightmare is brought to life with this horrifying yet poignant story of a man transformed into a monster.

SWAMP THING
Alan Moore/Stephen Bissette/
John Totleben/Rick Veitch/various
The writer and the series that revolutionized comics —— a masterpiece of lyrical fantasy.

Vol 1: SAGA OF THE SWAMP THING
Vol 2: LOVE & DEATH
Vol 3: THE CURSE
Vol 4: A MURDER OF CROWS
Vol 5: EARTH TO EARTH
Vol 6: REUNION
Vol 7: REGENESIS

Y: THE LAST MAN
Brian K. Vaughan/Pia Guerra/
José Marzán, Jr.
An unexplained plague kills every male mammal on Earth —— all except Yorick Brown and his pet monkey. Will he survive this new, emasculated world to discover what killed his fellow men?

Vol 1: UNMANNED
Vol 2: CYCLES
Vol 3: ONE SMALL STEP
Vol 4: SAFEWORD

ADVENTURES IN THE RIFLE BRIGADE
Garth Ennis/Carlos Ezquerra

BARNUM!
Howard Chaykin/David Tischman/
Niko Henrichon

THE BOOKS OF MAGIC
Neil Gaiman/various

**BOOKS OF MAGICK:
LIFE DURING WARTIME BOOK ONE**
Si Spencer/Dean Ormston

THE COWBOY WALLY SHOW
Kyle Baker

THE FILTH
Grant Morrison/Chris Weston/
Gary Erskine

GODDESS
Garth Ennis/Phil Winslade

HEAVY LIQUID
Paul Pope

HUMAN TARGET
Peter Milligan/Edvin Biukovic

HUMAN TARGET: STRIKE ZONES
Peter Milligan/Javier Pulido

HUMAN TARGET: LIVING IN AMERIKA
Peter Milligan/Javier Pulido

HUMAN TARGET: FINAL CUT
Peter Milligan/Cliff Chiang

I DIE AT MIDNIGHT
Kyle Baker

IN THE SHADOW OF EDGAR ALLAN POE
Jonathon Scott Fuqua/
Stephen John Phillips/Steven Parke

IT'S A BIRD...
Steven T. Seagle/Teddy Kristiansen

KING DAVID
Kyle Baker

THE LOSERS: ANTE UP
Andy Diggle/Jock

THE LOSERS: DOUBLE DOWN
Andy Diggle/Jock/
Shawn Martinbrough

**PREACHER: DEAD OR ALIVE
(THE COLLECTED COVERS)**
Glenn Fabry

PRIDE & JOY
Garth Ennis/John Higgins

PROPOSITION PLAYER
Bill Willingham/Paul Guinan/Ron Randall

**THE SANDMAN PRESENTS:
TALLER TALES**
Bill Willingham/various

SEAGUY
Grant Morrison/Cameron Stewart

SEBASTIAN O
Grant Morrison/Steve Yeowell

**SHADE, THE CHANGING MAN:
THE AMERICAN SCREAM**
Peter Milligan/Chris Bachalo

SWAMP THING: BAD SEED
Andy Diggle/Enrique Breccia

TRUE FAITH
Garth Ennis/Warren Pleece

UNCLE SAM
Steve Darnall/Alex Ross

UNKNOWN SOLDIER
Garth Ennis/Kilian Plunkett

VAMPS
Elaine Lee/Will Simpson

V FOR VENDETTA
Alan Moore/David Lloyd

WAR STORIES VOL. 1
Garth Ennis/Chris Weston/Gary Erskine/
John Higgins/Dave Gibbons/David Lloyd

YOU ARE HERE
Kyle Baker

Search the Graphic Novels section of vertigocomics.com for art and info on every one of our hundreds of books. To purchase any of our titles, call 1-888-COMIC BOOK for the comics shop nearest you or go to your local book store.